The Poet's Tale

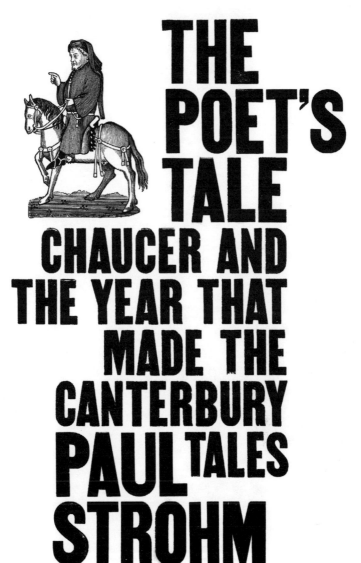

THE POET'S TALE

CHAUCER AND THE YEAR THAT MADE THE CANTERBURY TALES

PAUL STROHM

PROFILE BOOKS

First published in Great Britain in 2014 by
PROFILE BOOKS LTD
3 Holford Yard
Bevin Way
London WC1X 9HD
www.profilebooks.com

1 3 5 7 9 10 8 6 4 2

First published in the United States of America by Viking Penguin, a member of
Penguin Group (USA) LLC, 2014

Printed and bound in Great Britain by
Clays, Bungay, Suffolk

The moral right of the author has been asserted.

Illustration credits
Insert page 1: Ashmolean Museum
2, 3, 6 (top), 8 (top and bottom): The British Library
4 (top and bottom): Hatfield House
5 (top): © Bibliothèque municipale de Besançon (cliché CNRS-IRHT)
5 (bottom): Diane Heath, University of Kent
6 (bottom): Museum of London
7: Parker Library, Corpus Christi College, Cambridge

A CIP catalogue record for this book is available from the British Library.

ISBN 978 1 78125 059 4
eISBN 978 1 84765 899 9

The paper this book is printed on is certified by the © 1996 Forest Stewardship
Council A.C. (FSC). It is ancient-forest friendly. The printer holds FSC chain of custody

ACKNOWLEDGMENTS

This book is dedicated to Claire Harman, whose encouragement has sustained me throughout. For advice on London history I owe special thanks to Caroline Barron and Sheila Lindenbaum. Each has significantly influenced my thinking on a number of the matters covered in this book, although neither should be held responsible for any of my particular conclusions. Elliot Kendall designed the London map appearing at the beginning of this volume. In addition to the example of his own work, James Shapiro has offered valuable suggestions on several occasions. I have also received advice from Ardis Butterfield, Susan Crane, Carolyn Dinshaw, and David Wallace. In the longer perspective I have relied upon the cumulative efforts of many scholars who have worked during the past two centuries to identify, edit, and publish Chaucer's life-records, including Frederick Furnivall, R. E. G. Kirk, Eleanor Hammond, Edith Rickert, Ruth Bird, Martin M. Crow, and Clair C. Olson.

CONTENTS

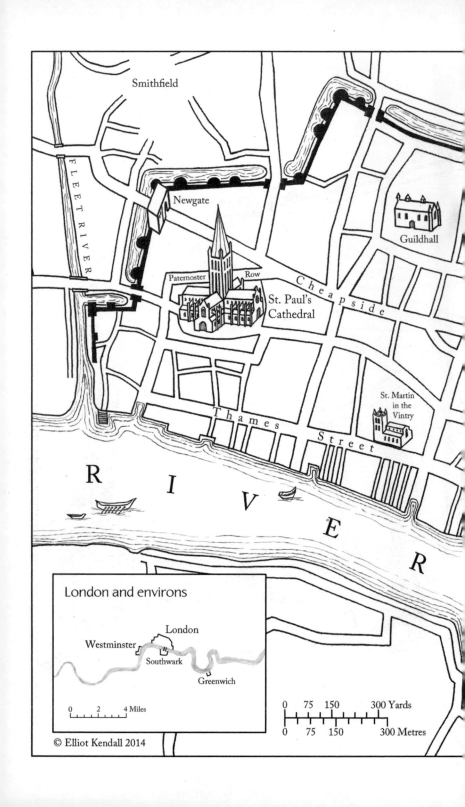

Smithfield

FLEET RIVER

Newgate

Paternoster Row

St. Paul's Cathedral

Cheapside

Guildhall

St. Martin in the Vintry

Thames Street

R I V E R

London and environs

London

Westminster

Southwark

Greenwich

0   2   4 Miles

0   75   150   300 Yards

0   75   150   300 Metres

© Elliot Kendall 2014

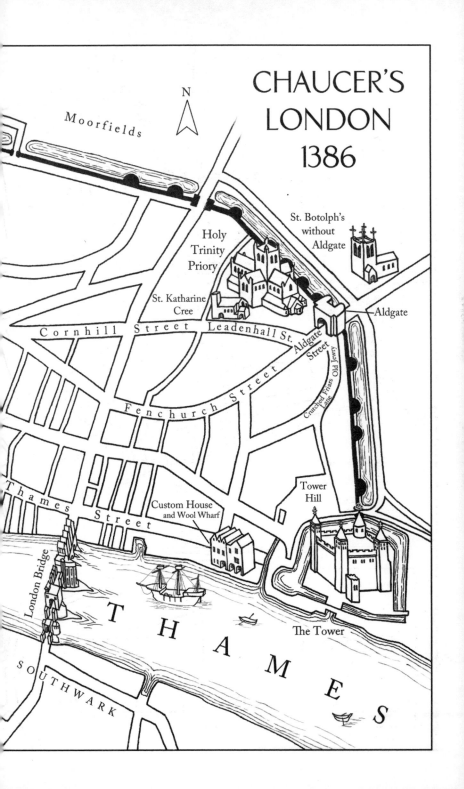

Anne of Bohemia. Queen of England, married to Richard II, 1382–94

Nicholas Brembre. Wool merchant, collector of customs, and four-time mayor of London; ardent supporter of Richard II

Sir Peter Bukton. Knight of the royal household; familiarly addressed by Chaucer in one of his short poems

Geoffrey Chaucer. 1343(?)–1400. Courtier, civil servant, and poet

Philippa Chaucer. Lady of Queen Philippa's household; wife of Chaucer and sister of Katherine Swynford

Thomas Chaucer. Chaucer's son and possible literary executor; prominent supporter of John of Gaunt and the Lancastrian household

John Churchman. London entrepreneur and developer of the 1382 custom house; later creditor of Chaucer

Sir John Clanvowe. Courtier and occasional poet in the manner of Chaucer

Sir Lewis Clifford. Diplomat and advocate of Chaucer's poetry

Edward III. King of England, 1327–77

Nicholas Exton. Fishmonger and mayor of London, 1386–88; Nicholas Brembre's more moderate successor

Jean Froissart. French chronicle writer and poet; well-informed contemporary commentator on the English scene

John of Gaunt. Duke of Lancaster; first marriage to Duchess

Blanche, second to Constanza of Castile, third to Katherine Swynford

Thomas, duke of Gloucester. Enemy of Richard II and head of the oppositional aristocratic party, 1385–89

John Gower. Fellow poet and friendly rival of Chaucer

Henry of Derby. See Henry IV

Henry IV. King of England, 1399–1414; also known as Henry of Derby, Henry Bolingbroke

Thomas Hoccleve. Clerk; early fifteenth-century poet and devotee of Chaucer

Richard Lyons. Corrupt London financier, slain by irate rebels in 1381

John Lydgate. Monk of Bury St. Edmunds and extremely prolific fifteenth-century poet; respectful imitator and follower of Chaucer

John Northampton. Draper; populist mayor of London, 1381–83, and adversary of Nicholas Brembre

Philippa of Hainault. Wife of Edward III and Queen of England, 1328–69

Adam Pinkhurst. London scribe; Chaucer's frequent, and probably favorite, copyist

Richard II. King of England, 1377–99

Paon de Roet. Knight of Edward III's household; father of Philippa Chaucer and Katherine Swynford

Sir Arnold Savage. Sheriff of Kent, possible Chaucer host and benefactor

Henry Scogan. Esquire of the king's household, occasional poet, eventual tutor to sons of Henry IV

Ralph Strode. London legalist and bureaucrat with possible previous career as an Oxford philosopher; literary friend of Chaucer

Katherine Swynford. Chaucer's sister-in-law; mistress and eventual third wife of John of Gaunt

Thomas Usk. Aspiring writer and ill-fated London factionalist

Thomas Walsingham. Monk of St. Albans and prolific writer of English chronicles

The Poet's Tale

Chaucer's Crisis

Geoffrey Chaucer often wrote about reversals of Fortune. One of his most frequent literary themes is the impact of sudden turning points and transformations, blows of fate that alter or upend a situation. Some of his characters withstand such changes, and even find ways to turn them to their own advantage. His Knight, for example, muses upon a young man's cruelly arbitrary death and still counsels his survivors to find ways of seeking joy after woe. The Knight's proposed remedy is one that will recur several times in Chaucer's poetry: "to make virtue of necessity" (*"to maken vertu of necessitee"*) by confronting bad circumstances and turning them to advantage if one can.

No wonder Chaucer favored this advice, since his entire career was a series of high-wire balancing acts, improvisations, and awkward adjustments. In his childhood he escaped the disastrous Black Death that ravaged all of Europe. As an adolescent he declined to pursue, or was discouraged from pursuing, his vintner father's secure career in the London wine trade. He entered the more volatile area of court service instead. Early in that service he was packed off on a military adventure in France, where he was captured and held prisoner until ransomed by the king. He found his way to an advantageous marriage and a reputable position as esquire to the king, but was no sooner accustoming himself to that life than his political allies decided to deploy him elsewhere. They sent him back to London, where he was reimmersed in mercantile culture in the awkwardly conspicuous and ethically precarious post of controller of the wool custom, charged to monitor the activities of some of the richest and best connected and least scrupulous crooks on the face of his planet. He was given occupancy of quarters over a city gate—the very gate through which the rebels would stream (probably under his feet) during the Peasants' Revolt. He was intermittently and undoubtedly disruptively tapped for membership in diplomatic delegations, including arduous trips over the Alps to Italy on royal business. Throughout, in court and then in the city, he maintained precarious relations with the most hated man in the realm, the overweening John of Gaunt. He was thrust into awkward and compromising dealings with the most controversial man in London, the unscrupulous wool profiteer Nicholas Brembre. He was in recurrent legal trouble, harassed over unpaid bills, and was the subject of a suit for *raptus*—abduction or even rape—brought on behalf of a young woman named Cecily Champagne. Briefly recalled to royal service in later life, he was exposed to dangerous travel and several times violently robbed, once in a Falstaffian location known as the Foul Oak in Kent.

Chaucer knew all about turbulence and change, but one brief period in his life posed a particularly severe challenge to his ideas about virtue and necessity. In the autumn of 1386 he was confronted by a clutch of adversities, not only disruptive of his personal and political life but potentially disastrous to his literary life as well. This was his crisis, his time of troubles. Its multiple origins, the hardships it imposed, and especially its remarkable outcome are the tale this book will tell.

In the perverse way of crises, this one interrupted a period of relative calm. For the preceding twelve years, between 1374 and

1386, Chaucer had lived in a grace and favor apartment over London's Aldgate and settled into something approximating a routine on the Wool Wharf. As the autumn of 1386 approached, he was enjoying a high-water mark in his civic career. His duties as controller of the wool custom had recently been eased by appointment of a deputy, without interruption to his salary. His socialite wife, Philippa, was comfortably settled in Lincolnshire with her sister Katherine, mistress to the formidable Gaunt. Earlier that year Philippa had been inducted into the highly prestigious Fraternity of Lincoln Cathedral, along with the future Henry IV and other persons of consequence. His political allies in King Richard's royal faction had just engineered his election as a shire knight, or county representative, for Kent in the Westminster Parliament. In both court and city he had proven and reproven his worth as a pliant and useful member of the group of literate civil servants comprising the administrative bureaucracy of later medieval England.

Although his selection as a shire knight was probably a result of his sponsors' wishes rather than his own desires, he might have taken some satisfaction in the position. Shire knights were the top tier of elected parliamentary representatives, enjoying higher status and privilege than those from boroughs and towns. Besides, members of Parliament (MPs) usually had a good time. The numerous inns and taverns along Westminster's King Street boomed. Despite civic attempts at regulation, prostitutes streamed toward Westminster and, especially, the freewheeling adjacent area of Charing Cross. MPs maintained an air of jollity, attending banquets and other collective events and also hiring private cooks and musicians to enliven private parties in their group accommodations.

Whatever its recreational advantages, though, Chaucer

joined this Parliament on behalf of other people's interests: those of Richard II, whom he had loyally served, and also the mercantile and political interests of the royal party in the city of London. And he joined it at a particularly unfortunate time. Richard was under unrelenting assault by the aristocratic followers of his uncle Thomas, duke of Gloucester, and this session was shaping up as an early and important test of strength. Its outcome would be disastrous for the king's faction. These bad results for his allies were closely intertwined with Chaucer's own life prospects. A petition approved and announced in Parliament encouraged his resignation from his patronage job on the Wool Wharf. Even as Parliament was meeting, previous city allies ousted him from his apartment in London; he could not return there, and would never again, in any settled or consecutive sense, be a resident of London. Other elements of his support system were crumbling. His controversial collaborator and associate, the high-handed London mayor Nicholas Brembre, was discredited. His volatile, aristocratic patron John of Gaunt was absent from the realm on a lengthy and quixotic and unpopular military adventure. Richard's own problems would multiply in the coming two years, culminating in his near deposition and the condemnation of his closest followers during the Merciless Parliament of 1388. To these movements of state may be added a list of more purely personal woes, including the ebbing of Chaucer's marriage (he was already living separately from his wife Philippa, and she would die the following year), a partial estrangement from his children (who were being raised in Lincolnshire, as young Lancastrians), and—puzzlingly, since he had worked among the most conspicuous grifters and profit takers of the realm—his own chronic insolvency. In what might have been a quiet time of personal consolidation, he suddenly found himself without a patron, without a faction, without a dwelling, without a job, and—perhaps most seriously—without a city.

From our vantage point we might suppose that his literary reputation would have bought him some time and temporary credit. From a young age, and throughout all previous changes of fortune, Chaucer had resolutely pursued his literary aims. By 1386 he had written more than half of his poetry, a body of work already sufficient to establish him as the greatest English author before Shakespeare. Why then, in his time of trouble, didn't doors fly open for him or admirers vie to provide him with support and succor? In fact, he was not yet a celebrated writer. His literary successes had been confined to a small and appreciative circle rather than shared by a more general literary public. He wrote not for hire or on command or, most certainly—prior to 1386—for fame, but simply because he wanted to. He had not made, and would never make, a penny from his verse. His supporters were few and private rather than numerous and far-flung. He had come to know some of them during his years of court service, and then others in the city, and they constituted a group of interested acquaintances rather than a national or international public. Moreover, in the years following 1386, many members of this circle were experiencing their own temporary privation, or even ruin. The end of 1386 would find him effectively on his own, adrift in Kent, without any of his customary life supports. His task, and opportunity, was to decide upon his own next course of action.

His responses to earlier trials had been practical and political, involving new posts, new alliances, new loyalties. This crisis found him temporarily bereft of practical options, and his riposte—his own attempt to make virtue of necessity—would be literary this time. His literary avocation would, in the years following 1386, become his principal area of endeavor, his full vocation, with results that we celebrate today. Already a successful writer, but among a limited circle of acquaintances, he would now accept the preconditions and burdens and excitements of public success. Previously fame-averse, he would embrace the challenges and implications of literary celebrity and perhaps even fame itself. He would set his sights on a career that didn't yet exist—in England at any rate—as what we now call a man of letters, addressing an audience that didn't exist yet either, a broadly constituted English literary public. For this trying moment in his life also provoked his most consequential literary stride. In the agitated circumstances of this difficult year, he would conceive and embark upon his masterpiece.

The 1386 crisis must be understood not just as an isolated event but also within the context of its antecedents and its consequences. The first section of this book will concern the run-up to crisis: Chaucer's marital estrangement, his rather awkward perch over Aldgate, the contradictions and difficulties of his post at the wool custom, and his dispiriting parliamentary session. The second section will turn to his response. Above all, it will consider the new artistic resolve he formed during and after the crisis, his commitment to the ambitious and startlingly unprecedented project of the *Canterbury Tales*.

Two Chaucers?

This book proposes a connection between an author's immersion in ordinary, everyday activities and the separately imagined world of his literary work. Every literary biographer faces the problem of bridging this practical and conceptual divide. But the problem is stretched to a breaking point in the case of a premodern writer who kept no personal diaries and maintained no regular written correspondence or other firsthand account of his motives and thoughts.

Not that the Chaucer biographer lacks evidence or material; the records of his official life and duties positively bristle with evidence, but of an exclusively public sort. His official duties are extensively documented in city records, accounts of the exchequer, grants and warrants of the king, John of Gaunt's household registers, and other sources—but with one remarkable peculiarity. As far as existing records go, Chaucer the *poet* remains all but hidden from history. Based on the 493 documents of his official life published in the *Life-Records*, nobody would have known he was a poet at all. For these official and attested documents contain no mention whatever of the accomplishment for which *we* know him, his contribution to English poetry.

One could go so far as to imagine, speculatively, the existence of "two Chaucers," the one busy in court and city and the other scribbling in obscure digs somewhere. The first with a public career conducted at a level of moderate visibility and the other as a private writer perfecting his art on his own terms. The records display a public man seeking advancement, forming political and factional ties, representing his king at home and abroad, and supervising the export of the most valued commodity in the land. The writer and private man is, by comparison, hardly to be seen. If that body of brilliant surviving literary works had not raised the question of authorship, and provoked a search to provide him with an identity and a life history, civil servant Geoffrey Chaucer might have escaped the mantle literary history has assigned him. As revealed in the public records of his career, this courtier and bureaucrat seems a busy enough man in his own right and hardly likely to have written all those poems, tales, scientific writings, and other treatises now credited to Chaucer's pen.

Speculation about separate Chaucers needs a quick quashing, though, before it opens the door to the host of crackpot theories of disguised identities and faux authorship that have dogged Shakespeare and from which Chaucer has been blessedly spared. Fortunately for our sanity in this matter, a few slight shards of literary evidence, originating outside the protocols of official record keeping, imply a connection between the two otherwise separate identities. The French poet Deschamps writes to hail Chaucer the poet for his literary translations, and their link could only have been Lewis Clifford, a knight of King Richard's chamber and an old friend whom the courtier Chaucer would have met while in royal service. Clifford, at least, would have had a simultaneous sense of "both" Chaucers, as would some other members of the court. Within the body of his incidental verse, Chaucer mentions the names of Henry Scogan and Peter Bukton and Philip de la Vache, all of whom the poet would have known in the first instance as members of the Edwardian and Ricardian courts. The "two Chaucers" also appear to merge at one moment within the body of the poetry itself. This is when, in his satiric *House of Fame*, the protagonist—one "Geffrey"—is described as completing his "reckonings" (that is, his work-related calculations) and going home at night to immerse himself in books. This Geffrey's duties would seem a counterpart to Chaucer's own record-keeping responsibilities at the Wool Wharf, and Chaucer can easily be imagined immuring himself with his books inside his rather garretlike apartment over Aldgate. At these few frail junctures, and hardly any others, the public servant and the private poet converge.

Aside from these few references, Chaucer's extensively documented public life and his virtually undocumented artistic life remain more obstinately separate than those of any major English writer besides Shakespeare. Nor is he an Augustine or Abelard or Rousseau or Rimbaud, canvassing his own life for narrative material. Just as medieval anatomists were more likely to read Aristotle or Galen than to dissect frogs, so was Chaucer more likely to turn to books and his sense of literary decorum than to personal incidents as his starting point when he set out to craft a tale. He never wrote a tale about a merchant's son who became a courtier, or a courtier who became a bureaucrat, or the wool trade and the Calais Staple, or a noisy apartment over a city gate, or a failed attempt to pack a Parliament, or any other subject demonstrably drawn from his life experience. Besides, even had he done so, we still wouldn't be able to distinguish between his faithful reportage and his indebtedness to a mixture of literary sources and pure inventions. His handful of apparent references to himself within his poems—as a wallflower at the dance of love or a hapless man ensnared by marriage—are far too conventional to be seized as literal life truths. Even the crucial reference in the *House of Fame* to "Geffrey" coming home at night from his day job and immersing himself in books occurs within a piece of literary invention and falls somewhere beneath the standards of hard evidence.

Literary biographers are always on precarious ground when they go prospecting in an artist's body of written work seeking nuggets of buried life experience. The temptation is especially great for the biographer of a premodern figure for whom life evidence remains scattered and inferential. Supposed links between art and life often prove a kind of fool's gold, alluring but deceptive. For example, Chaucer's actual parliamentary involvements might seem sufficient warrant to look within his literary parliaments for such connections. Chaucer does, indeed, write about unruly parliaments in his *Parliament of Fowls* and also in *Troilus*, but both descriptions turn out to have been written prior to his own parliamentary term. Besides, the parliament of birds was an established literary trope of the day, and Giovanni Boccaccio, Chaucer's partial source for *Troilus*, already had the idea of situating the decision about Criseide in a quasi-parliamentary council of barons. Or consider a tantalizing moment in Chaucer's *House of Fame* when the overbearing Eagle shouts "Awak!" in Geffrey's ear—in voice and volume, Chaucer says, of someone he might (but does not) name (*"Ryght in the same vois and stevene / That useth oon I coulde nevene"*). One influential critic made the plausible suggestion that this must have been a rendition of Chaucer's own wife, Philippa, waking him up in the morning. Except that he probably wasn't living with Philippa at the time. And then other critics came along and suggested that the voice must have belonged to an officious servant, or to Lady Philosophy, or to Christ on Judgment Day. In other words, we'll never know. Perhaps the voice simply belonged to this particular noisy Eagle, and Chaucer can't name his source because he invented it.

Alongside Chaucer's other personal reticences may be placed his general aversion to topical poetry or to poetry devoted to outside events or burning themes of the political moment. His Knight has been in numerous battles, but the account of his military experience avoids such hot-button instances as skirmishes in the Hundred Years War with France (despite his own experience in that intermittent war). Nor does he take the opportunity to comment on a subject of considerable personal importance, John of Gaunt's ongoing military adventure in Castile. The deposed king Pedro of Castile (Gaunt's father-in-law) and

Bernabò Visconti (whom Chaucer may have met, or at least seen, in Italy) are mentioned as victims of Fortune in his "Monk's Tale," but only in general terms and not in any way suggesting personal acquaintance. He alludes to the 1381 Peasants' Revolt and the rebels' shrill cries and their revenge on the Flemish community in his "Nun's Priest's Tale," but these were commonplaces. Besides, by comparing them to the din of the barnyard animals' pursuit of the fleeing fox, and by transposing these events into a mock-heroic register, he seems more interested in neutralizing their raw shock than in exploiting them for their own sake. His dour contemporary John Gower, seldom hailed for his contemporary relevance, is the one who tackles public events in his poetry and moves events like the Peasants' Revolt to the forefront as subjects of political commentary and moral observation.

Wishing to move past the bare details of Chaucer's official life but unwilling to ransack his literary works in a vain search for hidden clues, I have pursued a third option. Intermediary between a writer's public life on the one hand and fictional and literary creations on the other are those activities comprising what might be called the "writing scene": all those matters of situation and circumstance that permit writing in the first place, the essential preconditions and occasions of literary art. Why then rummage around in an author's work for purported life details when the known circumstances of an author's daily life bristle with significant information about his or her exercise of his or her craft? When, for example, did the artist find time to write, or a place to write, or an appreciative audience, or a means of addressing that audience? Chaucer shows an active interest in such matters throughout his writings, scenes of literary enjoyment, such as the ladies hearing a romance of Thebes read aloud in Criseide's garden; worries about manuscript production and scribal error in his poem to Adam the Scrivener; evidence of direct address and lively interaction with an intimate audience scattered throughout his poems. The connections I will draw between his poetry and his life will involve those life arrangements that hindered or helped his writing, that advanced or retarded his search for an appreciative audience of his poems.

The sequence of events unfolding in the autumn of 1386, would have an immense influence on the *circumstances* of Chaucer's art: on his writing scene, on his access to an audience, on the importance of audience to his work, on his ambitions for himself as a writer. In the end of it all, these altered circumstances will have an impact on the artwork itself, on its form and its means of presentation, and on what Chaucer hopes to accomplish by writing it. Within the practical details of Chaucer's ordinary life rests an explanation for his most extraordinary literary departure, the enabling idea of his final masterpiece, the *Canterbury Tales.*

In the closing months of 1386 Chaucer experienced a devastating cluster of reversals that has every appearance of defeat. But sometimes the grim particulars of a defeat can create a new opening, a fresh alternative. All these frustrations, this eclipse of career, this forced relocation, this abrupt termination of a London life that had suited him well will create the incentive for a new life through art. A new art requires a new audience, and Chaucer will seek and find one—first, fictively, through his company of Canterbury Pilgrims, and then concretely, through an expanded and diversified reading public. Forgoing the customary comforts of a familiar audience, and discovering a voice (or, more accurately, a multiplicity of voices) in which to address a broadened literary constituency, Chaucer will remake himself.

This partially compromised and marginally successful faction-alist and bureaucrat will set himself on course to become what he is for us now: a poet shaped by circumstance but who also found a way to place himself beyond circumstance, to become a poet for all time.

Chaucer may, in fact must, be seen in double vision: as the medieval poet that he was and as the poet of permanent themes and enduring stature that he aspired to be, situated in the "then" of his own time but also speaking to the "now" of ours. At one moment in his poetry he addresses this very issue. In his *Troilus and Criseide* he considers the predicament of Trojan lovers, long vanished in past time, and the obstacles to his own reconstruc-tion of their emotions and experiences. They are completely un-like us but bafflingly like us as well. So much time has passed, he says, that speech itself has changed; they didn't even use the same words for things, and words that then had value now seem wondrously silly and strange. But—and here is his crucial point—for all their seeming oddity of speech or custom they got on with the business of life and achieved practical consequences we can still appreciate and understand. In love, he says, they fared as well as we do now (*"spedde as wel in love as men now do"*). They are taking their own and different avenues to recognizable objectives, following, as he figuratively says, different paths to Rome but getting there nonetheless (*"For every wight which that to Rome went / Halt nat o path"*). Differences, he wisely suggests, must be acknowledged, but some human emotions and objec-tives remain recognizable across time.

My aim is to write an evidence-based account that respects the past as past, but that simultaneously seeks out linkages be-tween that past and our present. At various points in the pages to follow I will attribute motives to Chaucer that, with modest adjustment, are close cousins to our own: motives of love (and accommodation to its absence), ambition (and its curious lack), loyalty (and its limits), financial security (and an apparent indifference to wealth), a wish for fame (and a disdain for its requirements). Such conceptions, or *usages* as Chaucer calls them, have their own distinctive medieval inflections. Love might have been a bit more pragmatic in Chaucer's day; even in the age of courtly romance excessive love was regarded as a fever and disease. Loyalty stood somewhat more to the forefront than today, and lapses in personal commitment were more severely judged. Financial security was often equated with entitlement to property, to which Chaucer had no practical access. Fame was perhaps even more ardently sought than it is today, although also seen as a precarious and double-edged aspiration. But even when such differences are acknowledged, these *usages* are sufficiently elastic, and share enough characteristics of our own, to provide a common ground for appreciation of this remarkable man's travails and all that he achieved.

CHAPTER ONE

A Married Man

Those Aldgate mornings Chaucer awakened alone, or in any case without the company of his wife Philippa. She appears never to have lived with him there. Chaucer's lease was drawn to himself as sole occupant, whereas the previous lease for his London dwelling had been made out to a married couple—"to Walter Parmenter *and his wife Joanna*"—including both their names. Besides, a woman of Philippa's background would have been unlikely to enjoy such quarters in a fortified tower over a city gate. His relations with Philippa were companionate but, at least at this stage in their lives, distant, as a closer look at their particular circumstances will help to explain.

Any marriage, even when amply documented or lived out before one's eyes, will retain its areas of private reserve. The more so with Chaucer and Philippa, whose marriage is glimpsed mainly in public documents and records—grants and annuities, household affiliations, ceremonial duties—and no private communications at all. Carefully examined, though, even taciturn records of financial transactions and public ceremonies have their partial tales to tell. Several telltale pieces of stray evidence—including her presence at a Lincolnshire social event and an annuity payment via the sheriff of Lincoln and the intimacy of their oldest son's connections with the Lancastrian household—suggest that Chaucer and Philippa lived apart far more often than they lived together during their thirty-year marriage. Like some twenty-first-century "commuting" marriages, theirs was conditioned by demands of simultaneous careers, economic necessity, and geographical separation. Perhaps the real surprise is that, with so many competing pressures and agendas, they stayed together at all. But they did, just barely, and here is what can be known of their story.

A Squire of Lesser Degree

Son of a successful London citizen and vintner, the young Chaucer initially sought a career in aristocratic service. A normal career track would have had him following his father into the wine trade, becoming a member of the vintners' guild, and living out his life among the prosperous bourgeoisie who effectively ran the city of London. But he, or his father, had other ideas. John Chaucer had been on the fringes of royal employment as a deputy collector of customs at Southampton and other ports, and knew something about launching a career that would take his son at least partway beyond his mercantile beginnings. Beginning in 1357, when Geoffrey was in his early teens, probably through connections his father had formed and exploited during his periods of royal service, he was taken on as a page in the household of Elizabeth, countess of Ulster, and then in a merged household with her husband, Lionel, a son of Edward III. In setting on this track Geoffrey relinquished the comforts of a family home and economic security accompanying the path to guild master in a London trade. Awaiting him, instead, was a more socially prestigious but far less certain future as a participant in the court culture of his day.

A page might be a mere chore boy, currying horses and carrying firewood and turning spits in the kitchen. (A haughty damsel in Malory's *Morte d'Arthur* insults the humbly reared Sir

Gareth by claiming that he is a *"luske and a torner of broches"*—an idler and spit turner in a noble kitchen.) But a page might also be a young man with prospects, a more genteel and versatile kind of errand runner destined for better things—including the ranks of valet, esquire, or even knight. Geoffrey's post was of the latter kind. Early in his term of service he was fitted out with a "paltock" (a fashionable tuniclike garment) at the countess's expense, and one doesn't wear a paltock to grub out the stables. As a young man marked for possible future advancement, he was trusted to make local trips and conduct small business arrangements on behalf of his lord.

On the same roster of domestic servants is a young woman who also seems to have been on an upward trajectory, one "Philippa Pan." The question is, was she Chaucer's future wife Philippa? The designation Pan remains mysterious. Pan might simply be a surname, which would argue against the notion that she is Chaucer's eventual wife, since Philippa Chaucer's surname was "de Roet." Or Pan might be an abbreviation for *panetaria*—anyone from "breadmaker" to "mistress of the pantry"—except that the household already had one. This Philippa was probably no commoner; Philippa had been a popular name ever since Queen Philippa's marriage to the young Edward III and arrival in England in 1327, but mainly among socially aspirational women. Although Philippa Pan is not necessarily "our" Philippa, we may reasonably suppose her so. She, like Geoffrey, received household gifts that designate her as a young woman from whom certain things might be expected: a holiday tunic of similar worth to his, together with an ornamental corset, leather work, and other marks of recognition.

In any case, by 1366 doubt is resolved: There is a Philippa Chaucer. A document of 1366 names her as a lady, or *domicella*, of the queen's chamber. Even given the lapse of a half-dozen years since the Ulster household, this would have been a young marriage. Each was about twenty-two years of age. A popular impression, abetted by *Romeo and Juliet*, is that matches were always arranged and that medieval people married extremely young. These points hold true for dynastic marriages, when thrones or substantial properties were at stake, but not for most others. Granted, in 1396 Richard II married the six-year-old daughter of the king of France, whom he happily pampered and treated as a little girl, and, more proximately, Edward III was only fifteen when he entered into his arranged marriage with his Philippa, the thirteen-year-old daughter of the count of Hainault. But these dynastic marriages were exceptions. Richard II's marriage to his "expensive little morsel" of flesh was widely mocked, and Queen Philippa's youth was repeatedly commented upon. Early modern marriages, for members of the gentry (like Chaucer), suggest twenty-six as the average age for men, twenty-one to twenty-two for women. Chaucer's marrying in his early twenties was on the young side for the later fourteenth century, and this bare fact may suggest a relation initially marked by enthusiasm and free choice. In any case, it suggests an absence of reluctance, a sense that he considered this to be an advantageous marriage.

This 1366 document locates Philippa in the entourage of the queen. In 1367 Chaucer would closely align their lives by entering into royal service as well. He is first described as a *valettus*, or valet, and then, in another document of the same date, named as a *scutifer*, or esquire, of the king. This title of esquire—whether a hasty correction or mark of recent promotion—means that Chaucer, as well as Philippa, has achieved a "gentle" social rank, putting each on the same side of the line that defined the two great social categories of the later Middle Ages, that separating gentlepersons from the bourgeoisie and others.

Chaucer and Philippa were equals in the matter of gentility, but a gulf, and in fact even a double gulf, remained between them. Philippa's smooth accession to *domicella*, the female equivalent of knighthood, is easily enough explained. As the daughter of Sir Paon de Roet, a knight of Hainault who came to England in the entourage of Queen Philippa and remained, she was of a lineage that affirmed and secured her status. Her sister Katherine moved easily into the household of the Duke of Lancaster, beginning as an *ancilla*, or servant, to Duchess Blanche in 1365, and attaining the status of *domicella* soon after. Of course, both sisters brought a good deal to the table. Paon de Roet had been something more than a run-of-the-mill chamber knight. His title, in the entourage of Queen Philippa's sister Marguerite, countess of Hainault, had been Maistre Chevalier de l'Ostel, or chief knight of the household. In England, he would be given the title Guienne King of Arms by Edward III. These titles are undoubtedly somewhat pumped up, in lieu of other rewards. Nevertheless, Paon de Roet cannot be written off as a mere down-at-the-heels opportunist. Not simply a knight, he was granted some marks of special distinction within that privileged class. He executed tasks of trust and responsibility in England; Froissart, for example, names him as one of the knights delegated to provide safe conduct for the burghers of Calais on the occasion when their conqueror Edward III had condemned them to death. Furthermore, records show that Philippa Chaucer's nephew Thomas Swynford received an eventual inheritance in Hainault—suggesting that de Roet was no piker and had at least some lands to give.

As son of a London wine merchant, Chaucer started a notch below and never caught up. The thing about his status of lesser, or *meindre*, degree is that—unlike many of his fellow esquires (who would eventually become knights)—he earned his rank not through birth but through service. The *meindre* would fall away; he would be known as an esquire of the king's household and, after he left it, simply as esquire. But this court had a glass ceiling, and odds were against an esquire who had earned his rank through service emerging as a knight. He had to make do with the status available to him, which is elsewhere expressed as that of *mesnal gentil*—a household gentleperson—not a "menial," as in our modern usage, but a member of the king's *meynee*, or band of undifferentiated household supporters.

Their social differences are illustrated in a document of 1369, in which liveries of mourning are authorized for members of the household attending Queen Philippa's obsequies. Such ceremonial occasions served double duty as orchestrations and performances of social difference, and in this document differences are clearly displayed. Of black cloth for mourning garments, lords and ladies (*damoiselles*) receive a dozen yards, ladies of lesser rank (*souz-damoiselle*) receive a half dozen, knights receive a dozen, and esquires of greater degree (*de greindre estat*) and lesser degree (*de meindre degree*) receive three yards. Philippa, together with sixteen ladies of the court, receives her six yards; Chaucer is down there with eighty-eight esquires of lesser degree and just scrapes into the category of those receiving three yards. If he had been looking for a match with a social equal, the subdamsels—that is, a social notch below Philippa—would have been the category for him.

Such distinctions could be suspended or masked on some collective and ceremonial occasions. One can imagine a situation of provisional equity in which the entourages of the king and queen, mingling together in amity, might suppress their senses of small social difference—especially since all (although Chaucer barely) were on the same side of that divide of medieval society that separated the "gentils," or gentlepeople, from the immensely larger body of the ungentle with whom they shared the realm. The fifteenth-century household book of Edward IV imagines a social life for his esquires, in terms perhaps a bit old-fashioned for that century, but still evocative, and probably applicable to ladies of the court as well:

> The esquires of the household have been long accustomed, winter and summer, in afternoons and evenings, to gather into their lord's chambers within the court, there to keep honest company according to their knowledge and accomplishments, talking of chronicles of kings and other policies, or in piping or harping or singing, or military exercise, to help occupy the court and accompany strangers, until the time comes for departing.

Although Chaucer presents his invented self in the *Canterbury Tales* as reclusive and tongue-tied, his short and topical poems written for social occasions reveal him as convivial, playful, and given to easy social exchange. His poetry could only have been written by an alert and enthusiastic social observer, and he can easily be thought to have thrived in the atmosphere of gaiety, regular festivity, and situational equality that would have prevailed in the royal household.

Yet there's no doubt that, according to the social norms of the day, Chaucer "married up," that he would have had every reason to consider the alliance a social advantage. Contributing to Philippa's allure was the considerable prestige of her Hainault connection. This connection undoubtedly added a touch of glamour to the alliance, a hint of old family and Continental flair that surely intrigued a young and somewhat socially aspirant young man of mercantile and bourgeois origin. He could hardly have imagined at the moment of his marriage how important this connection was about to become.

Hainault Chic

Perched on the Francophone rim of what is now Belgium, scarcely a hundred miles from Paris, fourteenth-century Hainault enjoyed a reputation for high diplomacy, polished chivalry, and undoubted fashion. Militarily and politically it dominated the lowlands, and as a force in Europe it would have seemed, at least until Edward III's great victories of the midcentury, nearly equal to England itself. In fact, Hainault quite literally *made* Edward III the king of England, and by conquest at that. Here is the story:

Near the end of Edward II's clouded and ineffectual reign, his rambunctious queen, Isabella, deep into her affair with Roger Mortimer, sought to secure her own influence by assuring her son Edward's succession to the throne. She turned, unsuccessfully, to her brother Charles IV of France for aid and then, opportunely, made the acquaintance of Jeanne, wife of William, count of Hainault (and her young daughter, Philippa) while still in Paris. In 1326 Isabella visited Hainault and, abetted by other frictions between Edward II and Count William, gained the support of the count and his brother, John of Hainault. As a derivative aspect of this alliance, and a guarantee of its fulfillment, a marriage contract was drawn between Prince Edward and Count William's daughter Philippa.

The invasion of England transpired with the support of some

seven hundred men under the command of John of Hainault, comprising much of the chivalry of the land together with common soldiers. Edward II was dethroned, and Queen Isabella and her son Edward gained the upper hand. Her son was crowned Edward III on February 1, 1327, and Edward and Philippa were married on January 24, 1328. One measure of the puissance and centrality of Hainault in English affairs is that the initial marriage contract, drawn under supervision of Queen Isabella and her paramour, Mortimer, promised a substantial dowry *to Hainault*, guaranteed by an English forfeit of ten thousand pounds if the marriage did not occur. Dowries could flow one way or the other, from bride to groom or groom to bride, although usually from the bride. In this case, Hainault's prestige, and its worth to England at this difficult juncture, is clearly exemplified in England's willingness to pay handsomely for the privileged association. Nor was this association to end. Count William of Hainault would serve as Edward III's principal strategist and ally in his decision to claim the crown of France. Relations between England's new king and the French had begun on a more positive note and—without the mischievous existence of the Hainault connection—the Hundred Years War between England and France might never have occurred.

The Hainault demi-invasion in support of Edward III, and then the actual arrival of the new queen-to-be Philippa and the establishment of a lustrous court, meant that considerable numbers of Hainaulters crossed to England, first for battle, then for the wedding, and some to stay. The English and Hainault aristocrats seem to have merged with ease, but instances of strife marred relations between ordinary English and Hainault troops, including a particularly bloody riot in York at the time of, or soon after, Edward and Philippa's marriage. Nevertheless,

in official accounts, and among the elite, Philippa and her entourage scored success after success. She was hailed upon her
arrival in England as, among other things, *courtoise*, or possessed of highly refined manners, and she did not disappoint
this expectation. Her arrival set off a round of parties, the like of
which the English mainland had hardly seen. As the chronicler
Froissart has it, she was greeted with "great festivity, great no-
blesse of lords, counts, barons, knights, high-born ladies and
maidens, and there they held tournaments marked by beautiful
and grand attire, jousting and lance-play—all for the love of
her—and dances and carols, splendid feasts, continuing day after day." Forty knights and esquires were said to have escorted
her, and a retinue remained behind even after they departed,
including no less a figure than the young Gautier de Mauny,
who would become one of the most celebrated chivalric figures
of the midcentury, and, as Sir Walter Manny, found the London Charterhouse. Also lingering were, as Froissart says, "many
young esquires whose purpose was to dwell in England with the
queen." Her entourage even included a page—one Watelet de
Hainaut—whose job was to care for the queen's *leporarii*, or
hares. (Hares were sometimes decoratively employed in stylish
mock-hunting parties organized for women of the court.) Froissart, the principal informant in these matters, was himself a
Hainaulter, and came to England in his youth to serve the
queen, and to write poems in her praise. Queen Philippa's court
was a magnet for young women, too, and she surrounded herself
with a dozen *damoiselles* of Hainault as her constant companions.

The English, according to Froissart, could not get over prais-
ing their Hainaulter queen as *"si douls, si courtois, si amiable"*—so
sweet, so courteous, so amiable. And Philippa was thought to

be a person of moral substance as well. Her sagacity and her humility were lauded, and also her profuse maternity—bearing Edward nine children who survived infancy. She was praised on all these counts for her intercession with the angry Edward on behalf of the doomed burghers of Calais, whom the king had condemned to death in punishment for the city's resistance, and on that occasion her status as a woman obviously well along in pregnancy lent gravity to her plea. Froissart, exclaiming on his own behalf but also summarizing the views of her subjects, compares her with Arthur's Guinevere: "Since the time of Queen Guinevere, consort to King Arthur and Queen of England, then known as Great Britain, no such gracious queen had entered into the land, or received such honor."

Of course, this comparison with Guinevere cuts several ways, and one imagines Philippa both as a good queen and as one who knew how to have a good time. Edward and Philippa's court was marked by its penchant for lavish consumption and frivolous display. At great expense, she sought fabrics from Ghent, Ypres, Malines, and Louvain, and was a frequent purchaser of ribbons, taffetas, and other materials suitable for brilliant toilettes, rich headdresses, and outlandish coiffures. At one point Edward III paid five hundred pounds—the equivalent of several hundred thousand dollars today—for a single dress for Philippa in observance of St. George's Day, together with other lavish expenditures on embroidered clothes and fine jewelry. Later in the century, one English chronicler would engage in a rant on this subject, accusing men of the court of going about in gowns and looking more like women than men, especially when seen from behind, and wearing fancy paltocks (the garment with which the countess of Ulster rewarded the young Chaucer at the beginning of his courtly career) and pointy-toed shoes called "crakowes" that were more like demons' claws than proper male ornaments. From whatever perspective it is viewed, the Hainault-influenced court, itself enjoying Holy Roman Empire connections with the pretentiously elegant court of Bohemia, was undoubtedly a center of fashion and a point of dispersal for varied foreign influences.

These Hainaulters were, in other words, a racy crowd. As the Chandos Herald, an up-to-date commentator on the times and himself of Hainault origins, has it, Philippa surrounded herself with lively young women in festive circumstances: a gathering of ladies and damsels "Most amorous, spirited and fair" (*"Tres amoureuse, frike et bele"*). They amused themselves, he continues, with dancing and hunting and hawking, great festivities and jousts, just as in the reign of Arthur. He is describing an event of midcentury, Edward's triumphant return to the English court, and the celebrations that followed his military success at Poitiers, occurrences of the decade before Chaucer and Philippa joined the king and queen's chamber. But even though Philippa was not yet among the *frike* damsels, there is no reason to suppose that the atmosphere had much changed upon her arrival. *Frike* is etymologically connected with our modern English "frisky," and throughout the medieval centuries the ladies of Hainault were thought to play it fast and loose. Marie de Saint-Hilaire (whose name marks her as an immigrant from the region) was a member of the queen's household and an early contestant for John of Gaunt's favors, bearing his first illegitimate son. In the fifteenth century Jacqueline of Hainault alternately enthralled and bored Humphrey, duke of Gloucester, with her antics, imprisonments, cross-dressed escapes, military exertions, and legendary allure. In the sixteenth century Anne Boleyn, great-granddaughter of Renaud de Boulen, a knight of Hainault in the service of Edward III, made a mark of her own. But all this brings us to Katherine Swynford, née de Roet, Philippa Chaucer's sister, who was rivaled only by the senile Edward III's dissolute mistress Alice Perrers as the preeminently scandalous lady of her time.

"Katerina"

Philippa's sister Katherine gave crucial impetus to both Philippa's and Geoffrey's careers. Katherine established a beachhead in the household of John of Gaunt in 1365, followed by Philippa's ascent to the queen's chamber in 1366 as well as Geoffrey's nearly concurrent advancement to esquire of the king's household soon after. Philippa's and Geoffrey's initial appointments were probably on their own merits rather than owing to Katherine, but in the years following, Katherine would position herself to bestow some real family favors.

Katherine's leverage revolved around her relations with the powerful and controversial Duke of Lancaster, John of Gaunt. Gaunt was the most talked about and reviled man in all of England. So named because he was born in the city of Ghent and the third son of Edward III and Queen Philippa, he was in the absolute forefront of public discussion from the mid-1370s, when the death of the Black Prince and the prospect of his young son Richard succeeding to the crown raised the suspicion that his uncle Gaunt coveted the crown. As Edward's oldest surviving son and the wealthiest man in England, owing to his inheritance of the far-flung Lancastrian estates through his first wife Blanche, his was a formidable claim. Even when acting in sporadic support of the young king Richard, and even when off seeking the throne of Castile after his second marriage to Constanza, daughter of the deposed monarch Pedro the Cruel, he never escaped suspicion in his native land. He was controversial even in death, when Richard seized his estates and barred the return of his exiled son, Henry of Derby—the final, drastic miscalculation that would cost Richard his throne.

Already established within Gaunt's household, Katherine vaulted in influence in 1368 when she became governess and effective foster mother of his and his deceased wife Blanche's daughters, Philippa and Elizabeth. If she had not already caught Gaunt's eye by then, she and Gaunt would definitely become lovers soon after his return from Aquitaine, together with his new and dynastically important bride, Constanza of Castile, in 1371. Even as Gaunt presented Constanza to the city of London in February 1372, Katherine was his principal love interest, and their relationship was fully entrenched by the date of his and Constanza's daughter's birth in June 1372. The progress of their relationship is borne out in Gaunt's ducal records. His previously routine gifts and annuities to Katherine surge abruptly early in 1372 and steadily thereafter. A cash gift and two substantial annuities in March 1372 mark the new relation, followed by an expanded annuity in May 1372, title to her deceased husband's lands in June 1372, and the gift of a tun (954 liters!) of the best obtainable Gascon wine as well as additional wine of similar quality from the Rhine in January 1375, a grant of manors and tenements in July 1375 . . . and other gifts of materials, timbers, and items for the upkeep of her properties.

Gaunt's own marriage was not the only complication that the adulterous couple chose to ignore. When she became the governess of Gaunt's daughters, Katherine was already married: to one of Gaunt's retainers, Sir Hugh Swynford, a well-positioned and prosperous knight of Kettlethorpe in Lincolnshire, and they had a young son, Thomas. Froissart, who was a Hainaulter himself and well positioned to intercept relevant gossip, is quite emphatic on the commencement of the affair during Hugh Swynford's lifetime, observing that Gaunt started up with Katherine soon after his marriage to Constance, she being "also married to an English knight."

The inconvenient Swynford was a knight of Gaunt's retinue, on military service to the duke in Aquitaine in 1371–72. The Aquitaine campaign was a disaster from beginning to end, as the English lost town after town and castle after castle to the resurgent French under the leadership of the great commander Du Guesclin. Gaunt himself resigned his command and left Aquitaine in July 1371, salvaging a portion of his reputation but leaving some of his retainers, including Swynford, behind. Swynford's name appears for the last time in Gaunt's *Register* for March 1372, among those rewarded for service, and this must be reckoned the approximate date of his death. Remembering that Gaunt's romantic interest in Katherine quickened between October 1371 and February 1372—in any case, just prior to Swynford's death—we are confronted with all the elements of a David-Bathsheba situation. David is said to have urged his commander Joab to place Bathsheba's husband, Uriah, "in the front of the battle, where the fight is strongest," with instructions to "leave ye him, that he may be wounded and die" (2 Samuel 11:15), and Swynford would lose his life defending the interests of his absent lord in the muddled Aquitainian campaign. Whether his death was in some degree arranged cannot be known, but it was certainly allowed to transpire, and to transpire concurrently with Gaunt's courtship of his wife.

Katherine's term as governess to Gaunt's daughters continued for thirteen years. At some point during this term, or retrospectively, Chaucer seems to have decided to tease his sister-in-law a little. In his "Physician's Tale"—which may be one of the tales he wrote prior to the *Canterbury Tales* and then included among them—he pauses to address governesses. Speaking of chaste Virginia, he describes her youthful virtue and jocularly admonishes governesses that they should do their duty to protect such innocent charges, saying that they may have gotten their jobs because they are virtuous, or else, alternatively, that they have been frail themselves and thus know young women's deceits (*"knowen wel ynough the olde daunce"*). The past poacher of venison, he goes on to say, best knows how to guard the forest. Here we see Chaucer in a familiar vein: He loves to engage in the mock chiding of friends with whom he has the most amicable of relations. This is a familial and inner-circle variant of a style of banter at which he excels. We can take these lines, in other words, as an index of an intimate situation, one laced through with familiarity, affection, and—for added spice—a delicate hint of the edgy envy that must have accompanied the situation of mingled bounty and dependency that would have marked Philippa's and Chaucer's relations with their suddenly prosperous and prominent companion.

Chaucer's and Philippa's relations with Katherine were undoubtedly advantageous to them but involved unavoidable embarrassments as well. Katherine was a deeply unpopular, and in fact scandalous, figure throughout the realm. During the first two decades of their relationship Gaunt seems to have done little to mitigate the sensitivity of her situation and, indeed, to have seized every opportunity to throw it in the nation's face. Throughout his second marriage, to Constanza of Castile, Gaunt not only kept public company with Katherine but paraded their relationship in a series of ostentatiously public displays. The chronicler Thomas Walsingham has Gaunt courting disapproval, traveling about the country with his "Katerina," parading the relationship, throwing her together with Constanza to the latter's certain humiliation, and creating social crisis after social crisis by introducing her into the most stately households of the land.

The rudiments of Katherine's situation between 1372 and her surprising elevation through her late-life marriage to Gaunt in 1396 are clear enough, but how should her awkward position as Gaunt's publicly flaunted companion actually be captured in language? Chaucer himself thinks a lot about such things. His Manciple, on the way to Canterbury, says that he sees no difference between a cheating wife of high degree, who is nevertheless called a "lady," and a poor woman who engages in the same conduct and is called a "wench" or a *lemman*:

> There is no difference, truly,
> Between a wife of lofty social rank
> Who treats her body shabbily
> And a poor wench, other than this:
> If their behavior's equally amiss
> The gentle one of highly ranked estate
> Is still called "lady" in the terms of love
> And if the other is alone and poor
> She ends up being called a wench or whore.

> (*Ther nis no difference, trewely,*
> *Bitwixe a wif that is of heigh degree,*
> *If of hir body dishoneste she bee,*
> *And a povre wenche, oother than this—*
> *If it so be they werke bothe amis—*
> *But that the gentile, in estaat above,*
> *She shal be cleped his lady, as in love;*
> *And for that oother is a povre womman,*
> *She shal be cleped his wenche or his lemman.*)

Lemman—"lover"—is a word with common or lower-class associations, as of course "wench" is as well, and so nobody would have thought of Katherine as either. Yet, as the Manciple goes on to say, whatever she be called, "Men lay the one as low as lies the other." (*"Men leyn that oon as lowe as lith that oother"*).

Froissart says that the women of the court, scandalized by her and Gaunt's marriage, described her as his "concubine," a reasonable enough description—but Froissart is writing in French, and nobody seems to call her a concubine in either English or Latin. (It may be that in these languages the term "concubine" was restricted to a very particular situation—the female companion of a priest or other ecclesiastic who could not marry on account of his vows. She might—from the perspective of a monastic chronicler—not even have been thought worthy of this practical designation.) In any case, the monastic chroniclers who commented on her situation were prepared to mince no words. The *Anonimalle Chronicle*, written in Anglo-Norman French, describes her as *"une deblesce et enchauntresce"*—a she-devil and an enchantress, imagining her casting a spell upon the innocent, and at least sporadically repentant, duke. Walsingham chimes in with similar descriptions of devious or even impermissible arts, describing her as *pellax* (deceitful or seductive) or her conduct as *nefanda* (impious or even execrable). The best she ever does is achieve a description as "that woman" (*"illa foemina"*) or, the word "consort" not yet having entered the language, a neutral but knowing observation that Gaunt enjoys her company, or *consortium*.

The relationship with Katherine was one more provocation to a public sensibility already chafed by Gaunt's power and pride. In the tumultuous days of June 1381 now known as the Peasants' Revolt, Gaunt found himself an object of public condemnation and actual outrage from a series of causes. Only his absence from London saved him when the rebels destroyed his Savoy Palace, and he was humiliatingly forced to seek sanctuary in Scotland. He was most definitely one of the rebels' high-value victims and would have been put to death along with Chancellor Sudbury and Treasurer Hales, had they apprehended him. As it was, the rebels wasted his lands in Kent, stopped Canterbury pilgrims and made them swear to "accept no king whose name was John," burned and leveled his Savoy Palace in London, killed a Franciscan simply because he was said to be a friend of the duke, and considered him—according to the chronicler Henry Knighton—"as their most hated enemy of all mortal men."

Whether or not all the turmoil provoked him to any actual soul-searching cannot be known, but upon his return to England he certainly engaged in a demonstration of public remorse for whatever elements of his past behavior had so swung circumstances against him. One aspect of his public repentance was his decision to lessen the public visibility of his ties to Katherine. There can be no doubt that she was a significant irritant. Her foreignness, as well as her dodgy character, is what strikes chronicler Knighton, who depicts Gaunt as stewing over his relations with Katherine: "For he had, together with his wife in his household a certain foreign lady [*quandam dominam alienigenam*], Katherine de Swynford, whose relations with him were greatly suspect." That Katherine, reared if not born in England and a familiar figure in the court of Queen Philippa, should still be regarded as *alienigena*, an exotic from a strange and alien situation, might at first seem strange. But Queen Philippa's court was itself French-speaking and stylistically exotic, and must never have seemed anything but foreign to the English populace—a populace whose ordinary members had proven ready to murder dozens if not hundreds of Hainaulters and throw them in the river Ouse during the earlier disturbances at York in June.

Either from actual remorse or prudent policy, but undoubtedly more the latter than the former, Gaunt swore to remove Katherine from his household in order to restore at least one aspect of his public reputation. Certainly he went through some kind of public display of remorse. The chronicler Walsingham, who previously described Gaunt as arrogantly imposing Katherine on his subjects and peers, and even on his wife, now describes him protesting abhorrence of his consort—named as "that" Katherine or the "notorious" Katherine (*"illa Katerina"*)—and abjuring her, at least *seemingly*, with tears and expressions of grief to produce the fruits of true penance.

For all the theatricality with which Gaunt rejected his mistress, the evidence of his private conduct argues strongly that his actual feelings hadn't changed at all. Discharging her as governess to his daughters by Blanche in the late summer of 1381, Gaunt then provided her with a remarkably munificent golden parachute in the grant of a very handsome, two-hundred-pound annuity—an annuity suitable to a fully aristocratic style of life. Then, on the more sentimental or at least domestic side, he arranged for her to receive a magnificent silver *chaufour*, or chafing pan. In March 1382 he arranged for delivery of two more tuns—1,908 liters!—of Gascon wine. In October 1383 he arranged for her to receive confirmation of her right, in fee simple or without restriction, to her former husband's manor of Kettlethorpe—a consequence not easily achieved in the fourteenth century, when a widow was entitled to a third of her husband's wealth and possessions but rarely inherited land.

Katherine's acceptance in Lincolnshire, upon her return as

mistress of Kettlethorpe, was far from immediate. She confronted a full-scale local challenge less than a year after gaining control of her ex-husband's estate in 1383. In September 1384 a number of persons, including the mayor of Lincoln himself, Robert de Saltby, and two bailiffs of the city invaded her properties at Lincoln and Grantham and were later accused of carrying away goods and assaulting servants. By the end of the decade, however, Katherine was fully aboveground again and finally, when Constanza's death in 1394 created the opportunity, Gaunt took the remarkable step of marrying his former mistress. This was in 1396, when he was fifty-six and she forty-six. Soon after he secured the legitimacy of their four children, coining for them the name of Beaufort. Although the act of conferring legitimacy would not allow them succession to the throne, all of the children would be enormously important in the affairs of the realm, especially with the accession of their half brother, Henry IV, the first of the Lancastrian kings. Son John Beaufort would merge with the royal line, as great-great-grandfather of King Henry VII.

This marriage amazed—even stupefied—the whole country. Walsingham fulminated that, upon Gaunt's return from Aquitaine in 1396, he withdrew to Lincoln where "he married her, to the astonishment of all who witnessed the amazing event, since the circumstances of such a woman were quite inappropriate for marriage to a lord of such eminence" (*"quia fortuna talis femine tante sublimitatis heroi minime competebat"*). Froissart, who visited England in 1395, has the marriage gossip fully covered. He sees clearly enough that legitimization of their offspring is Gaunt's motive in this late-life marriage, and perhaps Katherine's as well. But the great ladies of the realm are scandalized, saying that the duke has massively forfeited respect and vituperated himself in this marriage and agreeing that disgrace will ensue if she is to meet the new queen of England (the putatively censorious queen in question is Richard II's deeply befuddled child bride, the six-year-old Isabella of France). They agree among themselves to shun Katherine's presence and, if she is allowed to meet the child queen and perform other duties of state, to refuse their assistance, avoiding her presence wherever she might be. Froissart re-creates the language of their haughty resolutions, in which they stand somewhere to the stern side of Cinderella's sisters:

> For great shame would come upon us if such a duchess, who comes from base lineage and was the duke's concubine through-out his marriage [*qui a esté concubine du duc ung trop long temps en ses marriage*], who, now that she is married, should surpass us! Our hearts should break with sorrow, and with good cause!

The more worldly, or more detached, Froissart sympathizes with Katherine against her detractors, observing that she remains married to Gaunt for the rest of her life, and he adds that she was "a woman who knew everything about matters of honor, because she had been well bred in her youth and throughout her life." A related anecdote conveys something of Katherine's actual savoir faire. When Katherine and Gaunt finally met with Richard's tiny bride, Gaunt gave her a lavish and high-value gift but Katherine gave her a small cup—a gift, Froissart approvingly says, befitting a child.

From a first-generation French-speaking *alienigena* and exotic to a celebrated courtesan to a duchess of the realm, grandmother of the queen of Scotland, and, eventually, ancestor of the royal family: By any standard, this is a remarkable ascent.

Striking, but not accidental; Katherine constantly managed the scaffolding of ascent with her gift for seizing advantage from any opportunities that might come her way. She repeatedly showed herself a capable administrator of her own affairs, and those of others. Once she secured her late husband's manor of Kettlethorpe and her other two manors, she was active in policing their bounds, frequently availing herself of legal remedies against trespass and hedge breaking. She became, quite evidently, a force in her community, accepting gifts from the mayor of Leicester for exerting her influence on his behalf, in 1375 and 1379. She understood ambitious schemes of consolidation and improvement, including gaining approval in 1383, in the very month in which she gained full control of her ex-husband's lands at Kettlethorpe, for the enclosure of three hundred acres of land and woods to make a park for herself.

The most remarkable evidence of her sound financial management rests in a document under the duke's own privy seal for 1386 in which Gaunt orders his receiver to pay Katherine £100, in partial settlement of 500 marks (some £350, or nearly a hundred times that in modern currency) that she "lent to the duke in his great necessity." Nobody in a position to lend money to Gaunt, the most lavishly endowed person in England, can be considered an unskilled manager of her affairs. Other evidence of her diplomacy includes her successful relations with the monks and divines who made up the governing body, or chapter, of Lincoln Cathedral. She made many gifts to the chapter, customarily bearing her personal emblem or device of the Catherine wheel, the emblem of her namesake (or else an allusion to her maiden name of Roet, Old French for "wheel," or "waterwheel"). She ended her life in a house rented from the dean and chapter, and she was buried near the high altar, where her tomb can be seen today. She arranged with the cathedral for an elaborate "Anniversary" service on the day of her death each year, and a mass was said for the repose of her soul in one of the Lincoln Cathedral chantries at 7:00 A.M. each and every day of the liturgical year, a practice still observed in cathedral records in 1545, at the brink of the elimination of all such observances in consequence of that sequence of revisionary events we know as the Reformation.

Collateral Benefits

Whatever combination of exoticism, managerial talent, sexual allure, and reliable fertility underpinned Katherine's long and apparently devoted connection with John of Gaunt, the relation was an undeniable engine of advancement for herself, for her sister Philippa, and for Philippa's husband Geoffrey as well.

Soon after the commencement of Katherine's affair, Philippa transferred her services to Gaunt's wife, Duchess Constanza. The affair had begun by spring 1372 and, on August 30, 1372, Gaunt instructed his receiver general to commence payment of an annuity of ten pounds to Philippa for services rendered, and to be rendered. This was the highest sum granted to any of the *domicellae*. For some perspective: Ten to twenty pounds was a gentleperson's good annual living in those days, and forty pounds annually was a requirement for knighthood. In May 1373 Gaunt presented Philippa (among others) with a more personal gift: a buttoner and six silver-gilt buttons. Other gifts would follow. But the most telling may be a second annuity of ten pounds. It is given jointly to Chaucer and Philippa. But in Chaucer's case for no noticeable duties: None of the common stipulations are made about service in time of war or daily household sustenance (or "bouge of court"). Nothing more was expected of Chaucer than "good and agreeable service," a catchall phrase that comes close to meaning nothing at all. The grant is undoubtedly aimed more at Philippa, who is singled out for service that "our good friend Philippa his wife has performed for our mother the queen, whom God pardon, and our much-loved companion the queen." (Gaunt is here referring first to Queen Philippa, whom Philippa Chaucer had earlier served, and second to his own notional "queen" Constanza through whom he claimed the kingship of Castile.)

This shift of responsibility to the Lancastrian entourage meant that Philippa would be spending most of her time at Gaunt's Savoy Palace in London, along with other locations in Kenilworth, Leicester, and, slightly later, Lincolnshire and Lincoln. Now alone in the royal court, principally at Windsor Castle, Chaucer appears to have taken this occasion to replot his future. Central to that calculation would be his new corridor of access to the otherwise utterly unapproachable Gaunt.

In the period 1369 to 1371—that is, just on the brink of Philippa's transfer to the Lancastrian household—Chaucer made what looks like one of his few attempts to gain favor or attract patronage through his verse. The poem, now called *The Book of the Duchess*, memorializes Gaunt's relations with his recently deceased, and evidently adored, Blanche of Lancaster, who had died in 1368. The poem's narrator, a thinly veiled stand-in for Chaucer himself, consoles an anonymous Black Knight for the loss of his dear companion, "White" (in evident allusion to Blanche). The narrator pretends to a certain obtuseness about the source of the Black Knight's sorrows, which permits the Knight to describe, and thus memorialize, her considerable array of virtues. Looking, perhaps, to his own aspirational relations with Gaunt, Chaucer's poem constructs a relation between the narrator and the Black Knight that is at once sympathetically familiar and respectful of social difference. The Black Knight, for example, addresses the narrator with the informal "thee," while the dreamer retains the more formal "ye" appropriate for a social superior. Who knows what, if anything at all, Chaucer might have felt himself able to say to John of Gaunt in real life, but the fact of the poem, and its implicit dedication to Gaunt at a time of sorrow, allow him to represent himself as a suitable member of a great lord's following, a person of discretion who can be trusted not to forget the subtle and not-so-subtle elements of tact that sustain connections between a lord and his followers.

Whether the poem was effective in securing Gaunt's interest cannot really be known. Although very possibly written with reward in mind, no reward can be shown to have resulted from it. But the poem would undoubtedly have been hatched within the atmosphere of heightened familiarity created by Katherine's incipient relationship, an atmosphere that allowed Chaucer to imagine a sympathetic tie between himself and the most powerful man in the land.

Chaucer's reward would come several years later, in 1374, but in a rather equivocal form—a patronage-based London day job (to be discussed in chapter 3) that required a good deal of work and represented something well short of unconditional bounty. Thus, while Katherine was raking it in and Philippa was doing pretty well, we find Chaucer striking out essentially on his own, but with a small and probably necessary boost reflecting Lancastrian favor. That this was *derivative* favor—mediated through Philippa and ultimately through Katherine—does not always occur to admirers of Chaucer's poetry, who naturally assume that a poet of his talent and stature would forge his own conduits of favor and grace. But recognition of Chaucer as a national poet, and hence as something of a treasure in his own right, was far away; his poetical talents would, in 1372 or 1376, or even in 1386, be little known and irrelevant to any quest for patronage or reward.

In Search of the Chaucers

Chaucer's new job in 1374 was accompanied by a lease to quarters over Aldgate (see chapter 2) but residence in a gloomy and spartan London gatehouse was hardly Philippa's style. All evidence suggests that she took advantage of the new family circumstances afforded by Katherine's relations with Gaunt by removing herself to Lincoln, and most probably to Kettlethorpe itself. In the company of her sister, Philippa would have had a receptive social circle of her own. Moreover, this location presented a ready-made educational and social opportunity for their three children, especially Chaucer's son Thomas, who would go on to become an intimate of the future Henry IV and an indispensable servant of the Lancastrian cause. Thomas, born in or around 1367, was the same age as Henry of Derby, and also close in age to another key Lancastrian, Thomas Swynford, Katherine's son by her first husband. In the environs of Kettlethorpe, and in Gaunt's nearby estate at Leicester, Philippa would, in fact, have had something like a family atmosphere, as Katherine gave birth to four slightly younger Beaufort cousins.

But even if Kettlethorpe and its environs offered something like a family circle, Chaucer appears not to have been much involved in its affairs. Of his and Philippa's three children, Thomas—a prominent Lancastrian and eventual speaker of Parliament—would never stray from the orbit of the extended Lancastrian household. The adult Thomas uses his father's seal on just one occasion (with the legend "S' Gofrai Chaucier") in a document connected with his residence at Ewelme, but his tomb bears the de Roet arms, and his identifications were more likely with his mother's and aunt's associates and ancestors. Chaucer dedicates his "Treatise on the Astrolabe" to a second son, Lewis—"Little Lowys my sone"—to whom he attributes an interest in sciences touching on numbers and proportions. A further record places Lewis in Lancastrian military service with Thomas in Wales in 1403, but nothing further connects him and his father. And an Elizabeth Chausier, who was probably his daughter, was made a nun in Barking Abbey in 1381 and received a substantial gift from John of Gaunt on that occasion—again suggesting that Chaucer's little household was something of a Lancastrian protectorate.

Evidence places Philippa in Lincolnshire between 1379 and her death in 1387, and nothing suggests that she shared a dwelling with Chaucer. An entry of November 6, 1379, from John of Gaunt's *Register*, authorizes Philippa (this time described simply as "damoiselle Philipe Chaucey" rather than as wife of Geoffrey Chaucer) to receive her annuity from Gaunt's receiver general in Lincolnshire. So too with her 1379 annuity from the crown, paid to "P. Chaucer" by W. de Spain, sheriff of Lincolnshire. She might, of course, have simply been in Lincolnshire on a visit. Later annuities were paid, as before, in London, with Chaucer picking them up on Philippa's behalf (with his own hand, *per manus Galfridi*), and this apparent arrangement argues for some kind of amiable, or at least beneficial, arrangement between the two. But the evidence points toward a long-term separation, with Philippa mainly in Lincolnshire and Leicestershire and Chaucer (except for a few periods of diplomatic absence) almost entirely in London.

A conspicuous event goes a long way toward explaining some

of the pressures on the marriage. On February 19, 1386, a distinguished group gathered in the splendid chapter house of Lincoln Cathedral. The ceremony that drew them there was an initiation of nine noteworthy candidates into the lay fraternity of the cathedral. Membership would confer tangible ritual benefits, including prayers, services, and intercessions after death. Moreover, membership in the fraternity was itself a considerable social distinction. Edward III had belonged, and his son John of Gaunt, and the very next year Richard II and Queen Anne would come to Lincoln expressly to join. The cathedral chapter house was an appropriately impressive venue. Built in the second quarter of the thirteenth century, this spectacularly vaulted structure had already been host to a century and a half of significant ceremonies, including a meeting of Parliament in 1301 and a notorious show trial during the early fourteenth-century prosecution of the Knights Templar. A description of the February 19 event, and its roster of participants, was deemed worthy of preservation in the records of the cathedral chapter.

Presiding over this event is John of Gaunt, arrayed in all his titles as duke of Lancaster and as king of Castile. His son—Henry of Derby, the future Henry IV—will be the principal initiate, together with a modestly distinguished group consisting mainly of young men. Although the group undoubtedly includes several friends, friendship with Henry is not its criterion of selection. A careful look at its composition reveals a different rationale: Most of its members are present by virtue of their tacit connection with Katherine Swynford, who appears to have had a strong hand in composing the guest list.

In addition to Henry, the initiates include his illegitimate half brother John Beaufort, oldest of the four children conceived within Gaunt and Katherine's long-standing relation. Also present is Sir Robert Ferrers, engaged to marry, or recently married to, Gaunt and Katherine's daughter Joan. This rather tenuous or provisional family circle is further enlarged by the addition of Sir Thomas Swynford, Katherine's son by her earlier marriage. Thomas would serve Henry throughout his career, ever available for tasks both legitimate and illegitimate, most notably his obliging murder of Richard II while serving as the deposed king's custodian at Pontefract Castle. Looking beyond Katherine's family circle into the sphere of her considerable Lincolnshire influence, the initiates also include Sir William Hawley, a mature knight of Lincolnshire and justice of the peace, who served worthily on local commissions. He might seem a slightly stodgy old-timer in this company, but surviving documents of Lincolnshire court cases record his good service to Katherine in varied and frequent litigations against recalcitrant tenants and trespassers on the Lincolnshire estates to which she enjoyed title by virtue of Gaunt's interventions. And, among this group of Katherine's close relatives and adherents, a further name remains.

Last named in this list of future *fratres*, or brothers, is Philippa Chaucer, a sole woman among men. Although Philippa enjoys a reputable social niche as a former *damoiselle* in Queen Philippa's household, that status alone would not explain her appearance in this elite company. Philippa is present not as the wife of the still obscure Chaucer but as Katherine Swynford's sister. Katherine herself may have been absent, or at any rate unnamed, for reasons of tact. Not yet possessed of the nominal or titular respectability and status she will gain after Constanza's death, as the third duchess of Lancaster, she may have been avoiding the limelight for reasons of reputation. This is all the more important because Gaunt has just gained parliamentary approval for his Castilian expedition, and his aspirational kingship—claimed on the basis of his relation with Constanza—is looming particularly large. In the meantime, with Katherine remaining behind the scenes, Philippa is an excellent placeholder. But where, on this signal occasion, is Chaucer?

The record names a dozen illustrious persons in attendance. Additionally, it mentions the presence of a great multitude of onlookers (*pluribusque aliis in multitudine copiosa*). Possibly Chaucer, up from London, is there, in this throng or "abundant multitude," but—as a former king's esquire and present minor official in the wool custom—too small a fry to warrant mention in any of this document's categories of consideration. Those joining the fraternity are all his social superiors, including a lord, knights, and esquires on a path to knighthood. Even Philippa, as daughter of a knight and a *damoiselle*, or lady of the court closely associated with the queen, outranks him. And so he might have been there, under the radar, taking advantage of standing room to witness this ratification of his wife's latest social advancement, but he more likely remained in London. Even though he now had the services of a deputy in customs, his life remained London-centered, and he still had unavoidable duties there.

Even if Chaucer had made the trip and was stationed somewhere in the crowd of miscellaneous onlookers, this is a moment when the divergence of his and Philippa's worlds was on full display. This was Philippa's apotheosis, the moment when the eminence of her connections was ritually confirmed and exhibited to the world. Chaucer stood on the brink of a year that would end in his disparagement and virtual exile. The remainder of his London year, with all its travails, would be lived without the consolations that a more intimate marriage might be imagined to provide.

Must this evidence of his and Philippa's divergent worlds be interpreted as proof of his marital unhappiness? This conclusion would become inevitable if we were to weigh the additional evidence of Chaucer's poetry in the balance. Within his poetry the liabilities of marriage are unsparingly explored, and its benefits universally derided. A prevailing theme throughout the poetry is, in the words of the Wife of Bath, "the woe that is in marriage." The Canterbury tales on marital themes—often called his "marriage group" of tales—are an unrelenting catalog of mistakes, misapprehensions, and woes. The Wife of Bath militarizes the marriage bed and requires spousal submission as a precondition for sexual favors and other forms of amity. Walter, the psychotically severe husband of the "Clerk's Tale," cruelly abuses his wife, Griselda, under the alibi of testing her virtue, driving her to passive-aggression and other weapons of the weak. The fulsome endorsement of marriage as a "great sacrament," spoken by the Merchant at the beginning of his tale of sexual exploitation and betrayal in marriage, morphs into embittered and ironic dispraise. The Franklin's knight Arveragus proposes that his wife, Dorigen, sleep with another man, as an ostensible vindication of an oath she has innocently made but in actual augmentation of his own honor. The most judicious commentator of all, the wise Justinus in the "Merchant's Tale," describes marriage as a purgatory on Earth.

Closest, perhaps, to a personal comment on marriage might be a verse epistle that Chaucer addressed to a friend considering marriage. It was evidently composed after Philippa's death in 1387—and probably, from its blithe tone, several years after that date—in which he swears never to fall into the "dotage" of marriage again. And of course he never did, spending the last months of his life within the precincts of Westminster Abbey, in one of the least marital possible situations. Still, this is an "occasional" poem, the occasion is a fourteenth-century bachelor party, and its motive is one of playful chiding rather than reportage. Even here, in this most apparently autobiographical of his pronouncements on marriage, the character of his sentiments is more closely related to the genre and purpose of the particular poem he is writing than to any kind of documentary or personally revelatory motive. Literary tradition rather than veiled autobiography seems to undergird most of Chaucer's antimarital sentiments. The strictures of the Wife of Bath's last husband Jankyn—wives as leaky roofs and sputtering fires and that sort of thing—are, for example, based on writings that go all the way back to the Sumerian *Epic of Gilgamesh* and the invention of writing itself. The realities of Chaucer's marriage must be sought in his own life details rather than in his literary creations.

Separation alone—especially voluntary separation in pursuit of different career objectives—does not necessarily argue for marital unhappiness. Chaucer and Philippa appear to have maintained a cooperative relationship, borne out in such matters as their arrangement for her annuity cheques. Cautiously appraised, their marriage must be judged a kind of détente, a cooperative alignment pursued for mutual convenience and advantage.

This is not to deny that Philippa might at times have experienced disappointment in the match she had made. Judged from the perspective of 1386, her social luster considerably exceeded that of her civil servant husband. Since leaving the royal court he had been living a rather bourgeois existence of waterfront connivance and record keeping by day and solitary poetic endeavor by night. In 1386 no evidence exists of his yet having circulated any of his verse, and if he had, it would have been to a handful of associates in highly select circumstances. In any case, he hadn't earned a documentable groat from his efforts. Besides, the poetry that he was writing had what some readers might have found an unnerving tendency to slide over into parody, jest, or other forms of belittlement. It was not for all tastes and not a certain success among Philippa's friends. Indeed, their literary preferences were more likely to be francophone than English, and they might well have maintained some reserve toward Chaucer's approachable and unforbidding style. Little wonder if, amid the atmosphere of social ascent and boundless opportunity with which she was suddenly confronted, Philippa concluded that her married life was holding her back, consigning her to a situation beneath her expectations and desires.

With respect to Chaucer's literary endeavors, the pattern of his writings (to be surveyed in chapter 5) suggests that he launched his first extended works in the dozen years of his and Philippa's separation, between 1374 and 1386. Then, conceiving the *Canterbury Tales* in the troubled closing months of 1386, he actually began to write in the year of Philippa's death, 1387. Theories might be spun from the relationship of these two events— Philippa's death and Chaucer's embrace of his most ambitious literary undertaking—but without any foundation in evidence. What *can* be said is that Chaucer's literary career appears to have been conducted independently of the marriage, flourishing and then surging in periods of absence and separation rather than during those of conjugal intimacy.

CHAPTER TWO

Aldgate

~~~~~~~~~~

For the twelve years prior to his departure for Kent in October 1386, Chaucer had lived over Aldgate, the easternmost and busiest of the city's seven gates. There, literally under his feet, passed royal and religious processions, spectacles of public humiliation, expelled convicts and sanctuary seekers, provisioners and trash haulers with iron-wheeled carts and vans, drovers, water and wood sellers, traders with Baltic and northern European luxuries, runaway serfs, Essex rebels flowing in on their way to burn Gaunt's Savoy Palace in 1381, and all the rest of a busy city's shifting populace. . . . Surely no residence more fitting could be imagined for a poet whose subject was soon to become, as Dryden would put it, "God's plenty."

Departing, he almost certainly knew that he wouldn't return. On October 4, the city's common council would act to repossess his gatehouse. By October 5 Chaucer was out, and a new tenant had been named. When Parliament ended seven weeks later he would withdraw to Kent, a move that had been a year in the making. He would never again live continuously in the city of his birth. Preparing to leave the city with which we identify him, he would have had good reason to wonder whether he had ever well and truly been a Londoner at all. Yet his twelve years at Aldgate had immersed him intensively in London affairs. Nothing tags him as an unusually ardent participant in city life; some evidence suggests the reverse. But he was an inevitable sharer and beneficiary of the complex and enveloping experience a metropole offers to each of its residents. A re-creation of his Aldgate life will suggest the extremity of the dislocation he was about to experience as a result of his removal from London after the crisis of 1386.

Above Aldgate

From Temple Bar on the west round to the Tower on the east (and intermittently along the north bank of the Thames), the city was encompassed by thick stone walls that dated to Roman times and were periodically repaired and augmented until they lapsed into military obsolescence in the seventeenth century. Substantial sections can still be viewed in the vicinity of the Tower, especially off Coopers Row, and to the north near the present Museum of London. (The visible section closest to Chaucer's location at Aldgate—a section he would have routinely passed on his way to work at the Wool Wharf—can now be seen at the point where Jewry Street gives way to Crutched Friars Street, in the Bar 2AD at 2 Crutched Friars, a slightly louche urban meet-up spot with couches for recumbent drinking and a colored light machine illuminating the wall itself.)

In facilitation of access and trade, the wall was penetrated by seven fortified gates, each flanked for defensive purposes by gatehouse turrets, or towers. These towers were built to enhance the security of the city, with no thought of providing rooms for people like Geoffrey Chaucer. The towers were secure points in their own right, with crenellated roofs that commanded the approaches, arrow and gun slits, and rooms for the storage of weaponry and, when necessary, accommodation of watchmen or soldiers. The connecting space between the towers was normally devoted to the operations of the portcullis—the latticed metal or wood grille raised at daybreak and lowered at nightfall that permitted a degree of oversight and control over who and what entered or left the city.

Aldgate served its military and strategic purposes well. From the time of its reconstruction in the early thirteenth century until its replacement in a more classical and less functional style in 1606–1609, it was breached only twice. One breach occurred during Chaucer's occupancy, during the Rising of 1381. Accusations flew at that time about various aldermen having betrayed the city, but the thousands of angry rebels streaming in from East Anglia and Essex, aided by numerous bands of journeymen and other angry sympathizers within the city, would have achieved entry one way or another. Chaucer, in residence at the time, probably knew the particular details of the intrusion from his well-connected city friends, and from neighborhood gossip, but he was not personally suspected or questioned in the matter. The other occurred in 1471 when a dissident styling himself the Bastard of Falconbridge assailed the city. He made inroads at Aldgate, but apparently by the design of its defenders. He and some of his men forced an entry through the gate before its portcullis was lowered to trap them inside, where they were taken and slain.

During the course of the fourteenth century the aldermen of the city got the practical idea of renting or leasing unneeded space over the city gates. Several motives might be served: either profit (from rent payers such as Chaucer's predecessors, Walter Parmenter and his wife, Joanna), or reward for city employees (such as Chaucer's friend Strode, the legal counsel or common pleader of the city of London), or else to curry favor with the royal party and other influential interests by providing rent-free quarters for sponsored persons (such as Chaucer himself). Like good London housing in any period, these rooms were certainly sought after, though they can hardly be considered luxurious. They were built for military occupancy and remained rough-hewn, nonprivate, and essentially unimproved in character. Chaucer's own habitation was cramped, cold, rudimentary in its sanitary arrangements, and (perhaps most seriously in the case of a writer) ill lit, even at midday.

Chaucer's Aldgate lease is preserved in those repositories of city business, the *Letter-Books*, as a matter of official record. The mayor and aldermen grant him lifelong and rent-free "the whole dwelling over Aldgate [*totam mansionem supra portam de Algate*], including the rooms built over the gate [*cum domibus superedificantis*] and with a cellar on its east side." So described, this dwelling sounds as if it might have been rather grand. Upon closer consideration, though, Chaucer's situation over Aldgate turns out to be far from lavish in its appointments.

The lease describes this dwelling as a "mansion," but in its Latin sense of "place to live" and without the connotation of grandeur attached to the modern word. *Domibus*, describing Geoffrey's actual apartment, is plural, and has an effect of something like "rooms," although its plural form is unspecific and may share the sense of words like "lodgings" or "quarters," which are plural in form but do not necessarily refer to more than one room. His predecessor's lease in fact refers to the dwelling in the singular and in its military sense, as one turret (*una turrela*), a single tower on the south side of the gate. We may suppose that this was Chaucer's dwelling as well. As a turret or tower it contained two rooms—one at ground level and one on the upper or first floor, but Chaucer's use would almost certainly have been restricted to the first-floor room, together with a *celarius* or storage area below and to the east of the tower. His own lease restricts him to everything *supra*, or "over," the gate, and necessarily so. Documents of the history and use of the gatehouse leave little doubt that the ground-floor rooms were strictly functional and unavailable for private use, affording practical space for the city Watch in peacetime, troops in wartime, armaments for the gatehouse itself, and, more than likely, accommodation for the wardens of the gate. Assuming that the ground-floor room was out-of-bounds and never considered for Chaucer's use, what then remains above?

The character and dimensions of the first-floor room can be reconstructed from a painstaking sketch map drawn for other purposes altogether. The great Holy Trinity Priory, adjoining the Aldgate property to the north and west, was slated for sale and liquidation following the sixteenth-century dissolution of the monasteries, and in 1585 one John Symonds (a joiner by trade but an exacting draftsman) was hired to prepare a map in order to facilitate the monastery's liquidation and either destruction or sale. A thorough worker, Symonds includes the city walls and moat in his drawing, and, unnecessarily for his purpose but usefully for ours, includes on its upper right-hand corner a scale representation of Aldgate's north tower. The two towers were presumably mirror images of each other, and information about the north tower room almost certainly applies to Chaucer's south tower room as well. The archaeological footprint of the Aldgate towers has them at some twenty-six feet in diameter, an apparently generous dimension. The thickness of the tower walls must, however, now be reckoned in. The Symonds map (together with measurements taken at the still surviving Westgate of Canterbury) permits a calculation. Aldgate's ground-floor walls would have been eight or nine feet thick and its first-floor walls at least five feet in thickness. Taking the exterior dimension as twenty-six feet, and subtracting ten feet for the first-story walls, an interior of about sixteen by fourteen feet may be supposed. Given the necessity of the portcullis and its mechanism between, and the difficulty of transit from tower to tower and probable needs of Aldgate to store weaponry and provide for an occasional garrison, Chaucer probably confined his activities to this single, modest-sized south tower room.

This was an undeniably spartan room. Perhaps the most striking revelation of the Symonds map is that its sole natural illumination would have been provided by two (or at most four) arrow slits, each widening within to some three feet to allow access and defensive use but then tapering to a very small aperture amounting only to four or five inches in the exterior stone wall of the tower. These slits may, by charity, be called windows, but only barely so. Light, even at midday, would have been extremely feeble. Arrangement for a small open fire might have been possible. Waste would be hand-carried down to the ditch that lapped against the tower and dumped there. Meals would not ordinarily have been cooked there; the London practice of the day was to eat on the run, at open kitchens or in taverns, with bread and other cooked food purchased directly from streetside ovens—in his case, probably alongside the city walls in the relatively open area on the city side of Aldgate.

Although modest in its comforts, the Aldgate accommodation did boast one possible amenity: access to the tower's crenellated roof, affording a view of open fields and the rather imposing parish church of St. Botolph's to the east, the Tower to the south, and the formidable spire of St. Paul's to the west. In his *Troilus*, completed earlier in 1386, Chaucer showed himself to be something of a laureate of gates and towers and their functioning and the vistas they afford—although, in that case, to rather somber effect. Troilus, counting down the days of his beloved Criseide's return from the Greek camp, climbs to one of the gates of Troy to look vainly out over the road stretching in that direction. In the process of his description, Chaucer shows several different kinds of rather precise familiarity with the tower and the gatehouse, and with city life. First, Troilus and Pandarus mount "the walles of the town" to see if they can view Criseide's approach. They strain their eyes on the distance, thinking each approaching person might be her, until they realize it is not. At noon—about an hour past the customary mealtime—Pandarus proposes that they go dine and then return, to which Troilus silently accedes. Upon their return, they wait until evening approaches, and, with it, the imminent closing of the gates. In his concern, he explains to Pandarus that he will speak to the porters, asking them by his prerogative as a prince of Troy to hold open the gate. But still no Criseide. Troilus deludes himself once; he thinks he sees her coming:

> "Trust me, I see her coming, there she is!
> Raise up your eyes, man! Can you not see?"

> (*"Have here my trouthe, I see hire! Yond she is!*
> *Heve up thin eyen, man! Maistow nat se?"*)

Pandarus answers that he sees nothing coming but a "fare cart," a provision cart or commercial vehicle. Finally, even Troilus must yield:

> The warden of the gates began to call
> The folk still lingering outside,

And bade them move their cattle all inside,
Or all the night they must remain out there.

(The warden of the yates gan to calle
The folk which that withoute the yates were,
And bad hem driven in hir bestes all,
Or al the night they moste bleven there.)

The porters, the warden of the gates, the closing of the portcullis at the end of day: Chaucer plainly knows a thing or two about the life surrounding a city gate and the traffic through it.

The down-to-earth touch of a provision cart or fare cart not only marks the death of Troilus's hopes but also serves as a reminder that the tower of a city gate (and especially a heavily trafficked one) exists for practical and commercial reasons rather than scenic admiration or touristic enjoyment. Soberly considered, Aldgate and its roof-deck would have presented its resident with numerous and challenging disadvantages.

One was sheer racket. The gates of the city, including Aldgate, were closed at darkness or by the hour of 6:00 P.M. in winter and by 9:00 at the latest in summer. They were reopened at first light and, in any case, even in winter by 6:00 A.M. Thereafter, the creak of iron-wheeled carts in and out of the city, drovers' calls, and the hubbub of merchants and travelers pressing for advantage on a wide but still one-laned road, probably made sleep impossible, five-foot walls or no five-foot walls. Moreover, merchants and drovers customarily stationed themselves for early morning access or exit, camping in the road outside the gate overnight, seeking precedence when opening time came. The city letter-books enable some reconstruction of typical traffic through the gates. Despite the presence of wells and conduits within the city, water was mostly trucked in, dispensed by specialists known as "water-leders." Other imports included varied construction materials, including tiles and sand and clay, together with produce, such as wheat, barley, bran, capons, and rabbits, and trade items, such as pewter pots. Special tolls and taxes were charged, with the proceeds to be applied to street repair, and an ordinance from 1376–77 specifies collection of:

> twopence a week on every iron-bound cart bringing victuals to the city by way of Algate, and every cart and car (*curtena*) bringing blood and entrails of slaughtered beasts entering the city or returning the same way; a penny a week on every cart or car not iron-bound bringing dung, etc; and a halfpenny a week on every horse laden with grain, etc, the money to be expended on the repair of the highway outside Algate.

This and other traffic would have passed under Chaucer's feet every day, starting at 6:00 A.M. or, in summer, earlier still.

Meanwhile, a stench wafted from the open sewer known in its northern extension as Houndsditch that ran (or festered) just outside the city wall, contributing modestly to the wall's deterrent force, since nobody in his right mind would consider wading it. (Although the city records do contain mention of one unfortunate who, seeking to bathe in the doubtful waters of the ditch, drowned there.) Now a paved-over street, Houndsditch retains its colorful name, alternately described as deriving from the kennels that were once located on its northern bank, adjacent to the hunting areas and open fields to the north of the city, or referring to the carcasses of dead dogs that were routinely dumped there. Either way, one may be certain that it stank to high heaven. Even aside from rotting garbage, dead dogs, and the occasional human corpse, it was loaded with fecal waste. The Holy Trinity Priory maintained an extensive latrine that ran alongside and jutted over the ditch, for its monks' convenience in relieving themselves, and Holy Trinity was, in the fourteenth century, a populous foundation.

And then there was the matter of felons' and traitors' rotting heads. Gatehouse towers were, in established traditions, the place for the display of severed heads of traitors and other notorious criminals. Aldgate was not the premier fourteenth-century place for this purpose; London Bridge was the preferred site. Yet any city gate could be put to this use, and in subsequent centuries Aldgate became a favored place for such displays. All the sixteenth-century sketches and renditions of the gate show it well arrayed in traitors' heads, mounted on special scaffolds for display. And so already in the 1370s and 1380s, Chaucer, taking the air, might have had problematic company there.

Nor did the apartment's interior promise much relief. Chaucer's lease reminds us that his quarters were subject to regular visits from the chamberlain of the guildhall to verify the state of maintenance (and to oust him in case of noncompliance). The city agrees not to use it as a jail during his occupancy but insists that civic officials shall have the right to enter the dwelling and its rooms for defensive purposes and to use them as they see fit ("*disponere et ordinare pro eodem tempore prout nobis melius tunc videbitur expedire*"). That is, Chaucer's flat, or at least all of its surrounding space, was available for quartering troops, storing provisions and military supplies, and the like. Even in times of peace and tranquillity, city regulations provide that six persons are to constitute the watch of Aldgate ward (undoubtedly using the gatehouse as their center of operations) and two sergeants keep guard over the gates by day, "lying by night in or near the gates"—most probably in Aldgate's own lower room, or else nearby. These sergeants were assigned a variety of duties, including preventing the entrance of lepers to the city, collecting tolls and monies for wall and road repair, and refusing admission to runaway serfs from the countryside who, if they successfully entered the city and dwelled there for a year, would have been granted de facto freedom of the city.

So much for routine. But in exceptional times, times of perceived military emergency, activity surged. The sergeants or wardens were responsible for mustering twenty-four men of the ward to be in arms to guard the gate. In 1377, for example, the death of Edward III sparked fears of a French invasion, and the common council hurried up and approved legislation mandating fortification of all city gates with portcullises and chains, and that extra fortifications called barbicans (*barbykanes*) be constructed in front of them. Residents were told to be ready to defend the city "in herneys," or military harness, and two persons were appointed from each neighborhood to keep the city gates. This latter precaution was not wholly fanciful. Perturbed over the entry of the rebels from East Anglia and Essex in 1381, London officials instituted additional security precautions during the meeting of Parliament later that year. The alderman of Aldgate was instructed to guard the gate with ten armed men, and daily guards were to be placed at all city gates during the open hours between 6:00 A.M. and 8:00 P.M., when the keys were to be placed in safekeeping.

In the months leading up to the 1386 Parliament all London was in a state of panic over a rumored invasion by the French. The chronicler Walsingham says that "they were timid as frightened as hares, and as timid as mice." They rush about for a siege:

Like men drunk with wine, they rushed to the walls of the city, wrecked the houses that were next to them, pulled them down, and destroyed them, and did everything in a state of panic . . . Not a single Frenchman had yet stepped into a boat, not one enemy soldier had put to sea, yet the people of London were in a state of such fear and agitation, that one might have thought the whole land in every region had been overwhelmed and conquered, and they were observing the enemy at their very doors.

All this occurred during Chaucer's last months in his quarters over Aldgate. Whether or not any adjacent buildings were demolished he would, according to his lease, have been responsible for quartering persons (six of whom had already been chosen) from the Aldgate ward who were responsible for the city's defense. His last days over Aldgate would have been crowded ones.

With all their discomforts, and the varied demands placed upon them, the gatehouse towers were certainly not built as luxury accommodations. Nor were they particularly needed for that purpose in the decades immediately following the midcentury Black Death, when numerous properties in the city stood vacant and the aldermen discussed various schemes for repopulation and in-migration. Occupancy seems to have increased in the last quarter of the century, though, and others were living above various gates when Chaucer moved to Aldgate. Some were rent payers and others were city employees of a middle status—common sergeants, pleaders, esquires of the mayor, and such persons. On a handful of occasions, including this one, king and council seem to have intervened on behalf of a member of the king's household and arranged for a favored party to occupy an apartment rent-free. We can get an impression of the worth of this perquisite from the cases of those who paid. The characteristic amount was 13s. 4d. per annum, a modest sum when compared with Chaucer's own normal income. Chaucer's friend Ralph Strode, a legal officer in city employment, was ousted from his apartment over Aldersgate in the course of a factional struggle and, when restored to favor, was awarded compensation of four marks per annum for his loss—a sum worth four or five times the apartment's apparent value but perhaps a form of political reward rather than a strict measure of his loss.

Chaucer's might be thought a middling property—something of a coup, in that others were paying rent for a similar privilege, but still short of luxurious accommodation. Nor does it appear to have been a "family" accommodation. Not only is Philippa's name omitted from the lease, but it seems not to have been her kind of establishment by any reckoning. Its rough-cut stone walls, its narrow arrow slits, its smelly ditch, and its generally defensive and civic character were ill-suited to the tastes of a classy and upwardly mobile lady, or, for that matter, to the emerging tastes of his socially ambitious son Thomas.

Around Aldgate

Chaucer didn't really choose his location over Aldgate. His supporters in the court and their counterparts in the city arranged it for him, and it happened to be one of the several properties that the city had within its gift. It nevertheless seems a convenient symbol of his entire London experience: rather blatantly public in some respects, yet quite private and defended in others. On the one hand, a site of intense activity—a noisy, vital conduit to the city and a focus of festivities, civil broils, and lively scenes of daily life. On the other hand, a place of withdrawal and retreat—a thick-walled, cold, and sparsely lit room up an awkward circular flight of stone stairs, perched on the edge of things, in an anything but fashionable quarter dominated by looming monastery walls.

To the extent that he portrays himself within his verse, Chaucer leaves no doubt about his inclination toward privacy. He announces, and finds mirth in, his own disposition as an onlooker and reluctant participant who removes himself from situations and avoids the public eye. In Chaucer's poem on the varieties of love, the *Parliament of Fowls*, his narrator hesitates before a description of love's perplexities above the gates of Venus's garden. His guide shoves him through, saying that he needn't worry, that this writing concerns lovers and therefore has nothing to do with him (*"this writing nis nothing ment by thee"*). He is, rather, like a spectator at a wrestling match who can enjoy the spectacle even if he is unfit to participate (*"Many a man that may nat stonde a pul / Yet liketh him at wrastling for to be"*). So too, in *Troilus*, does Chaucer disclaim any capacity for the passions he will describe, saying that he merely serves the servants of the god of love, that he wouldn't dare to pray for success in love, since he is so unqualified (*"I, that God of Loves servantz serve, / Ne dar to Love, for min unliklynesse / Preyen for speed"*). Among the Canterbury Pilgrims he is once again a bystander, a shy nonparticipant who has been observing much but saying little. Harry Bailly, as the pilgrimage's master of ceremonies, settles his gaze on Chaucer, whom he has evidently not previously noticed, and finds him an enigma. What kind of man are you, he asks (*"What man artow?"*) using, in the Middle English, the familiar "thou" rather than the more formal "you" to express a slight disdain. He goes on to suggest that Chaucer gazes at the ground as if he is looking for rabbits, that he is plump about the middle and as huggable as a little doll, with an "elfish" look that conveys a slightly mysterious reserve.

Closest to Chaucer's actual circumstances is the narrator of his *House of Fame*; he possesses a job keeping accounts in something like the customs house and returns home at night to a solitary dwelling. This narrator encounters an officious Eagle who calls him by name, Geffrey, and sets out to remedy his various deficiencies. One is that Geffrey simply doesn't know much, that he lacks gossip and "tidings," even of the people he lives among:

> You have no news at all
> About love's folk, how they have fared,
> Or anything at all that God has made.
> Not just events in foreign lands
> Remain mysterious to you,
> You don't know a thing—and hear
> Nothing else besides—about the folks
> Who dwell outside your very doors.

> (*Thou hast no tidinges*
> *Of Loves folk yif they be glade,*
> *Ne of noght elles that God made;*
> *And nought oonly fro fer contree*
> *That ther no tiding cometh to thee,*
> *But of thy verray neighebores,*
> *That duellen almost at thy dores,*
> *Thou herest neither that ne this.*)

This is, the Eagle explains, because Geffrey goes home after work and spends his time poring over books, reading silently to himself (the mark of a real bookworm in the Middle Ages, when readers usually declaimed books aloud, even if alone in a room):

> For when your labor is all done,
> And you've done all your reckonings,
> You hasten home without delay,
> And, just as dumb as any stone,
> You sit and read another book
> Until completely dazéd is your look.

> (*For when thy labour doon al is,*
> *And hast mad alle thy rekeninges,*
> *In stede of reste and newe thinges,*
> *Thou goost hom to thy hous anoon,*
> *And, also domb as any stoon,*
> *Thou sittest at another book*
> *Til fully daswed is thy look.*)

All these self-characterizations play into an idea of the artist as a dreamer or a partial recluse unfit for ordinary intercourse. But here arises the issue with everything writers say about themselves, or versions of themselves, in works of literary invention. Chaucer, a proven humorist, is plainly making fun of himself in this passage, but it's nevertheless hard to know which way the humor cuts. Perhaps he was a late-night gadabout and well-known party animal, and the joke rests in presenting himself as a recluse. More likely, though, he is telling the truth about himself: that he would rather stay in at night and ponder books than mingle with his neighbors.

This version of a privately inclined Chaucer receives additional support from his *Life-Records*, which suggest that, aside from work-related activities and his cultivation of a small literary circle, he was no joiner. Life in London presented a person of his attributes and attainments with a range of social possibilities that he leaves no record of having pursued. His failure to take up citizenship upon his return to London in 1374 is one indication of his private leaning.

To be a citizen of London in the later fourteenth century was a splendid thing. It guaranteed its possessor immunity from certain kinds of arrest and prosecution and conveyed other common rights about town, both social and commercial, as well as obligations of a typically civic sort: jury duty, ward meetings, election to common council, and the like. Citizenship was normally associated with membership in a craft guild, and craft guilds were fundamental to the social fabric of the city. Chaucer's father had been a vintner, and his father before him, and his mother, Agnes, married another vintner upon his father's death. He was raised, appropriately, in the London neighborhood known as the Vintry, consisting largely of modest homes above shops, on Thames Street, down near the river. St. Martin in the Vintry was his probable parish church. Guild membership, and progress to master, and London citizenship as a recognition of his status all presumably lay open to him, but he initially declined this option when he didn't pursue his father's trade. Even so, when he returned to London in 1374, he could have pursued any of several avenues to that goal, especially given his birth in the city and his father's status and his influential connections with Nicholas Brembre and other well-placed inhabitants. Citizenship could be purchased in a forthright arrangement and could also be arranged in connection with employment, like his job in customs. Yet he left these possibilities unrealized, declining citizenship's solaces and obligations.

And so Chaucer lived in London for a dozen years without the guarantees and emotional comforts of citizenship, in a city in which distinctions of citizen/noncitizen, freeman/nonfreeman, denizen/alien were attentively observed. Other forms of association also presented themselves, particularly those of ward (the primary unit of city government) and parish (the primary venue of London religious life). Yet in his Aldgate residence Chaucer enjoyed an unusually tenuous relation to both.

In 1386 London was governed principally via a system of twenty-four wards that varied in size and influence but each was responsible for delivering government services (and implementing taxation policies) for its residents. Nicholas Brembre and other of Chaucer's associates were endlessly interested in ward politics. Brembre and his associates intervened in 1384 to make the wards, rather than the city's crafts, the constituencies of elections to the common council, hoping the wards would exert a more conservative influence. Despite living on the boundary between two well-defined wards—Aldgate inside the gate and Portsoken beyond—Chaucer seems to have been interested in neither of them, or in the mechanics of city government that so absorbed his friends. Offices of a kingdomwide character seem to have had a bit more appeal. He would eventually serve as a justice of the peace for Kent and as a member of the county commission, and he agreed to serve one fateful term in Parliament, again for Kent rather than London. As national offices (even though constituency related) these promised contacts and rewards on a more generous scale. Mixing in city politics, even in what appeared to be the period of his associate Brembre's greatest successes, seems to have held no appeal.

Nor does any surviving evidence attest to his involvement in parish affairs. In its single square mile, among its forty thousand to fifty thousand inhabitants, London boasted one hundred parishes and parish churches, if we include a handful just outside the city walls. For most residents of later medieval England, the parish was a place of dense emotional signification. To be baptized in one's own parish church, at one's own font, was a matter of importance, and this is why the members of St. Katharine Cree, one of Chaucer's two possible parishes, were struggling with the Augustinian canons of Holy Trinity Priory to get their own font, which they would finally accomplish in 1414. Similarly, to be buried in one's churchyard was an important aspiration. A parishioner expected to pay tithes at his or her church parish, to be shriven there, to be married there, and to enact the other important stages and transitions of life there. Chaucer as poet idealizes, or perhaps sentimentalizes, the parish relation in his portrait of the humble Parson who preaches in his own church (a rarity, since many uneducated parsons were incapable of a sermon) and who cares for his own "parisshens," including the poor and sick. But, tellingly, in order to depict an ideal parish, Chaucer leaves London; in fact, he portrays the city as the enemy of the parish, opposing the virtuous Parson to the urban mass priests who flock the chantries or side chapels of St. Paul's to earn money saying prayers and services for the souls of the prosperous dead.

Chaucer's own London existence was cosmopolitan, in the sense of his having no single parish or evident connection with one. He had grown up in St. Martin in the Vintry but left there in adolescence for the courtly life he lived with the Duke of Clarence, and then in the king's rather itinerant household; he ended his life within the precincts of Westminster and was finally buried there (as a tenant of the abbey rather than as the poet around whom the Poet's Corner would ultimately be formed).

His residence in Aldgate again placed him exactly on another dividing line between two parish churches. If he faced cityward, to the west, St. Katharine Cree was there on Aldgate Street/King's Highway, its step-down entrance about three hundred yards from his door and just out of sight around the bend in the street. If he faced east, toward the countryside, he was even closer to the parish church of St. Botolph without Aldgate, barely seventy-five yards from his gate and prominently on immediate view. A sense of these spatial relations can still be derived from the location of these two churches today. St. Katharine Cree ("Creechurch," a slang abbreviation of Christ Church, the alternate name of Holy Trinity Priory) still sits, with its largely medieval tower, on the corner of Leadenhall Street and Creechurch Lane. The tower was heightened and its corners and upper elevations rebuilt with higher quality cut stone in the fifteenth century, but the body of the tower remains as it was in Chaucer's day, and is still available there to be seen on the site he would have known, one of the handful of surviving structures from his day. St. Botolph without the Wall—his other potential parish church and, if simple proximity is taken into account, his likeliest—was wholly rebuilt and considerably expanded in the fifteenth century. In sixteenth-century sketch maps and engravings of the city, it occupies a significant place on the skyline, higher than Aldgate itself and rivaling Holy Trinity. It was then torn down and rebuilt in a seventeenth-century style, but its footprint remains where it always was, close to the original location of Aldgate itself.

Chaucer was surrounded by such possibilities of involvement and social exchange, few of which he appears to have pursued actively. Even so, a city offers many of its richest experiences to all residents equally, including those who observe and appreciate its panorama without ever quite taking the full plunge.

Street Life

Accommodations in London were small, if not downright cramped, and much of life there was conducted publicly, in the street, for all to share and see. Even a resident in a tower surrounded by five-foot walls still steps out into the street to draw some water from the communal pump, or to enjoy a cup of wine or a measure of ale, or to pick up some bread from a streetside oven, or to visit a public latrine. Even the resident who skips a ward meeting will be governed by its ordinances, and the parishioner who skips mass will still divide the day by the sound of liturgical bells. The most solitary walker will jostle with fellow Londoners on narrow streets and hold a plethora of city sights in common.

During the daylight hours the public spaces of the city were jammed. The precincts around St. Paul's, the guildhall yard, and the principal streets teemed with people. Every kind of procession traversed the Cheap and other thoroughfares. Crowds gathered to view royal entries and other spectacles. Distinguished visitors received formal escorts and processionals from and to the port of London. Religious ceremonials and pageants issued from St. Paul's on feast and holy days. These grand civic events were augmented by a host of neighborhood equivalents. Corpus Christi and other processions were sponsored by London's hundred-odd parishes and innumerable religious fraternities. Groups of retainers roved in badges, caps, emblazoned tunics, and other marks of affiliation. Liveried guildsmen mustered and members of the London watch formed up in companies and patrolled the streets.

In the prologue to his fragmentary "Cook's Tale," Chaucer presents a devotee of such events, a young apprentice named Perkin, called "Perkin Reveler" because of high-spirited conduct. Careless of his duties, he needs no encouragement to desert his shop in order to enjoy street spectacles and disport himself on their fringes. He is especially attracted by "ridings"— all kinds of processions—and most of all when they proceed down the customary ceremonial street of Cheapside:

> He better loved the tavern than the shop
> For when there was a riding in the Cheap
> Out of the shop, that way would he leap;
> Until he'd seen all that there was to see
> And danced his fill, he would not come again.

> (*He loved bet the taverne than the shoppe,*
> *For whan ther any riding was in Chepe*
> *Out of the shoppe thider wolde he lepe—*
> *Til that he hadde al the sighte ysein*
> *And daunced wel, he wolde nat come ayein.*)

Perkin prefers street life to being indoors, and he and his friends meet up for dicing and other recreations at various streetside locations. If the streets offered revelry and fun, they also afforded disciplinary spectacles. Perkin himself has featured in more than one of them. Convicts were processionally escorted to Newgate and other prisons, often with musical accompaniment, and Perkin is one of those "sometimes led with revel to Newgate" ("*somtime lad with revel to Newegate*"). More serious crimes were treated at a higher level of processional formality; condemned traitors and celebrated criminals were "drawn" on hurdles to Tower Hill, Smithfield, and other places of execution, always before substantial crowds.

One or another procession was always forming up outside Aldgate, whether for purposes of honor (as when royals and dignitaries processed from the gate itself to Cornhill through Cheap and ultimately to St. Paul's) or dishonor (with offenders against the codes of the city led in procession to public humiliation at the Cornhill stocks or Newgate Prison). One frequent procession involved whores or common courtesans whose activities were statutorily confined to the stews of Southwark or other verges, but who frequently risked apprehension by chancing the lucrative city market. Provision was made in the *Liber Albus*, a venerable statute book of the city:

> If any woman shall be found to be a common courtesan . . . let her be taken from the prison unto Algate, with a hood of striped cloth and a white wand in her hand; and from thence, with minstrels, according to precedent, and there let the cause be proclaimed; and from thence through Cheap and Newgate to Cock Lane, there to take up her abode.

Whether for king or courtesan, for admiration or blame, the procession was likely to involve musical accompaniment, gawking onlookers, pop-up markets, and general hubbub.

But the people also filled London's streets on ordinary business. Most Londoners rose in darkness, around the canonical hour of Lauds (our five or six o'clock). By Prime (seven or eight o'clock) the sun was well up, and the business day had fully begun. From first light onward the streets were full. Any early morning nourishment, other than cold leftovers, would have been taken at food stalls, bakeshops, or communal ovens. This was, of course, a mainly pedestrian culture. Occasionally a lord and his entourage would force their way through the streets on horseback, stirring mild interest and some derision. But errands and work-related journeys and almost all travel for any purpose would have been on foot. After all, one could walk from the easternmost to the westernmost part of the city in a half hour, and from its top at Moorfields to its bottom at the Thames in fifteen or twenty minutes.

Even as Londoners rose with the sun, or before, the streets emptied at sunset. St. Mary-le-Bow and other churches rang a curfew bell at 9:00 P.M. in summer or at dusk in other seasons, whichever came first; the city gates were closed, and roaming the streets after that was a malefaction. The city watch was instructed to apprehend nightwalkers, whose purposes were automatically suspect, and lords and others on legitimate business were expected to bear torches at night in order to be easily seen and their business known. But until nightfall the streets remained clogged with pedestrian activity. This meant that people were accustomed to seeing one another, and to being seen.

In his *Troilus and Criseide*, Chaucer treats ancient Troy as a template of his contemporary London, and in that poem privacy proves almost impossible to attain. Everybody constantly attends to everybody else's business. Criseide, thinking about taking Troilus as her lover, is afraid that gossips will spy him entering or leaving her dwelling: *"Men wolde wondren seen him come or goon."* Privacy—in late-medieval London and in its imaginary counterpart, Troy—could be arranged, but at considerable effort and cost. Signs of the struggle for privacy are preserved in medieval legal records and statute books. As in many European cities today, civic legislation supported the right of gardens and enclosures not to be overlooked by neighbors' windows. Cases of "trespass," in which property owners asserted and defended their privacy rights, were among the most common legal proceedings. To be sure, some more securely private spaces did exist, although mainly for the already privileged: those in religious orders and for inhabitants of aristocratic town houses. In *Troilus*, the aristocratic inhabitants make full use of private gardens for solitude and rumination and on numerous occasions withdraw to private chambers or enclosed gardens. But such occasions for withdrawal were a matter of private privilege, a kind of fantasy possibility for the average Londoners. The very idea of a private chamber, for anyone other than a nobleperson, was a fourteenth-century invention, but it was out of reach for most, and the privacy even of noblepersons was often as not compromised. When Troilus and Criseide finally achieve their consummation scene—occurring in a chamber within a chamber within a larger hall or foyer—they share it with an observer, Pandarus, who discreetly pretends to read a book (appropriately, a *romaunce*) by the fire but does not leave the room.

Most London business occurred in plain view. Chaucer's London is a very public city, a place where people mingle together in crowded thoroughfares, where they post and publish their inner thoughts and broadcast them aloud, where different forms of street theater flourish, and where the public presentation of the self far overwhelms any gestures toward privacy or inwardness. Whether in small lanes and byways, or in processional and ceremonial places like the Cheap, in places of public assembly like St. Paul's Cross or in taverns and bakeshops, Londoners rub elbows with one another. More to the present point, they socialize.

Issuing directly from Aldgate and proceeding on through the city was its principal ceremonial and social street. First called

"Algate Street," it carried on as Leadenhall Street, then Corn-hill Street (with its markets and public pillory), widened to become the Cheap (its conduit flowing with fresh water on ordinary days and wine on days of celebration), and reached the gates of St. Paul's before proceeding northwest and leaving the city and stretching out into the realm beyond. Collectively these thoroughfares were known as the "King's Highway." City streets were notoriously cramped, of course, with a typical width of twelve feet, and that width itself compromised by protruding tavern signs ("alestakes") and other commercial signage. But the King's Highway, beginning with the generous twenty-foot space between Aldgate's two towers, was procession-worthy throughout its length.

Wider still was the open area just to the city side of Aldgate itself, forming a vital public space at the junction of Aldgate Street with Leadenhall and the branching of Fenchurch. At this junction was a popular public pump—which appears in sixteenth-century maps and was probably already present in the Middle Ages—that is still marked today by an inoperative drinking fountain and drain placed there in 1876 and adorned with a bronze dog's head. Unless he frequented the expensive water merchants, this is where Chaucer walked to draw his household water. Entrepreneurs gathered in this area, selling goods from market stalls; holy hermits in improvised cells took up occasional residence beside the gates and walls; and public preachers—together with the odd prophet or ranter—would have had their say. Flanking this courtyard and lining the King's Highway were two-story rental properties of a middling sort, as well as shops and other business establishments—many built adjacent to and managed as rental properties by the priory, whose walls loomed immediately behind. Tax rolls and court rolls attest to a range of vocational groups living there: fishmongers, butchers, potters, bakers, chandlers, goldbeaters, goldsmiths, fellmongers, vintners, saddlers, cordwainers, brewers, hatters, spurriers, cooks, janitors, armorers, fletchers, and the like, living in tenements, some with cellars, some with shops, some with gardens. Aldgate does not appear to be one of the racier wards. It contained six inns and taverns, to be sure, but this modest complement is to be compared with twenty-two in Breadstreet, twenty-five in Holborn, twenty in Smithfield, and fifty in Fleetstreet. Six taverns, though, combined with others just outside the walls, and yet others on Old Jewry and the streets leading to the Wool Wharf, together with the communal pump and shared ovens and other gathering points would have provided ample occasions of convenient or even unavoidable socialization.

Medieval street culture was inherently public and vocal in its own right. Chaucer does not give us anything in his poetry that sounds exactly like street cries, but his contemporary William Langland has an example of the kind of commercial chatter somebody stepping out on Aldgate's cityside would have heard:

Cooks and their knaves cried, "Hot pies, hot!
Good geese and piglets! Go we dine, go we."
Taverners spoke out in the same sort of way:
"White wine of Alsace and wine of Gascony,
From La Reole and La Rochelle, just right for your roast!"

Stepping from his dwelling in Aldgate, Chaucer found himself enmeshed in a web of words, starting with such commercial chatter but proceeding into an ongoing and collective urban conversation about people, manners, and other matters of opinion.

Street talk—slangy, impromptu, and unabashedly opinionated—would have been a scarcely avoidable fact of his life.

A typical conversational starter involved a request for an account of current novelties, to be caught up on what's going around or "what's new?" Nearly contemporary treason-trial records have one John Bernard getting into trouble in 1402 for soliciting loose talk from his friend William. He stops William at his plow, asking him for an account of any new things he has heard ("*quelx nouels*," in the Anglo-French of the trial record). William gives him a load of spurious gossip. That the recently deposed King Richard is still alive and raising troops to reclaim his throne, that the new king Henry is raising money so he can flee the realm and marry a duchess of Brittany, and such fancies. John does what one does with such "*nouels*": passes them on to two other friends in his village, and, as the rumor duly spreads, it lands the humble John in the middle of a treason trial.

The general hunger for spoken accounts of novelties and news abetted what might be called a gossip culture. The very word is a medieval English invention. "Gossip" is a contraction of "god-sib," or "good friend," with whom one shared private information or news. Chaucer's Wife of Bath explains that she—naturally—has a *gossib* named Alisoun, with whom she is more confiding than her parish priest:

> She knew my heart and private thoughts as well
> Better than our parish priest . . .
> She's the one I shared my counsel with.
>
> (*She knew myn herte, and eek my privetee,*
> *Bet than oure parisshe preest . . .*
> *To hire biwreyed I my conseil al.*)

She goes on to say that she tells her gossip everything, whether her husband had pissed on a wall (an utterly ordinary occurrence, that is, in fourteenth-century London) or (at the other extreme) had done something that could have cost him his life. So do Chaucer's Troilus and Criseide live in fear of gossiping tongues. Criseide, preparing to visit Pandarus's for the night of consummation, warns him to beware of "goose-like people's speech, / That dream of things that never were" (*"of goosissh poeples speche, / That dremen thinges whiche as nevere were"*).

Every fourteenth-century Londoner lived in a narrative or tale-telling culture. Anybody wanting to make a point about anything will cap it with a short tale or moral example. Sermons are punctuated with parables, examples, and illustrative tales. Even legal records abound in narrative reconstructions of events that serve a purpose but that also array themselves in zesty gossipy detail.

Awaiting resolution in the court of King's Bench in 1386 was a case with all the elements of a scandalously disturbing story. It seems, according to the findings of the jury, that a leper named Adam Matte came to the house of Maud Wheatwell in St. Clement's parish and bargained to lie with her for the sum of ten shillings. Maud refused but said that she had a lovely maidservant named Margaret who would serve. Maud collected the ten shillings, led Adam to Margaret's room, and, saying, "Do what you can," locked the door and took away the key. Adam is said to have thrown Margaret down and raped her. Following upon this distressing event:

> the maidservant was so hysterical by reason of the shame, the rape and the aforesaid Adam's disease that she at once went out of her mind and remained ill until the following Saturday, on which day she died.

Maud, by the way, evaded further prosecution by insisting that the absent Adam must first be found and convicted as the principal felon.

In another contemporary case brought into the guildhall for a hearing before the mayor, the aldermen, and the sheriffs of London, a bawd named Elizabeth Moring was accused of leading London women astray. In this instance she retained a serving woman named Johanna and diverse other women under a cover of their feigned employment as apprentices in the craft of embroidery. In fact, she incited them "to live a lewd life, and to consort with friars, chaplains, and all other such men as desired to have their company . . . for such stipulated sum as they might agree upon," she retaining the proceeds. In pursuit of these aims, she arranged for Johanna to accompany a chaplain to his chamber, under pretext that he needed a lantern borne before him, and she ended up spending the night with him but received nothing for her labors. Reproached by Elizabeth, she returned the following night under instruction to lay hold of some recompense for her trouble and found there a breviary (a service book like the one upon which the sexually scheming monk Daun John swears secrecy in Chaucer's "Shipman's Tale"), which she brought to Elizabeth, who pawned it for eight pence. Accused of many such intrigues, Elizabeth was convicted by a jury of twelve good men of the venue, who condemned her to the pillory and to expulsion from the city. This expulsion was itself accompanied by a highly visible ceremony in which she was taken to one of London's gates and made to forswear the city and its rights and privileges. Here we have plot, motive, reversal, denouement—all the elements needed for a good story, whether within or beyond the courtroom situation.

Racy narratives within Chaucer's own literary oeuvre—such

as the "Miller's Tale" and the "Reeve's Tale" within his *Canterbury Tales*—have literary sources in the Old French comic tales called fabliaux and elsewhere, and I do not mean to suggest that he drew them from surrounding life. If anything, Chaucer—working within literary rather than judicial traditions—tones his stories down a bit, tempering and redirecting their energies away from raw incident and toward more modulated points about mutual betrayal (the "Shipman's Tale") and displaced requital and revenge (the "Reeve's Tale"). But no one reading of Margaret's travails or Elizabeth's enterprising greed could fail to notice that Chaucer had the advantage of a London public that knew how to recognize and appreciate a well-told yarn. Chaucer's assumptions about tales and tale telling were formed within a society in which narrative exchange and the recital of racy incidents was part of the fodder of daily life.

Whatever claims of personal reticence he might make in his writing, he also supposes that strangers fall easily into streetside encounters and start talking. On at least one occasion, Chaucer represents himself as a participant in this talkative and convivial culture. While in Westminster for the 1386 Parliament, Chaucer gives a deposition before the Court of Chivalry. In this deposition he makes his point by relating a little story. The case involves the disputed right between two parties, one Scrope and one Grosvenor, to bear a particular coat of arms. In his story Chaucer says that he was in London and walking down Friday Street (a block of which still exists under that name). He sees the coat of arms hanging outside an inn, and asks a passerby about an inn displaying the arms of Scrope outside. The stranger replies, politely, "Not at all, sir" (*"Nenyl sieur"*), that these are the arms of Grosvenor, a knight of Chester. A small enough matter, but it suggests terms of easy intercourse, and that Chaucer himself was not hesitant to strike up a conversation when the circumstances were right.

The more fictional frame of Chaucer's poem *House of Fame* offers another account of a conversational exchange between amiable strangers. An unnamed bystander simply starts talking to the poem's narrator, Geffrey, interrogating him politely: "Friend, what is thy name?" (*"Frend, what is thy name?"*) And "Why have you come here?" (*"Artow come hider?"*) The stranger supposes that, since they are in the house where Fame's favors are erratically dispensed, Geffrey has come to seek renown. When told this is not the case, he persists: "Then what are you doing here then?" (*"But what doost thou here than?"*) When Geffrey explains that he is interested in hearing "new things" (*"newe tidings"*), the stranger offers to lead him to some. This stranger plays a familiar literary role as a tutor or guide, like Virgil in Dante's *Inferno*, whose task is to introduce the narrator into a new realm or set of experiences. But this amicable and inquisitive stranger is also behaving as persons of similar social station appear to have behaved on the London street: speaking without awaiting or expecting introduction, displaying polite curiosity and an aptness for information and exchange.

Approximations of the Sacred

Chaucer need not have been a noisy extrovert in order to participate in streetside conversation, and he need not have been a religious zealot in order to enjoy the solace of collective belief. Religious observance was vital to the texture of his London and neighborhood experience, even if elusively so.

The evidence of his writings must be weighed with caution, since many of his expressed perspectives—such as the orthodoxy of the Parson's harangue on penance, or the solemn wonder at the martyrdom of St. Cecilia in his "Second Nun's Tale," or the derision he directs at his irredeemably corrupt Pardoner—are adopted in furtherance of the particular kind of tale he has chosen to write rather than as the expression of any particular credo. Still, Chaucer's poetry permits a very rough and approximate religious profile, less in the literal statements that different characters make but rather in the tacit assumptions about religion that seem to underpin the body of his works.

He must certainly be considered a devout and orthodox Catholic, though (in his satiric treatment of his huntsman Monk or his sexually insinuating Friar) evidently of a mildly reformist persuasion. He does, after all, give the austerely orthodox Parson the last word on his Canterbury pilgrimage, in order to recite a treatise on penance painstakingly translated from two different ecclesiastical sources. And then, to cap it off, he ends the *Tales* with a personal response to the Parson, his own "Retraction," or expression of regret for any literary frivolities for which he has previously been responsible. An earlier fashion in Chaucer criticism used to attribute this retraction to the hand of an anonymous "monkish scribe" who placed sentiments in Chaucer's mouth that he wouldn't ordinarily have uttered. But more recent scholars have concluded that there's no reason to suppose these weren't his own words or that he was insincere in the matter. Even though he didn't head toward the fireplace with his disavowed manuscripts, a capacity for emphatic, if temporary, penitential response would have rested well within the range of his likely beliefs.

At the same time, the whole matter of belief is varied and responsive to time and situation; belief is never monolithic but is shaded and situational. If he articulates a particularly strenuous form of faith at the end of the "Parson's Tale," at other moments he expresses his religious views in a more supple and even wryly humorous way. At such moments he speaks of religion in the voice of one who believes, but unsolemnly so. In the prologue to his *Legend of Good Women*, Chaucer commences with a celebration of book learning, through which things we could not otherwise know are revealed:

A thousand times have I heard men tell
That there is joy in heaven and pain in hell.
And I agree well that it is so;
But, nonetheless, yet know I well also
That there is none who dwells in this country
Who's ever been in heaven or in hell,
Or knows of it in any other way
Than he's heard said aloud, or else found written.

(A thousand times have I herd men telle
That ther is joy in hevene and peyne in helle.
And I acorde wel that it ys so;
But, natheles, yet wot I wel also
That ther nis noon dwelling in this contree,
That either hath in hevene or helle ybe,
Ne may of hit noon other weyes witen
But as he hath herd seid, or founde it writen.)

And he adds a mildly jesting understatement, that we after all have no other ways of finding out, since nobody's ever tried it (*"by assay ther may no man it preve"*). Then another solemnity: Don't suppose everything is a lie unless you've seen it or done it (*"Men shal not wenen every thing a lie / But if himself it seeth, or elles dooth"*). And, finally, an all-out laugh: St. Bernard didn't see everything. (*"Bernard the monk ne saugh nat all, pardee!"*) A laugh, indeed, but a laugh by one who is easy with matters of faith, who has no need or use for tight-lipped hypocrisy.

Chaucer's comfortable but unsolemn stance toward matters of faith was silently abetted by the activities and structures of parish life. The parish and its institutions were prepared to do a good deal of his believing for him. The matter of Chaucer's particular parish—with nearby St. Katharine Cree and even nearer St. Botolph without the Wall as legitimate contenders—remains unresolved, as does the proportion of his active versus passive participation in parish affairs. But even if more a beholder or lurker than a regular communicant, he was a participant nonetheless.

There was room within a parish of several hundred Christian souls for various intensities of belief. Most thoroughly believing Christians confessed, at most, once a year, and rarely sat through a whole Mass. Mass was performed at least once a day, and usually more often in the parish church, always at first light and usually in late afternoon or Vespers, and parishioners were undoubtedly happy to know that it was being punctually observed without feeling particularly obliged to attend. Chaucer might have been content, like most, to glance in at the church door now and then, perhaps to view the elevation of the consecrated host (signaled by a ringing bell to draw the attention of those who might otherwise miss its spiritual benefits), without participating in the full ceremony. But, like most of his fellows, he would undoubtedly have been alarmed to learn of any interruption in the performance of morning Mass or the parish's liturgical cycle. He was, after all, its spiritual beneficiary. He would have gained this kind of derivative reassurance from the framing of his day by liturgical bells and by occasional processionals and other religious emblemata.

Even a London resident of Chaucer's rather tacit religiosity still lived in an encompassing environment of liturgical sound. Around Aldgate, any sound of ironbound wheels and drovers' cries was far outweighed by the holy racket of church bells. A Londoner would never have been more than two or three hundred yards from a frequently tolling bell, and in most cases closer than that. Most conspicuous by virtue of their enormity were the bells of Chaucer's immediate and looming neighbor to the north, Holy Trinity Priory. Just as the church and structures of the priory were the most prominent element of Aldgate's built environment, so were the priory's bells the most conspicuous in its soundscape.

A contract of 1312 survives for the casting of just one of Holy Trinity's nine bells, and not even its major one: to Richard de Wymbissh "to make one bell, good, entire, and well sounding, and as nearly in tune to the utmost of his power with the greater bell of the church aforesaid. And the said bell was to weigh 2820 pounds of good and befitting metal." And now imagine the deployment of that bell, and its eight companions, to punctuate and reenforce the hours of the liturgical day, as well as funerals and other ceremonial occasions.

Bells were not just tolled but pealed, rung in complicated successions, over extended periods of time. At medieval Lincoln, for example, the first of five peals began with the great bell tolling for half an hour, followed by a half-hour peal of a lesser bell, followed by the opening of the church doors, followed by another half-hour peal, then by two quarter-hour peals, and finally by a last peal introducing the service. This was for Matins, around midnight, and—however thick his walls—Chaucer's bed was some two hundred yards away from the Holy Trinity bell tower and its admired peals. Remembering that Matins is one of seven services on the full daily round (of which Matins, at midnight, and Prime, at daybreak, were the most prominent in lay experience), plenty of substantial (and ideally artful) noise was being generated around a traditional and monastic idea of the day.

Parish churches were also expected to punctuate this same cycle with their own chapel bells, especially at early morning Prime, the most popularly attended mass of the day, and at a late afternoon Vespers or Evensong. A single city church, St. Mary-at-Hill, might be taken as an example. The church records include a table of remuneration for the churchwardens charged with ringing the bells, and it provides that upon occasions of interment they will earn 6s. 8d. for a knell lasting the entire day, 40d. for a half day on the second bell, and 12d. for a truncated and low-budget performance lasting "no moor but the space of an hour." Those in financial distress could still have "the lityll bell" for 8d. for a man and 4d. for a child. The aspiration, though, was to have a daylong knell on the great bell, and other church accounts provide refreshment for bell ringers engaged upon this sunrise to sunset labor. Chaucer, at Aldgate, would have heard the bells of two different parish churches; he was three hundred yards from St. Katharine Cree (which most scholars identify as his parish church) but was even closer—just seventy-five yards across Houndsditch—to the bells of St. Botolph without the Wall. A century and a half later, but presumably referring to the same bell that would have rung closest to Chaucer's ear, the narrator of sixteenth-century author William Baldwin's brilliant satire *Beware the Cat* has this to say about an unexpected peal: "The greatest bell in Saint Botolph's steeple . . . came with such a rumble into mine ear, that I thought all the devils in hell had broken loose, and were come about me."

At their broadest extent, parish and abbey and cathedral bells merged to enclose London residents in an experience of liturgical time. Although the sponsorship and implementation of liturgical time was clerical, one need not have been a monk or a priest to live within its bounds. All one had to do was tacitly (and, prior to the last quarter of the fourteenth century, inevitably) internalize some of its assumptions and implications. As marked by the recurring patterns of liturgical bells, time is experienced as more cyclical or repetitive than linear. The different "hours" of the liturgical day are held within repetitive or recurrent structure. And the cycle of daily liturgical hours is, in turn, caught up within the larger recurrences of the liturgical year, with its long Lenten preparation and its climax in Holy Week, only to commence a new pattern of expectation and fulfillment. The rhythms of the liturgical year are additionally supported by the cycle of the seasons, as Chaucer himself so well observed in his general prologue to the *Canterbury Tales*, in which the Pilgrims are subject to an annual and recurring impulse, a stirring both natural and devotional, associated with the return of spring.

The progress through the liturgical order was the closest thing to an agreed-upon time scheme for the London day. Consequently, liturgical chimes served as keys to events occurring outside as well as inside monastery and church walls, striking a whole series of compromises with the practical and daily activities that occurred within its demarcation. Prime was not only the first of the daylight services but also the beginning of the civic business day, Vespers for the end of the civic as well as monastic day, Compline for the closing of the city gates. The six great gates of the city were shut at the first stroke of the curfew bell. Their wicket gates remained open for pedestrians, while the bells were tolling, and were closed at the last stroke. Lest there be any mistaking the matter, all of the city's belled parish churches—nearly a hundred of them—immediately commenced tolling. A thirteenth-century regulation of the city *Letter-Books*, still in force in Chaucer's lifetime, stipulated: "At each parish church, curfew shall be tolled at the same hour as at St Martin, beginning and ending at the same time, and then all the gates as well as taverns, whether of wine or ale, shall be closed, and no one shall walk the streets or places."

Just as Chaucer was a passive beneficiary of the Christian liturgical cycle, so did he live and thrive mainly in an environment of liturgical time. As with the sanctification of the Host: not necessarily deliberately present or primarily attentive but glad to know it was going on, and happy to live, as it were, beneath its protective umbrella. Customs within and without monastic walls and the yards of parish churches maintained a kind of easy and untaxing synchronicity. In the "Miller's Tale"—about as secular a tale as Chaucer could have imagined—the randy clerk, Nicholas, and his adulterous sweetheart, Alison, arrange to spend a hot night together, stretching from about curfew time (*"Aboute corfew-tyme"*), or sunset, until just before dawn: "Until the bell of lauds began to ring / And friars in the chancel began to sing" (*"Til that the belle of laudes gan to ringe, / And freres in the chauncel gonne singe"*). So the friars hear the bell for Lauds and get out of bed to pray; Nicholas and Alison hear the bell and know that their revels are drawing to an end. Has their time been sanctified? Well, not exactly. But it has been co-ordinate with a set of natural and liturgical rhythms that set an inescapable backdrop for daily (and nightly) activity.

Leaving Aldgate

Many elements of a city's life swirl around its residents, encompass them, without expecting or demanding their conscious assent. In this sense, a city and a culture are like a nervous system, directing heartbeat, blood circulation, and other physiological responses, without requiring the participant's will that they occur. Chaucer's involvement in his London neighborhood may have been a form of passive immersion rather than active engagement, but he was involved, and intensively so.

Now, as he set out for Parliament on that October morning in 1386, a time of severance was at hand. All that thick and involving texture of London life would be lost to him in Kent, one of the several extreme costs of his separation. Aggravating the whole matter is an additional possibility: that his departure from the Aldgate dwelling may not have been entirely voluntary. Evidence suggests that the collusive currents that got him his Aldgate apartment in the first place had now turned against him, that the current city adminstration now found him inessential, or even a liability, in London affairs. This evidence will be considered, along with other pressures bearing on his exit from London, in the two following chapters. In the meantime we may certainly suppose that an involuntary severance would have heightened his distress.

The precise date of his departure is a matter of conjecture. He could possibly have laid groundwork for his later removal to Kent by heading there some days or weeks before Parliament began; his Kentish involvements were already making modest claims on his time and might have required some looking after. But if any similarities are to be drawn between medieval and contemporary life, I would draw one here: I doubt that anybody, whether medieval or contemporary, would vacate a rent-free London apartment unless absolutely required to do so. September 30 was a holiday, the feast day of St. Jerome, and a tempting day to linger in one's neighborhood and parish. In any case by

October 1 he was gone. His parliamentary responsibilities required his presence in Westminster by that date, and by October 4 the mayor and aldermen and common council of London had reassigned his quarters, and he knew with certainty that he'd lost his right of return. The discomforts, but also the unfailing stimulation, of life over a busy city gate were now to become a memory rather than a reality. Any wishes for privacy he had entertained during his twelve years in crowded London were about to be granted, and probably exceeded, now.

CHAPTER THREE

The Wool Men

C haucer had arrived in Aldgate in 1374, as part of a conspir-
acy involving some of the most important men in the realm.
His post as esquire of the king's household had been a lifetime
appointment, with a modest but comfortable salary, and the occasional genuine excitements of royal ceremony, foreign travel,
and court intrigue. He would probably not have left it except
that an influential coalition of highly placed courtiers and mon-
eymen, including some to whom he was already deeply indebted, had decided that he would be more useful elsewhere.
This coalition was notable not only for the prominence of its
members but also for the fact that it exhibited a rare and highly
coordinated measure of collaboration between court and city, the
king's party in Windsor and Westminster on the one hand and the
mercantile elite of London on the other, to accomplish a common
goal. The members of this coalition settled on Chaucer—as a reliable Ricardian loyalist and king's man with family roots in
London trade—as the right person for their purposes: to fill a
critically important (and, unfortunately, deeply ethically compromised) post in the wool custom.

An explanation of Chaucer's ill-starred and ultimately frus-
trated years in the wool trade will require an extended look at
the trade itself, the operations of the Wool Wharf, the machinations of the collectors of customs (and especially the ubiquitous Nicholas Brembre), and the particular responsibilities of

the post Chaucer assumed. But first an account of the extraordinary machinations involved in getting him to London and placing him in the job will suggest the importance of his appointment to an opportunistic alliance of men accustomed to having their way in affairs of the realm.

Getting Chaucer the Job

Chaucer's new job in the wool custom is not one he would have dreamed up or sought for himself. It substituted a stringent daily routine and profit-driven associates for the relatively free and easy circumstances of court life. It has every appearance of a job that he accepted as a dutiful factionalist, because important people *wanted him there*. The machinations of influential people, in both court and city, were required to place him in the position, requiring the collaboration of persons across party lines and in different and normally incompatible spheres of interest. Certain minimum conditions needed to be achieved in order to reconcile him to the reassignment, and some of England's least scrupulous men worked in concert to see that they were achieved.

Chaucer's new responsibility as controller of customs would involve, putting it most simply, keeping an eye on things: overseeing the weighing of wool exports and the collection of wool duties; assuring himself and others that the collectors of customs performed their responsibilities honestly and reliably; and guaranteeing the arrival of the duties they collected into the king's coffers in the royal exchequer. His appointment as controller of the wool custom (bolstered by a concurrent appointment as controller of the petty custom) was recorded on June 8, 1374, and contains the stipulations normal for controllers at this time: He will serve in the port of London, keep his records in his own hand, perform his duties without a deputy, and be custodian of one of the two dies, or molds, used to form the wax seal called the cocket seal certifying that customs duties had been correctly assessed and collected for all exports of wool. But his letter of appointment was only the culminating step in a complicated transition requiring a collaboration across several different constituencies. A tight skein of consequential events surrounds this appointment and illuminates its significance. Unraveled, it shows how many people, in a variety of capacities, thought it important that Chaucer occupy this post at this time. Here is a brief chronology of events surrounding this appointment:

February 26, 1374: Nicholas Brembre is appointed collector of customs.

April 23, 1374: Chaucer receives a grant of a pitcher of wine every day, by gift of the king, to be collected at the Port of London.

May 10, 1374: Chaucer is granted a lease from the mayor and aldermen of the city of London for quarters over Aldgate.

June 8, 1374: His appointment to the controllership is conferred.

June 13, 1374: John of Gaunt grants a life annuity to Chaucer and Philippa Chaucer.

These dates are approximations, since they mark the entry of these actions into the written record rather than the precise dates on which the actions occurred. Nevertheless, they do suggest a sequence of events, and in this respect they have a story to tell:

Brembre's Appointment. Initiating the sequence is the appointment of Nicholas Brembre—already conspicuous as a representative of royal interests within the city of London—to the post of collector of the wool custom in February 1374. Everything known and suspected of his character, and his probable intentions of connivance in office, suggests that having a complicit controller of customs would be a matter of the highest priority for Brembre.

The Pitcher of Wine. Now follows a remarkable harbinger of Chaucer's prospects. He is granted, by privy seal, a pitcher (*pycher*) of wine each day, at the hand of the king's butler, to be collected each day at the port of the royal city of London ("*a prendre chescun jour en port de nostre citee de Londres*"). Because of the approximate nature of dating documents according to their entry in the record rather than their date of enactment, no conclusive claim can be made of this, but this gift appears to anticipate, rather than follow from, his coming appointment. Its unusual specification of a daily pitcher of wine (and not the annual or biennial "tun" of wine usual to such grants), and its regular collection at the port of London, suggest that Chaucer's appointment, and its specifics, were already in active discussion in and around the court prior to any official action being taken. Additionally, the form of the grant—by privy seal, the mechanism for expression of the king's personal wishes—suggests that, if not the king himself, at least persons in the royal orbit were involved in this machination.

The Aldgate Lease. And now, still prior to the appointment itself, we learn that the mayor and aldermen of London are on board. London was jealous of its chartered prerogatives, and, whatever the degree of his influence in the matter, the king had no authority over access to city lodgings. This was a responsibility of the mayor and aldermen of London, acting on behalf of the community or commonality of the city. Chaucer was granted his lease for the dwelling over Aldgate by action of Mayor Adam de Bury and the aldermen.

What prompted the London patriciate to act on behalf of this rather obscure esquire of the king's household? Two possible connections between the Edwardian court and the government of the city suggest themselves. One is Mayor de Bury himself, together with a cabal of merchant capitalists interested in wool profits and opposed to the forms of regulation and closer control that would be introduced in the period 1374 to 1377 with the formation of the Wool Staple. Bury and his closest associates—including the financier Richard Lyons and the wine speculator John Pecche—were temporarily riding high in 1374, and still clinging to some influence in the latter-day Edwardian court. (By 1376, all three of them would be overthrown, convicted in the Good Parliament of defrauding the king.) The simplest explanation for the consideration shown to Chaucer is that this unsavory trio might have exerted themselves as a favor to Gaunt, with whom they retained ties until 1376, and who even engineered their brief return to influence in 1377.

Even had this trio balked, however, Chaucer still had good relations with the rising faction of more respectable and restrained civic leaders, including Nicholas Brembre and his friends. The Brembre group had been steadily improving their position in city governance, and by 1374 would have had sufficient leverage to install Chaucer in his quarters with or without the concurrence of the mayor. Chaucer's lease was approved by the city's aldermen, and the serving aldermen in 1374 included all the members of the surging Brembre faction: three men who had served or would serve as mayor of London—William Walworth, John Philipot, and Nicholas Brembre—together with

Philipot's and Brembre's father-in-law, John Stodeye. Although there had been some mumbling about Walworth in and around the Good Parliament of 1376, and although contention with a coalition of lesser guildsmen led by the reformist John Northampton lay ahead, the members of this faction had managed to advance and enrich themselves without attracting the rancor that would dog Lyons (who would be violently slain by the rebels of 1381), Bury (who lived most of his later years abroad), and Pecche (whose political career was over). This is the year in which Brembre and Walworth would organize a substantial loan to the crown, and Brembre would soon be Gaunt's personal choice for mayor. In short, Chaucer's city prospects were in capable hands.

Chaucer's Appointment. The collectors and controllers of customs were, by tradition, native to or at least closely involved with the mercantile communities of the ports they served. Earlier in the century, and in some ports, the responsibility for nomination to these posts rested within the community itself. This was no longer true, but a local or community interest in his appointment was a certainty—as was, in the case of so vital a collectorship, the interest of the mayor and aldermen of the city of London. Appointment to such a post in the 1370s could have taken a number of forms: Appointments of his contemporaries and near contemporaries were made in the form of a bill from the treasurer of the realm, or else by the king. Or the appointment might be royal and issued in the name of the king through his privy seal. Chaucer's assumed the latter, and most prestigious, form. Although appointment through privy seal does not necessarily guarantee the personal interest of the king, it does, at minimum, suggest the involvement of persons centrally situated within the king's council or entourage.

Life Annuity. Finally, a familiar party enters the scene. Circumstances would have permitted Gaunt to hover supportively around this whole transaction. Gaunt had returned from the Continent in April 1374—in military disgrace, but at least on some terms with his father the king and, in the period before the Good Parliament of 1376, still on passable terms with the royal party in the city of London. Entered in the Duchy records for June 13, 1374, is John of Gaunt's grant of a life annuity of ten pounds for services rendered by Chaucer to the duke and by Philippa to Duchess Constance. I've already discussed this grant as a mark of Gaunt's interest in Philippa as sparked by his relation to her sister, but it also expresses at least a derivative interest in Chaucer as Philippa's husband. Gaunt's motive may have been to allow the pair to spend some time together, especially when she was serving at Gaunt's Savoy Palace, but Gaunt has no reputation for doing good deeds for their own sake. More likely he was throwing Chaucer a bone, a consolation for Philippa's extended absences in his service in Lincolnshire and elsewhere. In any case, this appointment gave Gaunt an opportunity to place a loyalist in city service, and thus to satisfy his own recurring desire to play a role in that London polity that (especially after 1377) would come to hate him so much.

And so considerable exertions—requiring cooperative ones by officers of the crown, John of Gaunt, Nicholas Brembre and others of Brembre's faction, and at least the consent of Adam de Bury and his soon-to-be-discredited gang—were used to install Chaucer in his new post. What remains to be explained is why so many different people, representing so many different interests, cared so much. On the face of it, and with respect to its rather modest remuneration, this might be mistaken for a minor posting. But it was a job that sat at the intersection of several urgently competing interests, and one in which a clumsy or overzealous appointee could wreak havoc upon a number of carefully poised and advantageous fiscal arrangements. In accepting this post he was acknowledging responsibility: to the exchequer, to which he reported for a full audit as many as four times a year; to Parliament, which considered itself responsible for the institution and performance of the controllerships; and to the crown, with its incessant and urgent need for a flow of customs revenue. Yet other parties remained to be satisfied as well. He would never have gotten the post without the approval of the all-powerful London wool men. They were currently flush with success, having achieved Edward III's agreement to their monopolistic control of the Wool Staple in the very years coinciding with Chaucer's first appointment to office, and they were accustomed to shaping national policy and priority in their own interest rather than the other way around. And finally, there can be no doubt that Nicholas Brembre himself, together with confederates like Walworth and Philipot, possessed veto power. His views would have dominated the aldermanic council, and nobody was going to come near that job without his personal approval.

The fact that multiple and rather discordant interests were responsible for his appointment contributed to Chaucer's workplace difficulties and increased the pressures culminating in his eventual resignation from the job. He was constantly confronted by contradictory situations that required him to satisfy the wishes of a revenue-hungry council and the exchequer on the one hand and a high-handed group of ruthlessly self-interested men on the other. As controller and nominal overseer of transactions vital to different parties for different reasons, he would find himself, quite literally, a man in the middle. If the crown could reward a loyal esquire with a patronage position, so be it; but its primary objective was to assure a revenue flow to the exchequer. If Gaunt could do a favor for his new companion's sister's husband, just as well; but his main interest was less in Chaucer than in the progress of his courtship with Katherine Swynford. If Brembre could please the royal faction by sponsoring a loyalist into a post in customs, so much the better; but his special interest was in the complicity, or at least the ethical nonchalance, of his controller.

Least evident of all here is Chaucer's own personal interest in this demanding, moderately compensated, and potentially ethically compromised post. He could not have failed to notice that the greatest fortunes in England were being made all around him. Was he a lamb among wolves or an ambitious coconspirator in the creation of wealth? The object is to form a judgment of Chaucer's own culpability or, to put it differently, of just how many compromises this new post would require him to make. And that, in turn, will require a grasp of some details— the particulars of port life, the machinations of his superiors, and the contradictory expectations surrounding the position he would assume.

The Wool Wharf

Relocating back from court to London in 1374 to assume his post in customs, Chaucer reentered an oddly familiar location and situation. He had been born on Thames Street, in the Vintry, just up from Fish Street, with its sailors' taverns and riverside holding tanks for lampreys and bream. His vintner father, John, was essentially a London guildsman, though with some mercantile experience as a shipper of wheat and some customs experience as deputy to the king's chief butler in Southampton

and other ports. When the son returned some thirty years later
to take up his post, his new workplace was also on Thames
Street, a scant half-mile east of his childhood home. He had
opted to become a slightly more elevated and better connected
version of what his father had been before him: a participant in
urban merchant culture, a habitué of the waterfront, an officer
of the king charged with the honest collection of tariffs, duties,
and customs.

What, one can only wonder, might Chaucer have made of
this rather circular course of events? After a dizzying youthful
whirl at courtly affairs and a promising marriage to a *damoiselle*
of the queen's household, and several promising diplomatic
postings, he found himself back in the city of his birth, following a vocational path already partly trodden by his father. Surely
this courtly sophisticate—having just completed a journey to
Genoa and Florence on the king's behalf—must have been at
least slightly bemused as he set out on his first morning's walk,
and subsequent walks, from Aldgate, down Old Jewry to
Crutched Friars Lane, and past the friary, skirting the Tower
precincts (and the notorious Tower Hill garbage dump), to his
new workplace on the London waterfront.

What, arriving at the Wool Wharf, would he have encountered there? An eighteenth-century commentator named Matthew Hale usefully described a port as defined by a convergence
of three different conditions or activities. It consists first of
"something natural": a convenience of access to the sea. And
next, of "something artificial": its built environment, concerning quays and wharves and cranes and warehouses and houses
of common receipt. And finally, "something civil": the civic administration of its activities, involving privileges and franchises
and, of course, the collection of duties and customs. This range

of attributes well describes the port Chaucer would have glimpsed in his boyhood on Thames Street, and then encountered in earnest when he took up his duties as controller of customs.

"Something natural." With respect to its natural setting, London benefited as the westernmost point on the Thames that seagoing vessels could easily reach. London's waterfront had been an important port since Roman times (with activity then centering around present-day Queenhithe and Billingsgate). The Thames was both wider and shallower in the Roman and early medieval periods, prior to wharf building and other channelings and confinements of the medieval period. As late as the thirteenth century the river was some 400 yards (365 meters) wide, as opposed to 300 (275 meters) now; Thames Street still marked the early medieval waterfront, and wool duties were probably imposed at the Wool House there, immediately behind the eventual Wool Wharf. Over the course of the fourteenth century the waterfront expanded a hundred yards to the south, and its riverfront abutment was rationalized and consolidated. One of several incentives for southern expansion was the construction of wooden bulwarks to defend against the French, which became less necessary after the Battle of Sluys in 1340, and were thereafter incorporated in the new and expanded line of wharves. The whole of the north bank of the river, from the Tower on the east to the Fleet River and city wall on the west, was thoroughly developed by 1374, with wharfs and quays, and "bridges," or boat landings, warehouses, and small factories.

The new-built hundred yards from the waterfront to Thames Street was an enterprise zone for commercial activity of every sort and for markets for foodstuffs and foreign goods. Specialized activities were arrayed both east and west of London

Bridge, captured in their medieval place-names: Oystergate, Hay Wharf, Wine Wharf (near which Chaucer was born), Garlickhithe, Salt Wharf, Fish Wharf, and the like. A drawbridge located in one of the twenty arches of the twelfth-century stone-and-masonry London Bridge permitted single-masted cobs and smaller vessels bearing foodstuffs and building materials to pass the bridge on the way to Queenhithe and the western wharves. Even with its drawbridge, though, passage through London Bridge was rendered difficult by formidable river tides and there is no doubt that Billingsgate, the Wool Wharf, and the nearby wharves surrounding the Tower were fortunate in the convenience of their location above the bridge.

The 1370s and 1380s were good years for the Wool Wharf. The advent of larger vessels by the century's end—multimasted carracks and enlarged Venetian and Genoese galleys—would cause some shipping to divert to Southampton and other more convenient seafront ports. (London's jealousy of its position and desire to retain it is indicated by an incident in 1376, when a Genoese merchant named Johannes Imperial, in town under royal protection to make preliminary arrangements for warehousing and port access at Southampton, was slain on the streets of London by thugs in the service of native merchants.) London's impending decline as a deep-water port would not, however, have been particularly evident in the fourteenth century, when it remained the locus of the wool trade—the kingdom's principal money spinner—and an altogether bustling place.

Something of the flavor of port commerce can be gained from a thirteenth-century account of regulations governing the activities of foreign merchants—in this case from Lorraine. Upon approaching the port they are obliged to identify themselves by raising their ensign. They are at liberty, if they wish, to sing their *kiriele* (a song of thanksgiving and praise, incorporating—or named after—the kyrie eleison of the divine service) until (but only until) they reach London Bridge. At the bridge they must wait for the correct tidal situation that will permit the drawbridge to be raised, after which they may moor at an appropriate wharf (perhaps the wine wharf in this case, since their cargo often consisted of the wines of Moselle), where they were entitled to dock for two tidal ebbs and one flow. During this period the king's chamberlain was entitled to board the vessel and inspect its cargo, selecting for the royal use such items of value as are deemed appropriate. Crew members were confined to the city and its environs, with additional encouragement to remain in the immediate vicinity of the port, below Thames Street. As a consequence, Thames Street, and the developing areas between it and the river, were lively environs. Documentary evidence for the late fifteenth century situates a "stew" quay devoted to prostitution just east of the Wool Wharf, together with two nearby brewhouses, the Hartshorn and the Ram's Head. But if the Lorrainers and other transient sailors wished to linger in the city for purposes of trade, they were subject to additional taxation. They were expected to have departed within forty days unless prevented by contrary winds, sickness, or debt, and were forbidden to engage in any trading of woolskins or unworked wool. Prior to departure, they were permitted to purchase foodstuffs (three live pigs are specified) for consumption at sea.

More enduring arrangements were, of course, possible, and London had significant colonies of Lombards, Flemings, and other foreign traders and artisans in the later fourteenth century; these are the Flemings who, as a result of sectional ill feeling bred by economic competition, were slain wholesale during the rising of 1381, and their bodies piled in the street. For all its

Flemish and Italian commerce, London was in most respects quite xenophobic with respect to "alien" traders from abroad and "foreign" traders from elsewhere in England. Continually depopulated by recurrent plague and other public health problems, London was heavily dependent on in-migrations of various kinds, yet it conspicuously discouraged foreigners and outlanders, jealously retaining privileges for its own citizens.

"Something artificial." The growing importance of the wool custom, and possibly the enhanced self-image of its workers, may be glimpsed in its built features. When Chaucer began work there, it was modestly housed on Thames Street, in what was probably a former dwelling on a onetime riverbank but now was separated from the river by several hundred feet of partially reclaimed land. In the course of his tenure its offices were moved to new and prepossessing quarters directly on the quay, with a spacious warehouse for the "tron," or scale, and the weighing of wool sacks, offices above for the collectors, the controller, the searcher, and other deputies and functionaries. This newly arcaded and two-storied customhouse was built squarely on the Wool Wharf itself in 1382 by an entrepreneurial citizen named John Churchman, in a joint enterprise with the crown. It was located immediately to the east of the present customhouse, now built slightly closer to the present river than its predecessor and separated from it by a highway, but still overlooking what would once have been the medieval waterfront. The building was an immediate success with all parties; the very next year Churchman provided further improvements, which led the crown to double its rent payment, comprising a third-story addition to the original two-story building: "a small chamber for the latrine and a solar [or further work-space] over the counting-house 38 ft. long by 21½ broad, containing two chambers and a

garret." Archaeological excavation also roughly corroborates this account, attesting to a substantial ground floor, larger in its dimensions (79 feet long and 30 feet wide) and also uncovering an addition to the east (56 feet long and 30 feet wide). Further confirmation of the accuracy of these details is the archaeological discovery of a "fine timber drain" on the east wall of the original structure, presumably belonging to the latrine mentioned in the Patent Rolls and a convenience undoubtedly utilized by Chaucer in the years 1382 to 1386.

Churchman's contract contains information about the interior of the building as well. Because this was a royal enterprise as well as a feat of private entrepreneurship, the crown supplied the working apparatus of the wool custom:

> The king has granted that during the life of John the tronage [or wool-weighing, an enterprise which Chaucer would have supervised in his capacity as controller of customs] shall be held during pleasure in that house, and the king shall have easement therein for balances, weights, and a counting-house [*computatorium*] for controllers, clerks and other officers of the tronage.

Chaucer would have spent his time between the weighing house below and the countinghouse and chambers above; and, from time to time, in this newly built latrine, with its sturdy timbered downspout exiting into the Thames. Excavations also offer some details of life as it was lived there: Mysteriously, a whole and remarkably intact buckler, or small shield, was found in the downspout of the latrine; also found there and about the site were knives, fishhooks, shears, buckles, needles, pieces of chain, a great quantity of sheaths (leaving no doubt that people openly carried an array of knives), combs, a wooden chessman, and many pieces of leather shoes, of which the most complete examples belonged to an adolescent and infants (no luck, that is, in finding one of Chaucer's own).

A sketched panorama of the 1540s by Flemish artist Anton van den Wyngaerde, now in the Ashmolean Museum, portrays the customhouse as a practical location where hard work took place. Consistently with the fourteenth-century records, his structure has five gables and its original three bays. The building's actual functions are suggested by a crane on the wharf for the loading and unloading of vessels. Its imagined activities and excitements are very much those of the real world. Showing up at the custom house—especially the new-built structure of his later years in office—Chaucer must have felt that, for better or worse, this was no ordinary place of work. Certainly, much was expected of him there, though by no means all of it for the best.

"Something civil." Following upon the port as a natural setting and a built environment is its true rationale and its centrality to the affairs of the kingdom as a whole: those legislatively sanctioned activities bearing upon the collection of duties on imports and exports, and especially the latter and especially the most vital export of all, English wool. The late medieval English wool trade was a magnet for contradictory hopes and suspicions, equally susceptible to glorification and condemnation. Chaucer is not given to writing "topical" poetry and, despite his twelve years of involvement in the trade, wool would not have occurred to him as a poetic theme. His contemporary John Gower has no such hesitations; in his satiric poetry he writes frequently and at length on different concerns and issues of the day. In his *Mirror of Mankind* (*Mirour de l'Omne*), a contemporary satire composed in French and the first of his three major poems, he offers a scathing critique of various contemporary abuses, with the wool

trade as one of his cases in point. Dominant among the figures he encounters there is a ubiquitous trickster figure whom he names Triche, or Fraude. This Triche (who, as Gower says, possesses the gift of turning up to down and top to bottom) rules all commerce but finds a particularly warm reception in the wool trade. The ubiquity and corrupting power of wool stimulates even the occasionally prosaic Gower to an unaccustomed poetic flight, in which he employs the device of apostrophe, or direct address, to wool as a seductress, and imagines her sway. Translating from the French in which his poem is written:

> O beautiful, o white, how delicate you are.
> Your love so wholly penetrates and binds
> The hearts of those who trade in you
> That freedom's a lost dream for them.
> They'll follow any scheme to fill their warehouse
> With every bit of you they can afford.
> And then they'll carry you across the sea—
> But you'll be mistress of the ship they sail.

Starting in the thirteenth century and peaking in the fourteenth, this risky mistress, wool, would certainly exercise her blandishments on the London mercantile establishment and the kingdom as a whole. Many lives would be changed by the prospect of acquiring great wealth through the wool trade, and neither the first nor the last of them was Chaucer's own.

The English crown was utterly dependent upon the wool trade as its most significant source of bullion and ready profit. Taxes on rents, fines, and payments for customary privileges, together with income from royal estates—that is, all the traditional or "feudal" sources of crown income—were effectively stagnant and vastly inadequate to national needs, amounting to less than a third of crown income. Special "subsidies," or crushing exactions of a tenth or a fifteenth of assessed personal or institutional wealth, were imposed throughout the 1370s and, augmented by equally unpopular poll taxes, amounted to another third—but were enormously provocative of public anger. Continental military adventures yielded occasional windfalls of ransom and booty, but since Edward III's astounding midcentury success at Crécy the costs of such attempts had far outrun any meager successes achieved. And so revenue from wool customs (together with revenue raised on the *expectation* of profit from wool customs) was the crown's, and the nation's, most important income source, regularly amounting to a third, or even more, of the exchequer's receipts in the second half of the fourteenth century.

Shorn and baled wool—together with wool hides and, as the century went on, rough-woven wool cloth—were in fact England's *only* significant export item. Records indicate occasional shipments of lead, tin, leather, cheese, butter, feathers and featherbeds, resin, frippery (whether rags or sewn clothing ornament), linen, wheat, woad (a source of blue dye), wax, and fat—exports, that is, of a miscellaneous character and decidedly modest profitability . . . but wool was the ball game. Excepting the odd peasant in a remote village or hermit in a cell, nobody in fourteenth-century England was more than one degree of separation from the wool trade. Revenues from the trade itself were creating fortunes—for wool growers in the countryside, of course, but even more conspicuously for the London merchant capitalists who acted as middlemen, purchasing the wool and wool hides and shipping them for sale abroad. So rich were the profits available to middlemen merchants that, even after payment of formidable duties and subsidies on each sack of wool or lot of wool hides, fortunes remained to be made.

Total crown revenues from wool duties and extra wool subsidies amounted to some forty thousand to sixty thousand pounds annually (figures that require a multiple of several thousand to approximate their value in today's currency). These revenues represented a staggering concentration of disposable wealth, and were naturally an object of multiple schemes, calculations, and designs. Collected in numerous ports of the nation, but especially in London, these sums made their periodic way by boat and road to the offices of the exchequer in Westminster, and thence to the royal treasury. And they were greedily observed at every stage, eyed up for personal profit. Like the giant marlin lashed to the side of Hemingway's old fisherman's boat, these revenues were vulnerable to various predatory inroads all the way from their point of first collection at the customs office to their final lodging in the treasury of the king.

So vital was this revenue stream, and so keen the interest in its apportionment, that a history of later medieval institutions could be written from its standpoint. The origin of the English customs service and even, in significant respects, Parliament itself can be traced to Edward I's interest in capturing a share of wool profits. The crown's constant fiscal duress required repeated appeals for special grants, taxes, and subsidies, and the need to legitimize such requests was a crucial factor in regularizing the periodic meetings, functions, and powers of Parliament. At a formative meeting of Parliament in 1275, the assembled commonalty of the realm authorized the crown to collect 6s. 8p. on each sack of wool shipped, with comparable amounts for hides. In its hunger for revenue, the crown kept coming back for renewals and augmentations of the wool duty, maintaining the original "ancient" rate but, in the course of the fourteenth century, augmented by an additional "subsidy" of 33s. 4d. Negotiations with Parliament were, however, unceasing.

By midcentury the domestic market for wool export (as opposed to foreign, and mostly Genoese) had been effectively cornered by a cohort of capitalists, numbering at most a couple of hundred members scattered throughout the kingdom and its ports, but heavily dominated by an inner group of London entrepreneurs numbering in the dozens and controlled by a smaller inner circle still. This amounted to a monopoly, and commensurately enormous profits, for the handful of major players. Earlier in his reign Edward III was suspicious of the monopolists, and he sought to avoid or suppress them in various ways—including at one point his attempt to exclude them altogether and to limit exporting rights to alien or foreign traders. Eventually, though, he and his advisers saw the advantages of stability and domestic control, vested in what came to be known as the Wool Staple, an organization of leading English merchants who controlled the wool trade. The staplers agreed to ship to a single destination (Calais, when political circumstances permitted and warfare did not intervene) and channeled wool profits to the exchequer in an orderly way. Parliament, representing native interests and urban capital, favored the staple and took the additional step of asserting its own right to control matters of staple policy; during 1372–73, it demanded that a single staple be recognized and claimed (somewhat fancifully) responsibility for its original establishment at Calais. By 1376, thanks to cooperation between Parliament and leading London capitalists, the staple was firmly reestablished at Calais, and its favored position would not again be challenged in the remainder of the century. The principal trading corridor was thus secured between London and Calais, with London wool exports roughly equaling, or slightly surpassing, the total combined exports of the other twelve ports participating in the wool trade. No wonder the staple policy was favored by the London mercantile elite as a confirmation and enactment of its own monopolistic proclivities, which protected the interests of the group without deterring London exporters from profit taking on a massive scale.

Fox in the Chicken Coop

Foremost among the monopolistic staplers, and a mover of Chaucer's appointment to customs, was the very man whose dealings he was expected to oversee. This was Nicholas Brembre, four-time London mayor, and a long-serving collector of the wool custom, as well as a man of dubious repute. A brilliant speculator, a ruthless political factionalist, an unswerving partisan of the king's London interests, Brembre was at the center of every major controversy arising in the city for a period of twenty years. Nothing in surviving records suggests that Chaucer and Brembre were friends, but for twelve years their relations would be absolutely crucial to Chaucer's well-being, and would prove fateful in the end.

Although a grocer by trade, Brembre had spent no time squeezing quinces or stocking shelves. He had already established himself as a precocious wool exporter, earning large sums as a young man in the 1360s, and he used his capital not only to buy land but also to extend his influence in city politics. He waded eagerly into the urban political fray on the side of the prosperous and well-situated victualing (food-providing) guilds that controlled the import and sale of foodstuffs and provisions in the city. His political wedge issues involved his partisanship on behalf of privileges for his fellow victualers, including the prohibition of aliens (including non-London Englishmen) from engaging in trade within the city walls, as well as the preservation of price fixing and other monopolies among native vendors. He was first installed as mayor in 1377 by virtue of a temporary alliance with John of Gaunt, who negotiated the ouster of the sitting mayor and replacement with Brembre as part of a rollback of reforms instituted by the Good Parliament of 1376. He served in that office during 1377–78, and then, no longer a particular ally of Gaunt's but as head of the royal and Ricardian faction in the city of London, from 1383 until his fall from grace in 1386.

He was embroiled in the murky circumstances surrounding the slaying of the insurrectionary leader Wat Tyler at the peak of the Peasants' Revolt in 1381 and earned a knighthood as a reward. His no-holds-barred contests with mayoral adversary John Northampton culminated in factional violence, Northampton's imprisonment, and an urban climate so poisoned by partisan rancor that as late as 1391 city authorities issued an ordinance "forbidding any one whatsoever to express opinions about Nicholas Brembre or John Northampton, former mayors of the city, nor show any sign as to which of the two parties they favored." By that time Brembre was long gone from the scene, condemned and executed in 1388 by the faction of anti-Ricardians who called themselves the Appellants (for filing bills of complaint and appeals of treason against the followers of the king). Following his turn of fortune and downfall between 1386 and 1388, to be described in the next chapter, Brembre stood in the dock alone, accused not only by his long-standing enemies but by members of his own erstwhile faction as well. But throughout Chaucer's term as controller of customs—with particular responsibility for oversight of Brembre's activities in his post as collector of the wool custom—Brembre was far and away the most powerful man, and least scrupulous profiteer, in the city of London.

Brembre belonged to a particularly vigorous and able group of merchant capitalists who dominated London affairs in the 1380s. Although their biographies need not be repeated here, his associates William Walworth and John Philipot lived lives remarkably similar to his own. All three served as mayors of London and as officers of the Wool Staple. All were knighted in reward for dispatching Wat Tyler and defusing the threat of rebellion in 1381. All balanced and extended their London interests by strong support of incumbent kings, first Edward III and then Richard II. Most centrally, all were involved in substantial loans, both personal and collective, to the crown.

Wool brought all three men into politics, dictated their relations with the king, and increased their personal wealth. Conspicuous for his particular focus on the wool trade was Brembre—tersely (and accurately) identified not as "Grocer" but as "Woolmonger" in the record books of the city of London. Records of wool exports are, of course, spotty, but those of 1365—when Brembre was still a relatively young man, probably in his late twenties—establish him as the biggest of all of the wool exporters, responsible for what one economic historian calls an "almost incredible" 1,432 sacks. Although not again reaching that height, he continued to deal steadily in wool, for instance exporting 286 sacks in the years 1380–81, and leaving 150 sacks when his goods were inventoried for seizure upon his death in 1388.

None of this would be remarkable except for Brembre's manipulation of his power position within the court and the city to gain appointment to the very post responsible for collecting the substantial duties imposed upon exporters of wool. Those responsible for appointments seem to have been either urbane or else highly cynical with respect to conflicts of interest, since the collectorship of wool customs was often held by a shipper in his own right. But rarely was a person so deeply immersed in the trade appointed for so long in the capacity of customs collector, or in a situation so blatantly marked by obvious and ineradicable conflict of interest.

Responsibility for the collection of customs and the transmittal of customs revenues devolved upon two collectors of customs assigned to each English port, first for wool alone and then for certain other duties (sometimes clustered as "petty customs"). These collectors were responsible for certifying that merchandise leaving the port had been properly evaluated (which, in the case of wool, meant weighing each bag in a tron, or scale, available there at the custom house), the duty had been duly paid upon it, and the merchandise cleared for export by affixing the collector's half of a seal, called the cocket seal.

An exchequer document of February 26, 1374, records Brembre's appointment to the collectorship of the London wool custom. His duties will be:

> to collect in the port of London and all ports and places from there on both sides of the Thames . . . [between Gravesend and Tilbury] the custom and subsidy on wools, hides, and woolfells, to wit, on each sack of wool 50s from denizens and 4 marks from aliens, and, in the performance of that office, to keep the cocket seal in that port.

Some longevity in this office was normally expected. But no sooner had Brembre settled into his post, marked by his reappointment the following year and that of his colleague Walworth, than he was summarily ousted. A document of November 15, 1375, revokes the two appointments and demands that they return "the seal called 'coket' and all other things affecting that office which are in their keeping, not meddling farther therein." But then, in a further reversal, in a specially amended document of August 24, 1377, the two are reappointed to their posts. The explanation was that Brembre had, in the meantime, been elected mayor of London, and had resecured his position by deftly arranging a mammoth collective loan to the crown. This loan—as recorded in the Patent Rolls for September 18, 1377, a month after Brembre's election—was from a syndicate of London merchants, including both Nicholas Brembre and John Philipot, as well as William Walworth and a fourth wool profiteer, their close associate John Hadley. It granted the substantial sum of ten thousand pounds to the crown. In addition to paving his way back to customs, this loan is notable as the first of the many instances in which Brembre would arrange loans and direct gifts for Richard II. Until then Brembre had been a conspicuous holdout. But now, following soon upon his restoration to the collectorship, he and his associate Philipot were credited with a loan to exchequer of £2,666 13s. 4d., in September 1378. Brembre is credited by himself for another loan of £1,333 6s. 4d., on August 23, 1382. He gave Richard II outright gifts totaling £233 6s. during 1386–87. All told, in the period from 1377 to 1389, Brembre is on the record for gifts and loans of £2,970 and Philipot for £3,076. During all this, collective loans continued to be made by the city itself, especially when it was under the control of Brembre's royal faction. As a Ricardian loyalist and consistent fund-raiser, he was able to influence the terms of his own loans, negotiating favorable interest rates and guarantees of his own prepayment ahead of other creditors who might be waiting in line. But the

primary advantage of membership in this fiscal loyalty club
came in the form of influential appointments to offices that lay
within royal gift, among which this return to customs in 1377
appears to have been particularly important.

But why, given Brembre's exceptional wealth and unquestioned position of power, would he have been so interested in
the collectorship of customs, a demanding job that required personal attendance and record keeping, and that paid little or
nothing beyond small reimbursements for expenses incurred?
Clearly, rather than a distraction from Brembre's pursuit of
wealth, the collectorship of customs was a vital element in his
acquisitive strategy.

Collectors of customs were expected to be men of substance.
Consequently, except for amorphous "expenses," they received
no other reward. Modest stipends were provided for other officials of customs in the various ports, including controllers,
searchers of vessels for contraband, and the troners who oper-
ated trons to determine the weight and hence the value of wool
shipments. The uncompensated nature of the collectorships
may be linked to their superior status, but it appears also to be
a tacit recognition of the various ways, some intangible and
some more tangible, in which they stood to profit from their
posts.

The earlier case of financier Richard Lyons offers a preliminary indication of the kinds of latitude a post in customs might
afford. A shifty foreigner, conniver, and wealthy capitalist almost universally hated in the city of London, Lyons was in-
dicted in the Good Parliament of 1376 for various forms of
self-aggrandizement and influence mongering. His indictment,
in turn, provides a quick tutorial in the abuse of customs procedures for personal profit. Most important, he is said to have ex-

ported wool illegally and without proper certification by the cocket seal, avoiding the Calais Staple, in order to line his own pockets. More specifically, he was accused of using his involvement as a "farmer" of the customs (that is, an agent working between the waterfront and the office of the exchequer to collect customs on behalf of the king) to aggrandize himself in a variety of ways: to allow illegal shipping of wool in avoidance of the Calais Staple; to set and collect unauthorized duties on wool for his own use; to avoid scrutiny of his actions by any controller of customs; and to remove various large and small amounts of wool from each sack shipped under his authorization. Members of Parliament can practically be heard sputtering with indignation as they describe his piecemeal but cumulatively enormous exactions: "And it is commonly said that he takes in particular 10s. in one parcel and 12d. in another parcel from each sack etc., which amounts to a very great sum for the whole time that he had been the receiver or treasurer." (Lyons, rehabilitated in the year following the Good Parliament, would serve with Chaucer on the waterfront as collector of the petty subsidy during 1374–75. Things caught up with him, though. He was murdered in Cheapside by enraged rebels during the Rising of 1381 for causes unspecified but that might fairly be summarized as arising from general detestation.)

All the deceptions practiced by Lyons were potentially available to Brembre, and a good many more, owing to his collectorship, his mayoralty, and his marital and other ties to the London mercantile elite. As collector he supervised the weighing of wool, and the weight of the wool (which could be greatly increased by the illicit addition of moisture) determined the amount of custom to be paid. Or a collector could simply wave a friend's shipment through, especially shipments with destinations less closely regulated than Calais. Such friendly favors would, of course, involve kickbacks, but more direct avenues to personal enrichment were available as well. Between quarterly (or less frequent) deliveries to the exchequer, a collector had access to the funds for his own investment and use; he could, in contemporary terminology, "live on the float." He could (a frequent accusation) charge covert fees, or accept bribes, for special handling. (Venetian merchants operating out of the port of Southampton included payoffs to customs officials in their regular budgets.) He also would have had the option of simply not reporting, and pocketing, collected funds. A collector of customs would have to be a bit stupid to fail to make money, if that were his aim. Yet the principal opportunity for profit taking has yet to be explained and deserves special attention because of its reliance upon the collector's relations with his subordinate, the controller.

Even when bolstered by wool income, the treasuries of Edward III and Richard II careened from one fiscal emergency to another. Cash poor on the one hand and spendthrift on the other, they were often in short-term duress. Here, too, wool revenues had a crucial part to play. When revenues fell short, the crown resorted to loans. In the first half of the century, this meant reliance upon Italian bankers, and these bankers were experienced enough, and shrewd enough, to demand something other than the English king's assurances as security for their loans. Such security might, and often did, consist of jewels, gold and silver vessels, and other valuables set aside to secure the transaction. The various royal crowns were themselves regularly pawned, and even hacked into pieces, in order to serve as piecemeal guarantees of royal loans. But even such valuables would not open the way to loans on the scale needed. As in so many other matters, the solution once again came to rest with the immense wool revenues passing through customs, and the crown's claim upon them.

From the earliest days of customs, at the end of the thirteenth century, a practice developed in which wool revenues were assigned as security for loans to the crown. But the ingenuity in this, and the temptation for all parties, is that loans were not simply made in the expectation of long-term revenues, but that revenues were assigned to the repayment of debts *at the point of their collection and prior to their delivery to the exchequer.* The Italian merchants' innovative practice was to loan money to the king in return for an advance assignment of customs receipts and for permission to install themselves as farmers of customs until they had recovered their initial outlay. As farmers of customs, they were not simply beneficiaries of the process but were installed *within* the process. The guarantee of their insider status was their custody of the newly created emblem of procedural integrity, the cocket seal itself. This was the two-sided device designed to be held in common possession by the collector and the controller of customs, one possessing its front and the other its back. Each was to separately certify the proper collection of the duty by attaching his half of the seal to each wool sack or bundle of hides—and each, of course, was to act as a check upon the honesty of the other. In normal times, the two halves of the seal rested with the collector and the controller of customs. Yet, as security for its debts, the crown instituted the practice of removing half the seal from the controller's custody and placing it with the creditor, who was thus invited to oversee his own repayment.

Various schemes involving the exploitation of the cocket seal would be canvassed, but all of them involve a relaxation of oversight in response to lenders' demands for security. In these cases, the creditor is installed in multiple (and self-evidently contradictory) capacities: as a merchant in his own right, but also as an overseer of the legitimacy of the transaction, and as a profit taker, collecting export revenues on wool—his own and that of others—until the debt is satisfied. Only a saint placed in such a position could be expected to behave honestly—and the wool trade was not a conspicuous location for the exercise of sainthood.

Now imagine the additional possibilities for chicanery if the creditor were not an Italian banker but an English wool exporter and, beyond that, were the collector of customs himself. For a lender serving as collector of customs would find himself in possession of *both* halves of the seal—the half received as a creditor of the crown and the half exercised by virtue of his official capacity—leaving him in sole supervision of every aspect of a complicated and highly lucrative financial transaction. For over a decade, Nicholas Brembre occupied this inherently compromised position of taxpayer, profiteer, lender, and loyal servant of the king. In four of these ten years his position was additionally secured by the fact that as mayor he oversaw all city loans to the king. In the collective 1374 loan, in which he participated as alderman of the city and collector of customs, provision was made that the creditors receive an immediate sum from receipt of exchequer, and that

> the mayor, aldermen, and citizens shall take 25s. of each sack of wool loaded in the said port until they be satisfied of the remaining £2,266 13s. 4d. due to them, and that they shall have one part of the cocket seal in the said part until [the sum] be levied by indentures between them and the collectors of customs and subsidies.

Because this loan embraced the period of his first collectorship, Brembre is, personally, one of the two collectors responsible for arranging payment to himself. This is the first of several occasions on which he might have enjoyed the unusual power position accompanying possession of both halves of the cocket seal. This position is repeated in the case of the 1377 loan of ten thousand pounds—this time from the city itself, and with Brembre now occupying the additional post of mayor. Once again, Brembre and the others are guaranteed repayment directly from the duty and subsidy on exported wool. According to the *Fine Rolls* for November 9, 1377, which records sums of money offered to the crown:

> On 18 September last the king, for security of payment of a great sum of money lent to him . . . by Nicholas Brembre, William Walworth, John Philipot and John Hadley, merchants of London, . . . granted that until the said sum should be fully paid to them they should take the whole custom and subsidy of wools, hides and woolfells in certain ports of England.

The "whole custom and subsidy of wools" was to be divided into two parts, with one portion to be paid directly to Brembre, Walworth, Philipot, and their associate Hadley and the other portion to go to the relevant collectors of customs at the time of the shipment. This meant that not only the first but also the second portion would go to Brembre and Philipot—that the entire game would be in their hands. They would be able to supervise their own terms of repayment, not only regulating the flow of proceeds to the exchequer, but directly pocketing some of the proceeds as well. In 1378 a further loan of five thousand pounds is overseen by Brembre as mayor and Brembre as "customer," and a parallel situation occurred in 1379, when five thousand pounds were loaned with Philipot as both mayor and collector.

This mixed situation, in which the collectors of customs were working part-time on behalf of the crown and part-time on their own behalf, remained wide-open to every kind of abuse. No mechanism, in this case, would have prevented the holder of both seal halves from skimming considerable sums of money under his own authority. Except, that is, for the presence of an appointee whose post was expressly designed to prevent such practices. The sole check on Brembre's license, once he was installed on the job, was the vigilance of the man who would be named controller of customs, who was charged to oversee and certify his accounts. In other words, all Brembre needed to assure his free hand in the conduct of his office was (depending on how we view the matter) a crony, a co-conspirator, a client, or a hapless dupe in the controllership. Yet to be determined is which of these roles Chaucer, entering upon his June 1374 appointment as controller of the wool custom, would choose for himself . . . or find himself assigned to play.

"Quis custodiet ipsos custodes?"

Nicholas Brembre clearly needed watching. But then, in the question posed by the Roman poet Juvenal in his sixth "Satire," "Who will watch the watchmen?" Juvenal directs this question to suspicious husbands who think they can secure their wives' chastity by vigilance. His point is that watchmen are as liable to corruption as those whom they are supposed to be watching, and this is certainly the contemporary view of controllers of customs. From the very beginning English parliamentarians had sought to quiet their own apprehensions by creating controllers of customs, in the hope that controllers might restrain collectors from abuse of their office, preventing them from dipping into the immense sums of money they were handling. But how, in turn, would the probity of this new cohort of watchers be guaranteed?

As early as 1275, with the institution of the wool excise itself, provision had been made for a controller to oversee the activities of the collectors in each port. The idea was that the controller would keep a separate set of accounts, against which the accounts of the collectors would be compared. Hence, the etymological sense of the Latin *contrarotulator* and French and Anglo-Norman *contrerollour* from which the English term is derived: a person who keeps or enrolls a separate or "counter-" record in order to ensure honest dealing on the part of the collectors.

The scheme of controllerships was implemented gradually and unevenly, but by the 1320s most of the wool ports of England had an appointee in place. It was a hopeful initiative, especially from the standpoint of the national interest, but appears in the main to have been a disappointing one. The controllers themselves usually had close ties to the very mercantile communities they were asked to scrutinize, were liable to be overawed by the wealth and prowess of the collectors they were asked to oversee, and had little incentive to place the interests of the crown ahead of their own security, comfort, and longevity in the job. Favoritism, expressed in the appointment of royal servants on the one hand and friends of influential merchants on the other, was rampant. No sooner was the system in place than an ambitious scheme of reform was undertaken, in 1331, with periodic further attempts throughout the century. The 1331 legislation, drafted in the exchequer and approved by the king's council, complained about absenteeism, negligence, and fraud, insisting that the controller be personally present for the weighing of each "sack, poke, and bale" of wool, and that the rolls of the collectors and controllers, with their seals, be overseen quarterly in the exchequer.

Such complaints, and attempted ameliorations, attest not only to grievances but also to affirmative hopes that controllers might prove equal to their job. Expectations for controllers and what they might accomplish had, nevertheless, been steadily declining. Accepting this dubious advancement in 1374, Chaucer would find himself within a settled and intransigent climate of negative opinion, a virtual guarantee of scorn, if not outright hatred, directed against anyone with the temerity to take the post.

The public at large held the entire personnel of customs in the lowest possible regard, and none of the various categories of customs workers escaped this tainted view. For all the prominence, and even glamour, of the new customhouse, it remained a broadly suspect location. John Gower, in his *Mirour*, again has something to say in the matter. Still addressing wool, he says (in this translated version of his original French):

> You had the advantage of an English birth
> But everybody says you're ill-behaved.
> For Fraud [*Triche*], his pockets lined with shady cash,
> Is Regent of the warehouse [*estaple*] where you live.

The *estaple* here has a twofold meaning, alluding at once to Churchman's building on the Wool Wharf, where wool was accumulated and weighed, and also to the management of the entire wool trade, or the Wool Staple. Gower concedes in his poem that some of the *brocours*—brokers or middlemen who facilitate

the wool trade, whether considered locally on England's Wool
Wharf or internationally in the offices of the staple—may do
their best to withhold themselves from fraud. Even so, Triche,
or Trickery, will always advance his goals in the end (*"Quique
s'en voet abstenir / Du fraude, Triche ades l'avance"*).

Collectors and controllers were, naturally enough, considering the nature of their job, universally mistrusted, resisted, and
defamed. Whenever Parliament voted a new tax subsidy for the
crown, its members routinely passed an accompanying resolution to the effect that none of them should be required to serve
as collectors in their own regions. The very language of the oaths
controllers were required to take upon assumption of office betrays unease about their ability to resist fraudulent practices. Although Chaucer's own oath does not survive, a representative
contemporary oath for controllers of petty custom in London in
1376 requires that they swear to conduct themselves without fal-
sity or fraud in any respect (*"saunz fauxme ou fraude faire en nul
point"*). Another template oath, this time for Queensborough in
1370, contemplates the possibility of illicit gift giving or bribery,
insisting that the appointee take no gift for his office (*"nul doun
ne prendrez pur vostre office"*) and that the appointee swear not to
allow merchandise on which customs are due to leave the port
without payment (*"ne nulles marchandises ne autres choses custum-
ablez ne suffrez passer hors du dit port sanz custume due paier"*).

That customs collectors and controllers were frequently unre-
liable in these respects is apparent from endless complaints
about corruption, graft, cronyism, and lost revenue registered
again and again in Parliament in dogged pairing with half-
hearted schemes for reform. In 1371, Parliament expressed its
suspicion that controllers of the wool custom were demanding
additional (and off-the-book) fees, petitioning the king that no

charges be set upon wool except those it had specifically approved. In 1379 the Commons, reasoning that "a great part of the profit of the kingdom pertaining to our lord the king is in the subsidy on wool" and taking note of the fact that sheriffs were replaced annually, petitioned that officers and controllers of England be limited to annual terms. In 1385, in a special "Bill" attached to the records of Parliament, its members imagined that potential profits were lost to the realm through slack enforcement and urged that custom collectors and other officers be appointed on merit rather than "special affection," and that they be subject to regular review and should perform their duties in person:

> Item, that the profits of [the king's] great custom and petty custom might be greatly increased, . . . the customers and other officers concerned with them should be appointed from good and loyal men, by the advice of his council and his officers, and not through pleading or special affection, to be removed according to their merits.

The tempo of such complaints built steadily through the century until, in a Parliament of 1410, we encounter a truly hysterical outburst, fueled by wildly inflated claims of the amount of income lost through inappropriate personnel, disloyalty, and personal profit taking on the part of officers in the wool custom, controllers included:

> Also, may it please our said lord the king and his said council to understand that in the time of Richard formerly king of England, now dead, around the fourteenth year of his reign [1390–91], £160,000 and more was answered for in his exche-

quer each year from the subsidy and customs on wools and woolfells. . . . Yet these are of much less value annually at present, because the customs officers, tax-farmers, searchers and controllers have often been appointed through bribery, and from among people who are not of good standing, who have not well or loyally fulfilled or performed their said offices in due form for the king's profit, but rather for their personal profit and advantage, which they still take for their own uses.

The framers of the petition urge that future officers of customs be appointed on the advice of the king's council through the treasurer of England (rather than the king's privy seal) from among those who will perform their duties in person . . . and that steep fines and imprisonment should be the penalty for dereliction. The complainants' fantasy figure of £160,000—more than double the revenues of customs in better years—suggests the heightened emotion surrounding this subject. But the point is that this Parliament—like those of the preceding century—was tormenting itself by imagining larceny on the grandest of scales.

Customs procedures, as already described, represent the utmost in ingenuity aimed at keeping collectors and others from skimming or diverting profits: the division into two parts of the cocket seal; the preparation of the controller's "counter roll"; the highly formal (and sworn) audit in the exchequer; a second check at Calais; and the possibility of further investigation of the cocket seals collected there. This would have been a foolproof system, *except* in cases where collectors and controllers were in cahoots. To say that such collusion *might* occur is not to say that it *did* occur, but it was certainly possible, especially when collectors and controllers were willing to make common cause. Ideally, from the point of view of the conspirators, such collusions would remain undetected, and hence be invisible to the historical record. But two cases do argue for the possibility— both from Ipswich, still in the fourteenth century an active wool port.

One fraudulent collusion involved two Ipswich collectors serving between 1307 and 1320. According to evidence produced at their trial, in the fiscal years 1315 through 1317 the collectors had concealed and withheld from the exchequer an astonishing £660 out of a total of £980 collected, or two out of every three sacks of wool. Furthermore, study of the exports from Ipswich in the years following the disclosure of the fraud suggests that, in the following decade, even with new collectors in office, equivalent sums continued to be diverted from the exchequer.

In this first case, the collusion was between the collectors, and a controller of customs appears not to have been on the job. In theory, an honest controller could have put an end to illegal practices, and evidence from 1327 through 1331 suggests that Ipswich collectors strenuously resisted the appointment of a controller to oversee their efforts. But suppose a controller had been on the job. Again in Ipswich, this time from the end of the same century, collusion occurs with a controller on the job—collusion, in fact, involving the controller in concert with the collectors, for mutual gain. In this case, one John Bernard was appointed controller of the wool custom in 1397, and colluded with collectors Thomas Godeston and John Arnald. Their collaboration commenced that very year, but it did not come to light because their accounts were collusively misreported. The conspirators would have gotten away with it had not Arnald either had qualms or fears of detection and informed the authorities of their illegal activities. Their case was heard in the exchequer in

1401 and revealed, by their own confession, that the trio had been immensely successful; in a single year they had skimmed the considerable sum of £525 from duties in the wool custom, which they divided among themselves, £250 going to collector Godeston (evidently the ringleader, or the most persevering of the three), £155 to collector Arnald, and £120 to controller Bernard. (If we remember that Chaucer's combined salary as controller of the wool custom and the petty custom amounted to less than £20 annually, and that his annual income hovered around £40, the temptations and rewards of larceny become clear.) Moreover, a considerable rise in customs duties in the years immediately after the three ceased their activities suggests that the sums involved might have been even greater than that.

In the latter case, each of the three made restitution for this confessed crime. None was additionally punished, and Arnald, the informer, was retained in royal service. In other words, with restitution thought to close the matter adequately, this crime was apparently regarded as something short of heinous—perhaps even rather routine. Certainly, the trial records suggest that their offense is a common one; the king's prosecutors themselves allow that "such deception [*talis decepcio*] by all the customs officers and controllers of customs and subsidies was occurring [*fiebat*] in every port of the king of England." This case, in turn, seems to have led to a general inquiry; in 1402 the searcher of Calais was instructed to turn in cocket seals from the various ports of England, and numerous discrepancies and several clear cases of fraud were uncovered as a result.

Scandal touched Chaucer's own Wool Wharf directly in 1380, when the collectors and controller were ordered to replace their four wool packers, who were accused of hiring deputies engaged in deceptive practices. But one other surviving record gives heart to those who would rather not believe that everybody is on the take: An early-fifteenth-century scandal at the port of London involved another wool packer (John Bowlas) and a dishonest merchant (John Somer), in which Bowlas tried to smuggle uncocketed wool cloths into a shipment. This evasion was discovered by a searcher's deputy, and the case was turned over to Thomas Prudence, collector, and his deputy. Confronted, Bowlas offered "to pay the controller faithfully the custom and subsidy due therefrom to the king"—that is, to bribe his way out of the situation by giving the collector the payment he had evaded. Proving honest, Prudence "answered him that he would not take any penny of the said custom and subsidy," ordering Bowlas to pay it to the collectors or their clerk. His wiles unexhausted, Bowlas then attempted to bribe the collectors' clerk, also without success, and then pleaded ignorance of the whole affair, saying that he had been unaware that the cloth had been uncocketed. Bowlas was found guilty and fined. On this occasion, the system seems to have worked: Prudence, his deputy, and the collectors' clerk seem to have stood their ground and resisted Bowlas's attempts to bribe his way to a cocket seal. But given the general reputation of the controllers, and a culture of bribery surrounding all aspects of the wool trade, the appropriately named Prudence appears to be an honorable exception to an almost general rule.

A bribery culture is back in full force in a Latin verse satire, aimed at the exchequer and its malevolent practices, penned at the end of the century by one John Bell, himself a controller of customs in the port of Boston. He sardonically rails, "Oh chamber of the exchequer, it's a marvelous place—that one. As I'll tell you, a thousand torturers lurk there." ("*O scacci camera, locus est mirabilis ille / Ut dicam vera tortores sunt ibi mille!*"). These torturers, as he tells it, lie in wait for gifts, which are expected to expedite each phase of the process of review, comparison, and entry of the collectors' and controller's accounts.

This is the very process in which Chaucer was involved several times a year, when summoned to the exchequer for those quarterly audits of his and the collectors' accounts. The auditor himself is "worse than a demon unless grand gifts are given to him"—together with more gifts to the baron of the exchequer, the clerk who enters the accounts, and various other greedy and expectant figures, right down to the usher who cuts tallies from hazel rods. A thin line separates gifts and bribes from customary fees. Although Bell's rancor may partially color his account, his poem is indicative of a climate in which money is customarily exchanged for favors. One must, additionally, pose the question of why it is that collectors and controllers of customs felt an urgent need to curry favor in the first place; to speed the process, perhaps, but a wish not to have accounts scrutinized too thoroughly might have been a partial motivation as well.

All this amounts to a body of suspicion and negative presupposition, one that Chaucer could hardly have escaped—and he seems not to have escaped it.

When You Swim with Sharks, Don't Bleed

Many of Chaucer's responsibilities there in the customhouse were quite routine in nature, and involved nothing nearly so dramatic as confronting the greedy and imperious Brembre. An enormous flow of work surged through the customhouse— from the hands-on work of tronage, or wool weighing, to the computing and gathering of many thousands of pounds in customs duties, to the storage and delivery of funds, all requiring meticulous record keeping and culminating with the ultimate auditing of those records in the chambers of the exchequer. According to one scholar who has studied two representative years in detail, Chaucer would have been responsible for an average of 15 cargoes a month during 1380–81, and 8.5 cargoes a month during 1384–85. These cargoes, of course, included the goods of numerous shippers, each of whom needed to have his goods separately inspected and weighed and sealed by the cocket. Chaucer would have been responsible for signing off on 109 seals a month during 1380–81, and 60 a month during 1384–85. This workload would have required his presence at the Wool Wharf on most days, often for the entirety of the daylight hours. Additionally, of course, full accounts had to be drawn up, including the names of ships and owners, the names of merchant shippers, the quantities of wool and wool hides, the amounts of customs collected, and issuance of the seal. Several times each year the collectors and the controller were then summoned to the exchequer for extensive audit procedures, which involved oath taking, the appointment of an auditor and an attorney for the collectors, a detailed comparison of the collectors' and controller's rolls, a reconciliation of accounts, and payments rendered to the servants of the crown.

He petitioned on several occasions for deputies, in order to accept commissions to travel abroad on business of the crown, and during 1383–84 to relieve the pressure of the work. In 1385 and 1386 he petitioned to have deputies on a permanent basis, suggesting either disaffection on his part or a recognition that his time at customs was drawing to a close (his Michaelmas 1386 petition for a deputy overlaps his term in Parliament and likely residence in Westminster). But even for those terms in which he had a deputy, Chaucer still oversaw important elements of his job. For example, he appeared regularly at the periodic exchequer audits, assuming we may take literally those records that required certification of his accounts "by view and by testimony."

This post might have been a coveted factional reward, but it was no sinecure. No wonder Chaucer says in the *House of Fame*, written during his incumbency in customs, that literary matters await the evening hours, after his "reckonings" are done. No doubt, he was a hardworking civil servant. But if so many of the tasks he performed were enumerative and potentially neutral in character, what might his temptations to misfeasance have been? Or, to put it differently, were there any reasons to suppose that Chaucer was anything less than honest in his job? Or, more bluntly still: Was Chaucer that rarity, an honest controller, or rather what most people supposed of controllers, something of a crook?

Suppose he wanted to do the right thing. Suppose that in a culture of habitual laxity and institutionalized evasion he had decided to be an exception who proved the rule—a "Thomas Prudence" of his office and a bulwark of good practice. Had this been so, he would still have found himself hamstrung in this post, with few and feeble tools of office available to his hand. A vigorous campaign against wrongdoing would have required his intervention in the activities of his puissant patron and fellow royal factionalist Brembre. He would, in the first place, have mounted his intervention from a position of extreme social and political disadvantage.

The collectors of the London wool custom were invariably men of considerable wealth and substance—men of the stripe of Brembre, Walworth, and Philipot, as well as the controversial Richard Lyons—the city's power elite. But the controllers of customs were men of modest means, citizens of London and modestly well-positioned guildsmen. One exception—one John de Hermesthorpe who also served in the exchequer and had a full-time deputy in his controllership, and who would eventually become a collector himself—is insufficient to overturn the general rule. In most cases, the controllership was a dead-end job, rarely leading to promotion or an improved position. Controllers were, in this sense, cannon fodder—thrown into the breach, asked to make the best of it, torn in loyalty between the crown and the local merchants, responsible for policing the actions of men vastly their superiors in wealth and social authority without any tools or sanctions adequate to the job. Any set of circumstances in which Chaucer might have been seriously expected to check any course of action pursued by Nicholas Brembre—Mayor Brembre, for half of his term—would be very difficult to imagine.

Perhaps more to the point, even in the unlikely circumstance that Chaucer had been bent on such an impractical intervention, he would frequently have lacked the *means* to do so. Here we return to the controller's primary symbol of authority, his half of the cocket seal, through which the controller established the fact of his own vigilance and testified to the honesty of the process he had overseen. Throughout its hundred years of employment, the controller's half of the cocket seal had as often as not been in other hands, taken from the controller and given over to major lenders to the king. Quite early in Chaucer's own tenure, for example, a mandate from the exchequer stipulated that three London merchants (including the ubiquitous and shifty Lyons), who had loaned £1,000 to the king, should receive two marks (26s. 4d.) from each sack of wool shipped from the port of London until the debt had been paid—"and that they or their deputy shall have one part of the cocket seal in the said port until satisfied." In some cases the collector's half might have been rendered, but in most cases it was the controller rather than the collector who gave up his portion of the seal. All in all, fourteen loans involving repayment through the wool custom, and relinquishment of the cocket seal, usually to Nicholas Brembre, were made to the king during Chaucer's controllership. These were loans of short duration, involving on average less than ten months, but the subtraction of as many as one hundred months from a twelve-year controllership represents a very considerable abridgment of Chaucer's effectiveness in office. Not only would he have had every incentive toward vice, but he was deprived of the rudimentary tools for maintaining virtue.

So he was unlikely to have proven a potent counterfoil to the machinations of his powerful patron. But, over at the other extreme of possibility, he doesn't seem to have been a particularly ambitious or enterprising co-conspirator either. Perhaps the most forceful consideration in favor of Chaucer's faithful (or at least actively uncriminal) conduct of his office is that he did not leave the controllership a wealthy, or even a prosperous, man. Many factors—including common sense, an awareness of Brembre's boundless acquisitiveness, and a recollection of the enormous and coordinated efforts required to get Chaucer into this post in the first place—suggest that his term in office was utterly compromised by considerations of personal profit. But the profit in question appears to have been Nicholas Brembre's, and hardly, if at all, Chaucer's own. Rather surprisingly, and perhaps unaccountably, Chaucer seems to have realized little personal profit in a post normally occupied by egregious profit takers.

The *Life-Records* suggest that Chaucer was in serious economic difficulties in the years immediately following his withdrawal to Kent. An action to recover a debt of £3 6s. 8d. was brought against him in April 1388 by John Churchman, the speculator and financier who rebuilt and released the custom-house in 1382, and who might be supposed a personal acquaintance, if not friend. Churchman launched simultaneous suits against others for sums ranging from £28 to £330; the derisory sum of his suit against Chaucer might suggest a more personal sort of quarrel, but also suggests that he was too hard-pressed to settle even a relatively modest claim. Another action for debt brought by an innkeeper and citizen of London in November 1388 would suggest the same. Chaucer's economic difficulties at this time would have been compounded by the termination of Philippa's annuity, last paid, as usual, into the "hand of Chaucer," on April 7, 1387. It was Philippa's annuity, but it represented a collective marital resource and, with her residence in Lincolnshire with her prosperous sister, it may have been partially available for her husband's use. But that modest income supplement was now at an end. No wonder that, in the light of all this, Chaucer embraces what appears to be an emergency measure to raise short-term capital at the expense of long-term financial prudence. On May 1, 1388, he assigns his exchequer annuities to one John Scalby. Such annuities to followers of the king were, in fact, coming into question by the Merciless Parliament, and the reassignment might possibly have been another prudent mitigation of Chaucer's Ricardian ties. But, more likely, they were sold for immediate cash in hand as a result of his straitened financial situation there in Kent.

Chaucer appears neither as an active criminal nor a virtuous reformer but as a mildly complicitous, and rather under-rewarded, fellow traveler in the slipstream of Brembre and other more greedy and less principled players. His shortcomings appear to have rested less in the commission of actual crimes than in the omission of certain forms of strenuous inquiry; less in dreaming up schemes for personal profit than simply in turning a blind eye to certain of Brembre's self-interested schemes; less in performing feats of criminality on his own behalf than merely in remaining untroubled, or at least unconsternated, by the knowledge that serious and underhanded profits were being made. He would have had the opportunity and the motive to satisfy the greediest and most extortionate schemes of Brembre and his cohorts simply by looking the other way; working to rule; keeping his head down; knowing when to keep his mouth shut; and allowing his superiors a free hand in their exercise of office.

This is less an argument for his innocence than a simple observation that he was neither more nor less innocent than we would suppose a controller of customs to be. A hundred years ago the most distinguished of modern Chaucer scholars, George Lyman Kittredge, refuted the prevailing view of Chaucer as a fun-loving naïf by describing the resources of tact and guile he would have needed just to get through the day. Addressing the Chaucerians of his era, whose frequent error was to mistake what he called the "effect of artlessness" in Chaucer's poems as a mark of naïveté, he dryly observed that a naïve controller of customs would be a "paradoxical monster" indeed.

A balanced view of Chaucer's performance in office would have him neither as a hero nor a villain but as a man who kept his head down, an enabler. Unfortunately, the activities he was enabling were those of Nicholas Brembre, a grasping, faultily principled, and ultimately deeply unpopular man. The day would come—and on Monday, after the feast of St. Jerome in the ninth year of Richard II, a day *had* come—when his reputation as an enabler would do him no good in the city of London.

CHAPTER FOUR

In Parliament

~~~~~~~~~~~~~~~~~~~~~~

The 1386 Parliament was going to be a contentious one. Richard's ambitious young uncle Thomas, duke of Gloucester,
had emerged as the head of an aggressive and intransigent reformist faction and its adherents arrived in Westminster primed
for a fight with the king. The reformists' hands were strength-
ened by a broadly shared sense of national malaise.

The country was on edge. England had been on the defensive, both militarily and economically, ever since the resumption
of the French wars in 1369. The English had experienced defeat
after defeat, most recently the failure of skirmish-minded
Bishop Despenser's Flemish "crusade" in 1383. More recently, in
the summer of 1385, Richard had exposed all his shortcomings
as a military leader with a tactically obsolete, overceremonial,
and utterly ineffective military incursion into Scotland. Now
Gaunt, who had quarreled with Richard over his passivity in
that campaign, had just set out himself on his similarly expensive and more protracted and equally unproductive quest after
the kingship of Castile. The additional effect of Gaunt's departure was to deprive the country of needed military resources at a
most unpropitious moment. Throughout the summer of 1386 a
substantial French force was gathered and prepared to embark,
prevented only by unfavorable winds from mounting a substantial invasion of the English mainland. Invasion panic swept the
country, particularly London, where rigged bastions were

thrown up against the city walls (including one just outside Ald-gate), garrisons were mustered, and the French were expected daily, right up to Parliament's opening when the hope that adverse winds might prevent invasion had just begun to dawn.

Coupled with these dissatisfactions was mounting distress over King Richard's own maddeningly spendthrift ways, the costs of his court, and his maladministration of finance. The year 1386 had already afforded one egregious example of Richard's extravagance. He played host, and arranged a state visit, for a truly outlandish scammer, Leo, the deposed king of Armenia. Leo had ruled Armenia for barely a year prior to his expulsion by victorious Moslems in 1375. He then roved Europe for the rest of his life as a distinguished guest and, eventually, self-styled ambassador of peace between England and France. King John I of Castile granted him, for a time, the city of Madrid, and King Charles VI of France made him a gift of Saint-Ouen Castle. Although stopping short of such bounty, King Richard received him with full monarchic panoply and gifted him at a level that entailed some strain on the English treasury. The chronicler Walsingham is particularly salty on the Armenian's motives and Richard's susceptibility. In his *St. Albans Chronicle* he observes that Leo posed as a peacemaker, but "he desired gifts rather than peace, and was more in love with money and the gold of the kingdom than with the people or its king." Upon Leo's departure in mid-February, Richard escorted him with pomp to his vessel and gave him a waxed and sealed letter of patent guaranteeing him a thousand pounds a year if he achieved peace between France and England.

Especially since 1376, Parliament itself had become the primary forum for the airing of economic discontents. It called for commissions of inquiry in 1379, 1380, and 1381. It advanced a petition for change in the highest appointive offices in 1383, and then embraced a sweepingly ambitious scheme for restraint of royal power in the Parliament of 1385. In this last, the customary grant of tax subsidy to the crown (to be devoted primarily to Gaunt's quixotic expedition) was approved only subject to ominous curtailments and to "certain conditions." The crucial wool subsidy was approved only on condition of its expiration between June 24 and August 1, 1386; this central element of royal finance would be withheld "lest such subsidy, resulting from a free and spontaneous grant by the lords and commons, if by chance it continued without interruption, should be demanded or claimed as a right or custom."

If all this weren't enough, the parliamentary participants of 1385 returned in 1386 bearing a special grudge. The 1385 Parliament had created a special commission, consisting of eight lords and knights, to oversee every aspect of royal finance. The king was obliged to appoint such a commission as one of the "conditions" of continued cooperation. The Parliament concluded with the adoption of a special bill listing the eight noble and knightly commissioners, and its language is significant. These are the "names of the lords who were ordained by the king to view his estate . . . as the commons have demanded." The parliamentary French of the original document is *come les comunees cryeount*, from *crier*, to proclaim, or even to shout out. This is exceptional language, and whether it is understood as something demanded or some other kind of outcry, it represents an unusual level of parliamentary assertion, especially when confronting a king of Richard's high pretensions. And this demand was coupled with others: that the king give credence to his own council; that he spurn inappropriate "information" or partisan influence; that the committee of lords oversee the income and expenditures of exchequer. Consistently with these positions, the bill also touched a topic important to Chaucer, insisting that customs collectors, controllers, and weighers (the officials, that is, of the wool custom) be appointed from good and loyal persons by advice of council, "and not through private pleading or affection."

The hope had been that the commission's appointed representatives might exercise a measure of restraint upon Richard's inclinations toward favoritism, fiscal excess, and arbitrary rule. Such hopes were bitterly disappointed. In the ensuing year, Richard and his chancellor, Michael de la Pole, granted no recognition of the commission's existence. This slight, and its attendant frustrations, were a prior irritant and affront in 1386. More than half the members of the new Parliament had been present in 1385 and had enjoyed the hopes attending the commission's creation. They and their fellows entered the chamber in a state of increased suspicion and heightened vigilance.

Gloucester's party already knew one thing they wanted: the resignation of the king's chancellor and favorite Michael de la Pole. They were also primed to contest a range of other issues, including disappointing receipts of the wool custom. Constituting a slight plurality of the seventy-four shire knights upon arrival, the dissidents grew in strength and confidence, developing into a substantial (and full-voiced) majority in the course of the session. But what about their fragmented and embattled Ricardian opponents?

Prevailing scholarly opinion has the 1386 Parliament as uniformly anti-Ricardian and supposes that the king's party had made no special effort to pack it with members sympathetic to their position. But the story is slightly more complex than that. To be sure, in and after 1388 Richard would become an ardent electioneer, and his tampering would become one of the causes of his deposition argued by Henry of Derby and the Lancastrians in 1399. Because efforts along these lines were less ambitious in 1386 does not mean they did not occur. Upon closer viewing, a handful of persons did show up in response to pro-Ricardian efforts, just not very many of them, and in any case too small a number to make their presence effectively felt.

Conspicuous in this respect was a member like Sir James Berners of Surrey, a chamber knight of the royal household and one of the Ricardian adherents condemned by the anti-Ricardian Appellants in the Merciless Parliament two years hence. Or Sir William Wingfield of Suffolk, a close associate and apparent friend of Chancellor de la Pole; he seems to have made his peace with the Appellants by 1388, but the Parliament of 1386 could not have been a comfortable one for him. Or Sir Richard Waldegrave, also of Suffolk, a member of the court party and an intimate of Nicholas Brembre, with whom he frequently dined in London. In these cases, we may see the faint outline of strategy. Just because the strategy was only partially realized does not mean it was no strategy at all.

Here is where Chaucer, shire knight representing the county of Kent in the Parliament of 1386, comes in. Chaucer biography normally involves looking for external evidence that will elucidate his career; in this case, however, Chaucer *himself* is the one who provides the evidence, because his presence in Parliament affords the strongest confirmation that the king's party made at least a partial attempt to assert the royal influence there. His presence argues that Richard's council or other followers did indeed make an effort to pack the Parliament—albeit a failed one—because there is no other conceivable reason for Chaucer, as the least qualified shire knight in the whole assembly, to have been there.

His qualifications were so dubious when compared with those of others in his category of representation that only a special interest in his election by supporters of the king can explain what he was doing there. On August 8, 1386, a writ had gone out from the king's council to the sheriff of Kent mandating the election of two knights to represent the shire at an upcoming parliament, to be held at Westminster on the first day of the coming October. This category of representation, seventy-four knights of the shire or two from each of the recognized shires or counties of the land, consisted theoretically of sworn knights (or knights "girt with sword" in the language of the writ). A majority of them actually occupied that rank. A significant minority, including Chaucer, did not: They were instead esquires of the realm, together with a small scattering of gentlemen. But, with Chaucer as the only apparent exception, the knights and esquires representing the shires and counties held one characteristic in common: the ownership of land.

Virtually the first thing anybody with sufficient cash in hand or influence in court ever did in fourteenth-century England was acquire land; even urban merchants such as Brembre and Philipot strove to dignify their station with rural manors and estates. Yet Chaucer, scraping by in his controllership of customs, enjoyed no such latitude, and would thus, upon his selection, become one of the few shire knights—possibly the *only* one—serving in the 1386 Parliament without a landed base. His lack of land raises a related issue, that of residence. The custom was that each of these shire knights should actually be resident (and not just a rent payer or somebody's guest) in the county represented. The writ of summons, reasonably enough, supposes that those elected should be *de comitatu*, or "of the county," in question. Only in the fifteenth century was it conclusively established as an absolute requirement that members had to live in the counties they represented on the date of the election, but it was already a normal understanding in Chaucer's own era. Even so, within the climate of assumptions surrounding land ownership in the fourteenth century, he must be considered a nonresident. He could, that is, be renting or borrowing a place to stay, but this would not have made him a resident in the vital landowning sense.

So Chaucer was to be seated among a body of shire knights overwhelmingly composed of hereditary landowners, most of whom were genuinely sworn and "girted" knights, and almost all having deep local associations in the constituencies they served. He would, to say the least, have found himself marginally and atypically situated in this group. Son of a bourgeois, owning no land, holding his barely gentle title as a result of loyal service rather than birth, nonresident or barely resident in the county he would be called upon to represent, Chaucer would have had much more in common with Parliament's outer fringe of citizens and burgesses than with his fellow shire knights— and without even enjoying a typical citizen's or burgess's level of economic success. Compared with his fellows, he was earning a paltry income. The *History of Parliament*'s analysis of shire knights from Kent in the period 1386 to 1421 has eight with annual incomes over £120, eighteen with incomes between £40 and £70, and only six of them (including Chaucer) worth under £40 per year.

Chaucer, in other words, would find himself in a familiar position within this group. Familiar, that is, in its marginality, in the tenuous hold it would have given him on the status of shire knight. As a courtier, he had achieved the rank of esquire, but esquire of *meindre*, or lesser, degree, responsible for useful tasks and services. In the city he had been associated with Brembre and the most powerful members of the ruling elite, but, again, in the capacity of useful servitor rather than policy maker or fellow strategist. Now, in Parliament, he will belong to the more select and prestigious group of shire knights, but only barely, and (as a one-term member of a body in which service was usually for long duration) fleetingly as well.

The anomalies of Chaucer's social position are illustrated in an event occurring during the parliamentary session. The celebrated Scrope-Grosvenor trial, in which two knightly claimants clashed over the use of a single coat of arms, was in progress, and the prestigious court of chivalry held a special session in the refectory of the Westminster Palace, at the convenience of the eighteen shire knights called to testify. Chaucer was among them, an undoubtedly pleasing summons for its recognition of his gentle status. But the other seventeen shire knights were all knights in fact, and invited to testify first. As an esquire of slightly dubious status, Chaucer cooled his heels, the last of the eighteen to testify. When he gave it, though, his testimony was apt and self-possessed; representing himself as a Londoner, walking down Friday Street, he described a conversation with an amiable stranger about a coat of arms displayed outside an inn located there. Here we see Chaucer conducting himself in what must have been a familiar way: with calm self-possession in an uneven social situation, discharging his responsibility with grace and a modicum of charm, and even telling a bit of a story in the bargain. But he was a junior partner, a lesser figure in the affair.

How did somebody so marginally qualified find himself as a shire representative in the first place, in a body dominated by hereditary landowners, many of whom were special pleaders

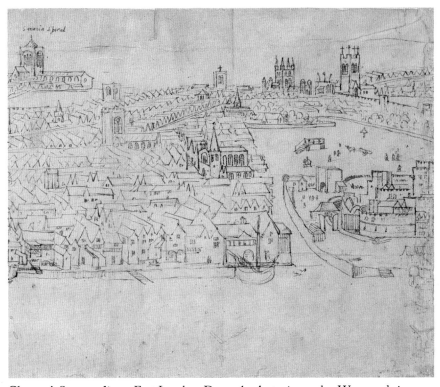

Chaucer's Surroundings: East London. Drawn by Antonis van den Wyngaerde in 1544, but the disposition of major buildings remains similar to that of 1386. On the upper horizon, at center, with a cross on its top, is St. Katharine Cree parish church. To its right is Holy Trinity Priory. Right of that is Aldgate, with three traitors' heads on scaffolds for display. At the extreme right is St. Botolph's parish church (considerably exaggerated in scale). In the foreground, on the riverfront, at center is the five-gabled and two-arcaded customhouse, identifiable by the crane stationed immediately outside its entrance. To the right are the environs of the Tower. London Bridge would have been located to the left of the scene illustrated here.

Four Courtly Youths: Four gentlepersons, holding ribbons, in a festive dance. The dancer to the right wears a garment similar to the "paltock" given to the young Geoffrey early in his courtly service.

John of Gaunt Claims the Throne of Castile: Gaunt, accompanied by Constanza of Castile, upon whom his claim was based, and his daughter, who would wed the King of Portugal, arrives in Galicia on his 1386 adventure of conquest. A messenger bows to him. Few medieval depictions of Gaunt exist; this one from a fifteenth-century chronicle suggests his haughty demeanor.

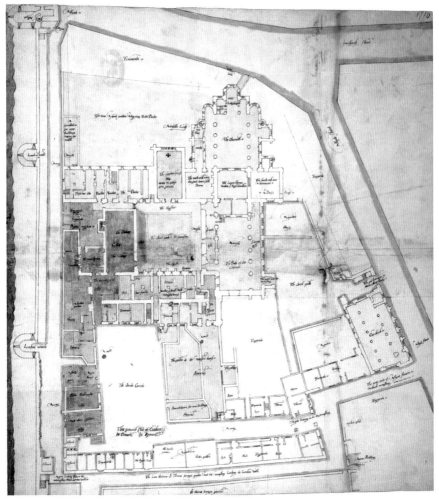

Plan of Holy Trinity Priory, with Aldgate North Tower: Sixteenth-century plan of Holy Trinity Priory, ground floor. Aldgate's north tower is at the upper left-hand corner. Chaucer lived in the similar south tower from 1374 to 1386. The Houndsditch was to the left of tower along the city wall. St. Katharine Cree, Chaucer's possible parish church, is at the lower right.

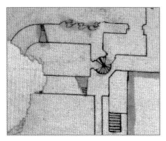

Tower, Upper Floor: This partially damaged inset represents the upper floor of Aldgate's north tower, equivalent to Chaucer's own south tower room. Illumination is provided by two (or possibly four) arrow slits.

1381 Rebels Assail Aldgate: This rather fanciful illustration from Froissart's *Croniques* imagines the 1381 rebels as a well-equipped army assailing Aldgate. In a further imaginative elaboration, Richard II, rather than Chaucer, cowers within. But Chaucer was probably at home, and possibly cowering, at the time!

Tower Window with Arrow Slit: This is an upper-floor window opening from the Canterbury Westgate Tower, constructed during Chaucer's lifetime according to plans by architect Henry Yevele (with whom Chaucer associated during his renewed period of royal service in 1389–91). It is the closest surviving counterpart to Aldgate. The grillwork is a Tudor addition, when the tower was used as a prison. The larger archer's opening is in the foreground; the arrow slit, about 5" in width, is in the background.

Chaucer's King: Richard II, King of England during most of Chaucer's mature years, enthroned with crown and symbols of majesty. This portrait is on permanent display inside the main entrance to Westminster Abbey.

A Cocket Seal Matrix: This is one side of the two-sided die or matrix used to form the wax seal certifying a bale of wool for export. The four loops fitted into four pegs in the other half-seal to allow the casting of a complete, two-sided wax image. This die, found in Billingsgate on the banks of the Thames, is identical to the one Chaucer would have possessed (at least part of the time!) in 1374–77, during the reign of Edward III. At the center of the die are the arms of England, accompanied by the inscription LORD EDWARD KING OF ENGLAND IN THE PORT OF LONDON.

Chaucer Reads Aloud: This frontispiece, from a sumptuous edition of *Troilus and Criseide* dating from the first decade of the fifteenth century, imagines Chaucer reading his poem aloud to the court of Richard II. This image celebrates the recently deceased Chaucer's new status as father of English poetry. Although it is a polite fiction—he is unlikely actually to have addressed so elevated a group—it conveys contemporary assumptions about the oral presentation of poetry and the importance of a "live" audience.

Cprologue

Ꝇret chere made our oste to vs euerychon
And to souꝑer sette he vs anon
He serued vs wyth vytayll at the beste
Stronge was the wyne ⁊ wel drynke vs lyste
A semely man our oste was wyth alle
Forto be a marchal in a lordes halle
A large man he was wyth open eyen
A fayrer burgeys is ther non in chepe
Bolde of hys speche and wel was y taught
And of manhood lacked he right nought
Eke therto was he right a mery man
And aftir souper to pleyen he began
And spak of myrthe amonge other thynges
Whan that we hadde made our rekenynges
He sayde thus now lordynges treuly
Ye be to me right welcome hertly
For by my trouthe yf þ J shal not lye
J saw not thys yeer so mery a companye

c iiij

The Pilgrims Dine Together: This illustration from Caxton's second edition of the *Canterbury Tales* imagines an amicable Pilgrim band. The hooded host figure is presumably Harry Bailly, although the artist may have taken this occasion to represent Chaucer himself in that role; the centrality and solemnity of the hooded figure are consistent with respectful fifteenth-century representations of Chaucer the Poet.

Chaucer the Poet: This manuscript illustration, commissioned by fifteenth-century admirer Thomas Hoccleve, depicts Chaucer as a mature and fully arrived poet. His somber attire, the inkhorn around his neck, the rosary, and his instructive gesture all contribute to an effect of gravity, appropriate to the stature he achieved in the decades following his death.

with a personal or regional ax to grind? The answer is that *he* was something of a special pleader, or at least representative of a special interest, in his own right. The shire elections were conducted by the county sheriff, a figure of considerable substance in later medieval England, and the sheriff was a royal appointee. In this case, the incumbent was Sir Arnold Savage, a confirmed Ricardian. One must assume that, given Chaucer's evident lack of other qualifications, including even such basics as residency itself, the word had somehow come down from the king's inner circle to Savage that he would be a good man to have.

Once in Westminster, he might have wished himself back in his room in Aldgate, writing poetry, or even back on the Wool Wharf keeping his accounts. But his mentors had a way of dragooning him into things, of putting him where they wanted him or supposed he would be useful. Once again, as with the job in customs, he seems to have been in Parliament as a result of other people's designs. In this case, the design of Richard's advisers or his followers in Kent that he be there, along with a small cohort of fellow partisans, to shore up the faltering royal position in a manifestly hostile legislative situation.

In Westminster

Had Chaucer, accepting this position, any notion of how many embarrassments lay in store for him there? Whether or not, for the next two critical months his residence would be Westminster, and Parliament would be the horizon of his experience.

Westminster was still separate from London in those days, with a half mile of clogged footpaths discouraging travel between the two. The easiest way to get there was by water taxi, but this route was hampered by tides, river traffic, expense, and overbearing boatmen. It was more a village than a city, though boasting fine structures like Westminster Abbey itself, a flour-ishing monastery in those days, the royal palaces, and stately Westminster Hall. Especially when the courts were in session, the king and his entourage were in the palace, and Parliament was meeting, Westminster became a crowded, exciting, and raucous place. Although enjoying only some three thousand permanent residents, it doubled or tripled its size on such occa-sions, with an influx of a thousand or more (including retinues of leading ecclesiasts and lords) at Parliament time, augmented by a half thousand semipermanent members of the royal house-hold, another half thousand lawyers, accountants, and scribes on the payrolls of the chancery and the exchequer, not to men-tion minstrels, tapsters, prostitutes, and other roving members of the service and entertainment industries. The profit-making citizens of Westminster were, in effect, at the parliamentarians' service, practicing various schemes of predation and entrapment to earn their livelihood at the expense of these hardworking but also fun-seeking visitors. Westminster enjoyed the status of a "liberty"—liberated, that is, from the strict curfews, antiprosti-tution ordinances, and restraints upon trade and consumption typical of the straighter-laced London upon which it nearly abutted. To be sure, the precincts of Charing Cross to the east and Southwark across the river were wilder still, with licensed and unlicensed brothels, unregulated brew pubs galore, and ev-ery kind of con game imaginable. But Westminster itself was very nearly an open city, and that is how the visiting MPs would have found it.

A look inside Georgetown bars, and Pimlico equivalents, when the U.S. Congress or the British Parliament are in session still gives a hint of the goings-on that might be expected when so many well-funded, short-term out-of-towners arrive on such a basis. Think of 250 potentially rowdy parliamentarians away from home, on expense accounts. Chaucer, for example, would continue to receive pay as a controller until just after the end of Parliament; during Parliament he would receive 4s. a day for his expenses as shire knight, a home county supplement of 6d. a day, and any contribution Kent might make to his parliamentary expenses, totaling something above £20, a sum equivalent to more than half his normal annual earned income. He was probably living in a shared room somewhere and husbanding his threatened livelihood, but some of his fellow parliamentarians were living large.

The expense account of the four London representatives to the 1388 Cambridge Parliament survives in the *Letter-Books*, and it is an eye-opener. Cities and boroughs sent their own representatives to Parliament, usually chosen from among the more prosperous merchants and tradesmen. Although they were technically of lower rank than the shire knights, they normally had plenty of money to spend, and (as in the case of the Cambridge Parliament) received additional subsidy to maintain themselves in fitting style for out-of-town events. This high-living group claimed for lodging (including cleaning and refurbishment of the house in which they stayed), £6 9s.; for kitchenware and tableware, £6 16s. 8d.; for firewood, £5 13s.; for hiring of horses and transport, £20 3s. 8d.; for wine, £9 2s.; for clothing for themselves and their servants, £22 15s.; for miscellaneous per diem expenses, £23 5s. 9d.; and for payments to servants, £7 13s. They paid for a steward, a butler, a cook, and kitchen boys, as well as for grooms to look after their horses. Most notably, they claimed for special payments to royal minstrels—evidently hired on a temporary basis for private parties in their own refurbished dwelling. In all, they laid out a hefty total of £112 7s. These were persons of substance, including three of aldermanic rank (they attended a total of twenty-five Parliaments among them), and London obviously had its own points of pride to be observed. Even so, the suggestion from such accounts is that a member of Parliament was expected to acquit himself well, and that his constituency had a responsibility for contributing to his estate. Chaucer presumably received nothing like this, and possibly nothing at all, from Kent, but his stipend of £20 on top of his regular salary would have meant that he could create conditions of comfort—perhaps exceptional comfort—for himself during his term.

King Street, between the palace yard and the bar marking the city's ultimate jurisdiction, angled north toward Charing Cross along the route of present-day Whitehall. In loose analogy with Las Vegas, it may be thought of as "the strip," a busy and raucous thoroughfare crowded with places for food, drink, and entertainment. By the turn of the sixteenth century this quarter-mile-long stretch boasted over a dozen taverns and alehouses, including the Saracen's Head, the Black Eagle, the Maiden Head, the Rose, the Peacock, the Lamb, the Red Lion, the Bell (three of that name), the Sun, the George, the Swan, the Boar's Head, the King's Head, and more, including a host of brewhouses too small or casual to possess names and signs. The Boar's Head, and other establishments, were already up and running in the fourteenth century, and there is no reason to doubt that 1386 boasted as many places of refreshment as 1508, when the population of London and its environs was still about the same. Besides, when one continued beyond the bar marking the Westminster limits and toward Charing Cross, things really got rowdy. In this unincorporated area, prostitution and related activities thrived, without even the nominal regulation that partially curtailed notorious Southwark brothels in

Parliament time. Chaucer and his friends would have had no trouble getting a drink of an evening, or at any other time of day. Their ease in consumption would have been abetted by the presence of "tipplers," or small retailers, with 127 operating in the parish by the fifteenth century.

For lodging Chaucer might have joined with associates to let a house (though presumably at considerably less expense than that of the 1388 Cambridge delegation), or he could have stayed in relative style at an inn like the Boar's Head. More likely still, he could have stayed in a let room in a private dwelling, although such accommodations were not problem-free. Consider the story of John de Whalley, a monk of Lancashire who sought lodgings at the home of one Alice Hull while prosecuting cases in the courts of Westminster:

> The night was an eventful one for Brother John, who (by a ruse, according to his account) was found naked in bed with Alice by her friend and pretended husband, Thomas Worsop. Crying "False monk and traitor!" Worsop dragged the hapless visitor by his legs out into the street, where he spent three cold hours before a payment of 5s. 8d. was accepted for his readmittance.

As to what an evening on the town would have looked like for Chaucer, we'll never know. But Thomas Hoccleve—a poet of the next generation who considered the artistically mature Chaucer his master—has given us a vigorous representation of a literary man's Westminster nightlife. Hoccleve was a clerk in the offices of the privy seal, employed in the palace, and he commuted the mile from his quarters near Temple Bar, between Charing Cross and the city. After work he lingered in the taverns around Westminster Gate. His account is awash with the self-reproach of a reformed man of late middle age, but nevertheless the allure of the strip shows through. He is tempted, he says, by the tavern signs: "The outward sign of Bacchus and his lure, / That at his door hangs day by day / Exciting folk to taste his moisture, / So often that one hardly can say nay." ("*The outward sign of Bachus and his lure, / That at his dore hangith day by day / Excitith folk to taste of his moisture / So often that man can nat wel seyn nay.*") Once settled in his chosen tavern of Paul's Head, he was also enticed by amicable women:

I dare not say how that the gathering
Of Venus' lusty children dear,
That were so goodly shaped and fair,
And pleasant of comportment and manner,
And could supply the world with cheer,
And were surpassing in attire,
To Paul's Head so often summoned me
To talk of mirth and fool around and play.

(*I dar nat telle how that the fresshe repeir
Of venus femel lusty children deere,
That so goodly so shaply were, and feir,
And so plesant of port and of maneere,
And feede cowden all the world with cheere,
And of atyr passingly wel byseye,
At Poules Heed me maden often appeere
To talk of mirthe and to disporte and pleye.*)

Sweet wine was on offer, which he especially enjoyed mulled "to warme a stomak with," and he explains that, in the hope of love and gratitude, he was the one who paid for everything. His additional hope was to be hailed as a "gentil man," although he knows well enough that this was purchased favor. Chaucer, bolstered by his status as a shire knight, wouldn't have had to scramble quite as much as Hoccleve, and would have been treated as a gentleman in consequence of his rank and parliamentary status. But he was neither lord, magnate, patrician, nor even landowner. He might not have had to pay for companionship, but he would have had to earn it by ingenuity, persistence, or personal charm.

Political specifics aside, six or eight weeks in Westminster on an expense account seems to have been regarded as an attractive prospect, and the majority of MPs returned again and again (among Chaucer's fellow London factionalists, John Hadley served eleven terms; Adam Carlisle, seven; and John Organ, six, for example). As for their legislative effectiveness, opinions were mixed but (as today) generally skeptical. Professionalism among the MPs was discouraged, and several Parliaments actively ruled against participation by lawyers, who were thought over-prone to press petitions on behalf of clients who had retained them. Most of the shire knights were military men who took occasional administrative posts in their localities in order to guard their own interests, but they were hardly legislators in any thoroughgoing sense. Many of them were, in the temper of the day, violent, with records of trespass, home invasion, rape and forcible detention, judicial combat, and occasional murder.

Some Parliaments appear to have risen above the calibre of their own personnel, as when, for example, the Good Parliament of 1376 chose Peter de la Mare as its speaker and demanded substantial reforms in the court of the doddering Edward III. At least one, the Merciless Parliament of 1388, went into a violent hyper-reform mode when the Gloucester faction, first visible in 1386, achieved a commanding position. Assuming brief governance of the kingdom itself, Gloucester's anti-Ricardian faction voted itself substantial rewards and condemned opponents such as Nicholas Brembre, Chaucer's fellow parliamentarian Sir James Berners, and his fellow littérateur Thomas Usk to death. (In this troubled year, Chaucer could only have congratulated himself for the safe haven—chosen or not—he had found in Kent.) More often, though, Parliament was a humdrum affair, in which participants, primed for legislative action by their constituencies, settled for modest concessions in return for their own acquiescence in the crown's incessant monetary demands.

The generally low regard for Parliament is effectively captured in a poem composed at the very end of Richard's reign, which described him as feckless and irresolute, and Parliament as ineffective. Its title is *Richard the Redeless*, alluding to his inability to receive *rede*, or good advice. Its account of Parliament shows a fair knowledge of its procedures and a keen eye for its failings. In its account, knights and citizens meet to figure out how to accommodate themselves to the nobles' wishes (the wishes, that is, of the magnates who normally dominated the king's council), and also how to betray the wishes and instructions of their own constituents. In this case, the reasonable but vain wish of the constituency is that no special taxes be granted for defense of the realm in the absence of an actual external threat. The foregone conclusion is that the tax, in the form of a tenth and a fifteenth of assessed clerical and lay possessions, will be given, even though the war in question is a rhetorically invented one. The parliamentarians are not too stupid to see this

ruse—for it is blatant—but simply too lazy and venal to do anything about it. Here are some of this poet's remarks on the low
calibre of these public representatives:

> Then sat some like a zero in arithmetic
> That marks a place and adds nothing.
> And some had supped with Simony in the evening
> And now, bribed, let slip the business of the shire.
> And some were tale-tellers, and went to the king,
> Branding as foes even good friends
> Who spoke for the best and merited no blame
> From king or council or commons either,
> Whoever cared about the truth of things.

And it gets worse:

> Some slumbered and slept and said but little;
> Some mouthed mumblings and knew not what they meant;
> Some were paid off and kept quiet accordingly,
> Wouldn't say a word for craven fear;
> Some were so sullen and clogged in their brains
> And couldn't come to a conclusion if they tried. . . .
> Some were so clotted with counsel that they knew
> The end of a matter before it even began
> And wouldn't have wanted it any other way.
> Some held with the majority however matters went,
> And some went just so far and never any farther.
> Some spoke out boldly, then were revealed
> To speak more for money promised by the king
> Than to comfort the community that paid their way.

One cannot imagine Chaucer as loutish as these. But he had made his own compromise. Rather than deserting the interests of his nominal constituency over the course of the parliamentary session, he arrived at Parliament already in the camp of the king. His problem would not be a conflict of loyalties, for his loyalties were clear. The problem would be that, for a man of his loyalties, this was the wrong Parliament to join. This would be a reformist Parliament or, at any rate, one in which ostensible reform would be pushed to the forefront as a motive and explanation for the pursuit of more personal agendas. Beginning in 1385, and then pivotally in 1386, and conclusively from 1387 to 1388, the king's youngest uncle, Thomas, duke of Gloucester, came determined to play a role, to enlist Parliament as a vehicle for his plans to restrain the power of the king. Whether truly reformist or simply arrayed in the trappings of reform, this was a program to which he had no difficulty in rallying larger and larger majorities of MPs.

Geoffrey Chaucer was no reformer, or certainly not in any terms that Gloucester and his faction would have recognized. His dim personal view of reform finds a counterpart in his poetic treatment of parliamentary institutions. His portrayal of the Trojan Parliament that hands Criseide over to the Greeks, and also of the squabbling birds in his *Parliament of Fowls*, is uniformly derisive. In these renditions, the loudest talkers, and squawkers, dominate each gathering, and the voices of reason and moderation never prevail. Nor does his own presence in Parliament suggest any personal inclination to associate himself with reforming or democratic impulses. Given his factional affiliations, such motives as increasing parliamentary authority and curbing royal initiative would have had no place on his personal agenda. The words and acts of individual MPs are rarely reported in the parliamentary rolls or in chronicle accounts, so his positions on particular issues cannot be known. But the record is punctuated by the repeatedly awkward and inopportune situations in which he, as a king's man, would have found himself as a member of this most unfriendly body.

The Session, October 1, 1386

The first session of the new Parliament convened in the Painted Chamber of Westminster Palace at 8:00 A.M. on October 1. These apparently mundane details contain a story in their own right, a story suggesting the climate of change in which this meeting occurred.

Until 1376 Parliament had moved by the stately measures of liturgical time, convening at half Prime, or somewhere between eight and nine o'clock. But for the previous decade it had convened by mechanical or clock time, at 8:00 in the morning. This new and more arithmetic form of timekeeping applied to the date of the meeting as well; by tradition the Parliament of 1386 would have convened on the first Monday after the feast of St. Jerome, but now it was announced for October 1, 1386. This new system of reckoning even applied to the computation of its year. For most people in England it was the ninth year of King Richard, second of that name—an effect of computing the years by regnal time, or the space of a king's reign—but for purposes of parliamentary record keeping, it was now 1386. Upon his arrival in Westminster, Chaucer would have been able to check the time on a mechanical clock that had been installed by Edward III between 1365 and 1367 on a bell tower facing Westminster Palace. This shift from liturgical and regnal time to clock and calendar time is one small but indicative component of a less traditional and more pragmatic attitude toward affairs. Liturgical and cyclical time schemes were at least tacitly complicit with repetition and status quo. The new, mechanical systems of temporal measurement bespoke a commitment not just to accurate measurement but also to pragmatic assessment and an empirical view of political and social issues. The framing of a parliamentary event within liturgical time (in relation to a holy festival) and on a regnal year (marked by its location within a given king's reign) bespoke a presumption of continuity not to be found within a clock-and-calendar system of reckoning. Certainly, kings were overthrown in earlier centuries, within liturgical and regnal time. But the position of an anointed or sanctified king is subtly enhanced by these traditional systems of temporal measurement, with their presumption that his reign is to be considered part of the established order of things. Richard was a great proponent of sacerdotal kingship, the view that kingship was not only hereditary but was divinely sanctioned as well. Shakespeare was typically acute in his *Richard II*, in which he develops Richard's inability to imagine the overthrow of a divinely anointed king. But the Parliament of 1386 would be marked by many insults to the idea of foreordained and sanctified kingship—insults of which its new conceptions of mechanical and calendar time were modestly but significantly predictive.

Despite such modernizing innovations, this Parliament was still shadowed—haunted, perhaps—by the partly effaced but still traditional date by which most delegates also knew it, as the Monday after the feast of St. Jerome, in the ninth year of the current king. Jerome was one of the four ancient fathers of the Catholic Church. Today he is known mainly for his translation of the Vulgate Bible from Hebrew and Greek into a flexible and accessible Latin that endured for a thousand years. In the fourteenth century, however, he was popularly known for his emphasis on the inevitability of Judgment Day. He was closely associated with the fifteen signs by which Doomsday would announce itself, and his inability, sleeping or waking, to avoid hearing the trumpet announcing the end of the world. If nothing quite so portentous as a final judgment was on the minds of the parliamentarians gathering in Westminster that Monday morning, an ominous sense of showdown, of serious reckoning, was definitely in the air.

The Painted Chamber, in which Parliament convened, was a room of sufficient size (seventy-five feet by twenty feet) and enormous symbolic resonance. The room itself was built in the late twelfth and early thirteenth centuries, and its extensive program of murals that surrounded the upper walls dated from the reigns of Henry III and Edward I. This room was originally the king's own bedchamber, although even at the outset more ceremonial than practical in its uses. It was used exclusively as a reception and meeting room after the reign of Edward II, whose actual sleeping and other nocturnal activities went on in a smaller adjacent chamber. The room in 1386 may still have contained the massive and curtained royal bed, or "bed of state," flanked by depictions of the coronation of Edward the Confessor—an object richly emblematic of election and anointment, dynastic continuity, and ancient traditions of consultation in the royal chamber. This highly charged repository of royal symbolism was, in turn, augmented by the chamber's ambitious program of wall paintings depicting the triumph of virtues over vices, together with a vast selection of politically admonitory representations of good and bad kingship drawn from the Maccabees, Kings, and Judges.

King Richard, having ample opportunity for inspection of the room, might well have noticed the depictions of Edward the

Confessor, one of his own exemplars and a subject of reverential treatment in the Wilton Diptych that he commissioned and carried as a personal altar. Members of a newly convened and contentious Parliament were less likely to spend much time pondering the iconography of the wall paintings that surrounded them. A continuation of the *Canterbury Tales*, entitled the *Tale of Beryn*, describes the bafflement of the Canterbury Pilgrims who try to interpret the stained-glass windows of the cathedral, and the parliamentarians were probably no more penetrating in their analysis of the painted walls. Perhaps, though, these murals of good and bad government were not entirely lost on the more intellectually curious members of the gathering. If his mind wasn't entirely on other things, Chaucer himself might have found matter for reflection. He was, after all, the author of the "Monk's Tale"—a series of tragedies in which protagonists, mainly secular rulers, fall from high to low estate by the intervention of Fortune—a work that he probably completed prior to commencement of the *Canterbury Tales* and thus had in hand by 1386. Some of his own subjects even coincide with the exemplary paintings that surrounded him on that morning of October 1386: King Antiochus (whom God bodily afflicted as punishment for his pride); Nebuchadnezzar (chastised by God for tormenting the Hebrew people); and Alexander (overthrown by Fortune despite his martial virtues).

For those parliamentarians whose eyes strayed toward them, these murals could have served various motives, depending upon point of view. Richard's opponents would have welcomed their emphasis on castigation of imperial pride. Richard's supporters might have taken heart from his appearance among such virtuous depictions. This desire to be viewed as a prince of sufficient gravity to school himself in matters of administrative virtue was prevalent among monarchs of the day, no matter how high-handed their actual conduct. This symbolic purpose caused every medieval English king from Edward III through Richard III to stock his library with at least one book of advice to princes or treatise on statecraft, whether he read it or not. Even for the undoubted majority of knights and burgesses who paid the specifics of these murals little heed, the chamber's decorations must have functioned a bit like the mural of good and bad governance in the Palazzo Pubblico, or town hall, of fourteenth-century Siena: to reconstitute this onetime bedchamber as a public place, a domain in which matters of public interest would be addressed.

Meetings of Parliament customarily began with a routine piece of business, the announcement of those lords chosen to receive and decide upon the disposition of parliamentary petitions. Then would follow a formal, and potentially rather ponderous, address by the chancellor of the realm (or in some cases by a prominent churchman) about the reasons for summoning Parliament and the most salient issues confronting the realm. This address was known as the *pronunciatio*, or pronunciation, and it carried a dual sense: It was at once a declaration, in that it outlined the king's wishes for Parliament, and also a proposal, in that it constituted a request for parliamentary action. When the chancellor was a churchman, this address was likely to contain what might be described as sermonistic elements, embracing a vision of divinely ordained national destiny. In any case, it was likely to be consensual, laced with pieties and conventional platitudes, and unlikely to present much of a challenge to the assembled body.

In the normal parliamentary state of affairs, the completion of this opening address would be followed by working sessions, with the magnates or lords of hereditary summons withdrawing to an adjacent room called the White Chamber for their sessions, and the shire knights and the citizens and burgesses withdrawing either to the abbey's chapter house or its refectory. Except in the most unusual circumstances, the total body would not meet again until the end of the session, when petitions were read together with their disposition by king and council. This time, however, Richard or his advisers made a serious mistake at the outset, using the *pronunciatio* to announce an unprecedentedly exaggerated demand on the public purse, cloaked not in broadly acceptable platitudes but in a completely spurious rationale.

Chancellor de la Pole, who delivered the *pronunciatio* on behalf of king and council, stood before Parliament as a thoroughly discredited man who had already forfeited any expectation of personal parliamentary favor: He had been associated with Richard's recent (and reviled) overtures of peace with France; he was blamed for the recent loss of Ghent to the French; he was regarded as one of Richard's most obnoxious favorites. Gloucester and his supporters were particularly irked by his advancement to the earldom of Suffolk, during that overceremonial and ineffective Scottish debacle the summer before. Despite his unpopularity, and the inevitable mumblings accompanying the occasion of his address, the lords, divines, shire knights, citizens, and burgesses were probably expecting some conventional rehash of the familiar themes: the climate of military necessity and the crown's need for supplemental funding to meet the costs of defending the realm. Instead, he brought with him a speech bristling with irrational claims and unfeasible ambitions. Even as it touched on familiar matters of financial necessity and the kingdom's needs, it did so with demands so strident in their articulation and so exaggerated in scale as to seem virtually idiotic. At any rate, whether through obtuseness or in deliberate provocation, de la Pole plunged ahead.

Parliament had been summoned, he explained, to ratify a recent decision of the king, who had "recently, of his own initiative and bravery [*sa proper mocione et corage*] proposed to cross the sea in person with his royal power to injure and assail his enemies in the parts overseas." One can only imagine the incredulity with which the knights of Parliament received the proposition that Richard—this completely unmilitary, peace-seeking master of hollow ceremonial—was thinking of invading France. This resolve, de la Pole went on to say, would disprove a prevalent *esclandre*, or slander, involving Richard's lack of military prowess or inclination (and which, in that regard, is no slander at all but a simple iteration of observable fact). Then, in contradiction of the militarily aggressive proposal he had just made, de la Pole veered into the truth of the matter: Substantial aid will be needed for the situation in which England actually finds itself, "for the defense and keeping of the kingdom against the enemy, who strives daily with all their power to invade England and destroy the kingdom." That is, far from ready to seize the initiative against France, the nation will be hard-pressed to defend itself in the months to come.

Petitions, the chancellor blandly concluded, should be submitted within the next two days. So much for the official summary contained in the *Rolls of Parliament*. The absurdity of requesting extraordinary funds on so risible a pretext as an invasion of France, at a time when England itself was fiscally tapped out, economically overextended by Richard's extravagances and Gaunt's expedition, and cowering with fear of a French incursion can only have enraged a body already dominated by skeptics and opponents of Richard's rule. Yet, if we believe even half of what the chronicles say, the rather bland summary of de la Pole's address in the parliamentary roll far understates the absurdity of his request.

The fullest chronicle account of the Parliament is that of Henry Knighton, an engaging and unusually well-informed canon of Leicester Abbey. He composed his description retrospectively—near the end of the century, some twelve years after the event—and his account includes the usual amounts of hearsay, distortion, and monastic prejudice. But he also wrote from a comprehensive knowledge of Richard's flawed kingship (or most of it, since he died the year before Richard's deposition) and with a keen eye for his characteristic failings. One must demur from time to time from his observations and interpretations and resist the foolish but frequent error of simply treating his account as factual in nature. But, if opinionated and occasionally exaggerated, his account is quite revelatory of the dynamics of this exceptional Parliament. Knighton expands, for example, upon the sheer outrageousness of de la Pole's request, not just with respect to its arguments, but also to the scale of the proposition he put forth:

> The chancellor had asked the commons in the king's name for four fifteenths, to be paid in a single year, and for a like number of tenths from the clergy, saying that the king was so much in debt that he could not otherwise pay what he owed nor meet his other commitments, whether for the war, or in his household, or to discharge other business.

This, after a year in which Richard had squandered a fortune on his expedition to Scotland, created unpopular dukedoms and earldoms requiring grants of royal lands and funds in support, squired around and preferred the absurd king of Armenia, and supported a bloated household of which nobody approved. The sum mentioned (very likely an exaggeration but still indicating a settled public memory of what had been asked) is outlandish. A fifteenth represents literally that proportion of the assessed value of all a secular citizen's movable goods; the clerical tenth represents the same in the ecclesiastical sphere. Rather than being reevaluated each time a tax was granted, the assessments on goods were passed along from year to year, and the fifteenth and the tenth solidified as traditional demands that, in the course of the fourteenth century, came to represent around thirty-nine thousand pounds in crown revenue, or around a quarter of the typical annual revenue of the kingdom. In exceptional circumstances, as when Gaunt's expedition was being funded the previous year, as much as one-and-a-half fifteenths and tenths might be granted. But a request for *four* fifteenths and tenths, if de la Pole really had the cheek to make it, would have amounted to a sum equal to, or even exceeding, the entirety of the exchequer's income from all other sources combined for the year in which it was collected.

Whatever the particulars of his request, it was obviously flagrant. Even the restrained language of the parliamentary roll records the vehemence of the response. All the commons, it says, reacted promptly, vocally, and of one accord:

All the commons, of a single accord and unanimously assembled [*touz les communes d'un accord et unement assemblez*], came before the king, prelates, and lords in the chamber of parliament, complaining grievously about Michael de la Pole, earl of Suffolk, formerly chancellor of England, then present, and accused him orally [*par demonstrance de bouche*].

The initial outburst might have occurred right there in the Painted Chamber or may equally have occurred in a follow-up session; but, given the rarity of the occasions on which the full body of lords and commons met together in the presence of the king, it probably immediately followed de la Pole's injudicious address.

In his retrospective account, the author creates a sense of unanimity that could not have pertained at the time. However cowed they may have been by the situation, a dozen or so Ricardian shire knights and some like-minded citizens and burgesses (including all four members of the London delegation) were present in the room. They may well have been drowned out and intimidated into silence but would presumably have withheld themselves from the anti-Ricardian tumult and its accompanying demand for de la Pole's impeachment. Whatever behavior they did adopt was, however, unavailing. Even with a minority of the members remaining silent or undemonstrative, Parliament gave itself over to general clamor in the wake of de la Pole's singularly ill-judged proposals.

This kind of upsurge, especially in its orally demonstrative character, appears to have been endemic to the English Parliament. After all, even today, in what appears to be a continuing tradition, the British Parliament surprises strangers who, expecting a high level of decorum in debate, are taken aback with the verbally rowdy character of the prime minister's questions and other unruly aspects of parliamentary demeanor. Certainly, Chaucer understood such verbal volatility as a prevailing parliamentary characteristic. He takes note of the expressive flagrancy of parliamentary debates in two works written prior to his own parliamentary experience.

In his *Parliament of Fowls*, the lower fowl (whom we might

liken to the parliamentary citizens and burgesses of Chaucer's day) listen with increasing impatience to the lengthy spoken protestations of three noble windbags and then interrupt with a vengeance:

> "Stop it!" they cried, "alas, you'll ruin us now!
> When will your cursed pleading ever end?"

> (*"Com of!" they criede, "allas, ye wole us shende!*
> *Whan shal youre cursede pletinge have an ende?"*)

These parliamentary birds are so agitated that, in fact, they desert speech altogether and lapse into cackles and quacks:

> The goose, the cuckoo, and the duck as well
> Cried out, "Kek kek! Cuckoo! Quack quack" so high . . .

> (*The goos, the cokkow, and the doke also*
> *So cryede, "Kek kek! kokkow! quek quek" hye . . .*)

So much for reasoned debate. And another verbal tiff, not much more reasoned in character, arises in Chaucer's *Troilus and Criseide*, a work probably concluded early in 1386. Here the question is whether to send Criseide to the Greek camp in exchange for Antenor. In this case, with the Trojan lords meeting in Parliament, Hector speaks against the exchange, on the reasonable ground that she is no prisoner in Troy and they have no right to barter her away. Supporters of the exchange lunge into strident opposition:

> The noise of people started up at once,
> Fierce as a blaze of straw just set on fire . . .

"Hector," they said, "What spirit might inspire
This choice; to shield this woman and lose
Sir Antenor? You couldn't be more wrong on this . . ."

(The noise of peple up stirte thanne at ones,
As breme as blase of straw yset on fire . . .
"Ector," quod they, "what goost may yow enspire
This woman thus to shilde and doon us leese
Daun Antenor? A wrong wey now ye chese . . .")

Noise again. By expressing the opposition as a form of precipitate oral racket, the narrator suggests his own disapproval of rhetorical excess and ill-considered action. The decision to exchange Criseide carries, nonetheless:

The parliament decided then and there
To swap Criseide for Antenor.
The president announced the deal
And overrode all Hector's urgent "nays."
And finally, whatever anybody said,
It was for naught; it must and should occur.

(For which delibered was by parlement
For Antenor to yelden out Criseide,
And it pronounced by the president,
Altheigh that Ector "nay" ful ofte preyde.
And finaly, what wight that it withsaide,
It was for nought: it moste ben and sholde.)

This undeniably aroused Parliament is blind to the implications of its actions and their longer-term effects. Little do they know,

Chaucer says, where their true interests lie. Antenor will, in one of the poem's deeper ironies, be Troy's ultimate betrayer. To the extent that a conclusion can be drawn from his verse, Chaucer believes the "cloude of errour" to be endemic in parliamentary situations.

De la Pole can be cast neither as the vain noble fowl nor as principled Hector. His follies belong to himself and the king, and Parliament's vocal outcry issues from its own particular annoyance, both at de la Pole's diversionary reasoning and his mistake in addressing them as potential gulls and fools. Given his dim view of parliaments in general, Chaucer might have derived some bitter mirth from this debacle, but hardly of a pleasurable or comfortable sort. In the first place, his own party was being decried. In the second place, and beyond the particular politics of faction, he clearly does not believe that *"demonstrance de bouche"* and verbal pyrotechnics are the way decisions should be made.

Chaucer shows an awareness in his writings of the rights of a silenced minority: Hector in the Trojan Parliament; the turtle dove of the bird Parliament, whose meek voice is drowned out by that of the churlish duck; and an old wise man in his "Tale of Melibee" who fails to achieve a hearing in debate and, shamefaced, sits himself down again. So must the several dozen partisans of the court party have felt in the course of the initial outcry against de la Pole. They might also have sensed a certain amount of stage management in the whole event. Gloucester and his anti-Ricardian adherents, after all, arrived at Parliament already angry: angry at Richard for ignoring the restraints demanded in the Parliament of 1385; angry at de la Pole for abetting his recalcitrance; and angry over a hodgepodge of more specific accusations. Impolitic as de la Pole's speech had been, his and Richard's partisans undoubtedly thought he had walked into a loaded situation, that he had been, in effect, set up.

Outnumbered and outshouted, de la Pole's parliamentary allies had no recourse but to simmer in silence. But Richard was no silent simmerer. A standoff appears to have ensued in which Richard violated custom by walking out in a huff and withdrawing to his palace at Eltham, with no stated intention of return. This withdrawal was a severe affront to the dignity of Parliament and to settled understandings of regal propriety as well. The near-statutory *Manner of Holding Parliament* supposes that the king will be present and presiding throughout the parliamentary session, available even if not publicly speaking to issues arising, and cites past "clamor" on those occasions when the king absented himself. "It would be a damaging and dangerous matter for the whole community of parliament and the realm should the king absent himself from parliament," this document insists.

Richard's intransigent withdrawal solidified and emboldened the opposition. The dominant elements of lords and commons sent word that they would proceed with no business whatever in his absence (a political stance, but also a practical admission, since no business could in fact be concluded in the absence of the king). They not only demanded the king's return but also the removal of Michael de la Pole as chancellor. These demands had hardened, according to Knighton, into a matter of "common assent" and were certainly majority views, although surely somewhere short (in the case of Chaucer and others) of unanimity. Always one to inflame a situation, Richard, in turn, replied to Parliament (by intermediary, from his Eltham retreat) that he would not dismiss the merest garçon on his kitchen staff at its request—a pronouncement that sounds so entirely characteristic of Richard that it can probably be accepted as an accurate representation or, if an invention, at least a truth-saturated one.

The *Manner of Holding Parliament* turns out to be prescient in its description of the consequences of a king's absence. Subsequent to Richard's withdrawal, "murmur" does indeed arise. The word "murmur," in both Latin and English, is closely related to the word and concept of "rumor," and at this juncture an extremely damaging rumor about Richard made the rounds, described, though with considerable variance, in several chronicle accounts. In Knighton's version, the king invited forty knights from among the commons to come to Eltham to treat with him. (Forty sounds like an outlandish number, but it is not entirely arbitrary. Forty is roughly equal to the number of actual knights among the shire knights, since it would presumably have been inappropriate for Richard to invite merchants and other commoners—or even, in this case, Chaucer himself—to treat with him on terms of equity or even of feigned equity.) Richard's purported plan was to then entrap and kill them. The whole accusation was obviously trumped up but gives a hint of the climate of near hysteria in which the whole parliamentary session proceeded.

What Richard actually got, instead of forty knights, was a delegation headed by his principal aristocratic rivals, the Duke of Gloucester and Thomas Arundel, bishop of Ely (and eventual chancellor of the realm under Henry IV), who apparently threatened to dissolve Parliament without having granted a tax or subsidy in the event of the king's continued absence. As Knighton tells it, the whole exchange quickly escalated, with Richard issuing an outrageous threat to make common cause with his kinsman the king of France, it being "better to submit ourselves to him than to our own subjects." Whether or not Richard actually proposed anything so extreme, Gloucester and

Arundel responded with an audacious threat, claiming that if a king should so estrange himself from his people, an ancient law would justify his removal: "Then it would be lawful with the common assent and agreement of the people of the realm to put down the king from his royal seat, and raise another of the royal lineage in his place." This would seem a wholly improbable suggestion had it not happened to Edward II earlier in the century, and would actually come close to happening to Richard himself in 1388, and then really would happen in 1399.

Perhaps owing to such a threat, or more likely the practical necessity of gaining Parliament's assent to some kind of tax or subsidy, Richard gave way. De la Pole was dismissed from his office as chancellor and delivered over to the impeachment proceedings, which then became the principal business of the 1386 Parliament. Several weeks later Richard returned—no doubt sulkily—to Westminster. By the time of Richard's return, the charges against de la Pole had been codified in a detailed seven-article indictment, the crucial parts of which were his failure to institute the reforms of 1385 and his irresponsibility in handling funds destined for Ghent, together with the subsequent fall of the city. De la Pole was, inevitably, convicted, then immediately rehabilitated by Richard, only to find himself eighteen months later, among those key followers of the king (together with Nicholas Brembre as well as Chaucer's fellow shire knight Sir James Berners), found guilty of treasonous collusion with the king and put to death by the Merciless Parliament of 1388.

The Parliament of 1386 ended on November 28, 1386, on a generally sour note, or actually on a succession of sour notes. It did finally grant Richard an extremely parsimonious subsidy—of a half tenth and a half fifteenth (an eighth of what de la Pole had, according to Knighton, brazenly requested)—as well as an extension of the wool subsidy, but these somewhat grudging provisions were made reliant upon the king's acceptance of oversight by a continual council headed by the Duke of Gloucester and others bent on restraining him. Richard was no more ready to accept the oversight of this council than he had been its predecessor in 1385, and thus the foundations of his defeat and near ouster by the Parliament of 1388 were set firmly in place. Moreover, the king's ill humor led him to an exceptional and ill-judged disparagement of Parliament's powers. With the entire body of commons and lords gathered there in the White Chamber, on its last day, to hear the recital of its actions and the disposition of its petitions, Richard, in violation of precedent, spoke. One commentator has observed that no parliamentary speech by a medieval king in Parliament *ever* came to a good end. This speech was no exception. There in the White Chamber, according to Knighton, "The king, in full parliament before its end, made open protest with his own mouth that he willed that nothing done in the said parliament should be to detract from him or his crown; and that his prerogative and the liberties of his crown should be preserved and protected." This maneuver may be likened to the recent practice of American presidents—most notably George W. Bush—of issuing "signing statements" when they sign a bill into law but accompany it with a personal statement restricting its application. Richard indicated by his signing statement that he meant to give no ground. Despite such prickly resistance, Richard and his handful of followers had been thwarted at each turn in the course of this Parliament, and their situation would only become worse.

Bad Aftermath

Parliament would next convene in the White Chamber in 1388, and its business would be the condemnation of de la Pole, Brembre, and other figures of importance to the royal faction. Chaucer was obviously well out of it. Those at his level of factional importance slipped just under the bar unless—like fellow writer Thomas Usk or the young attorney-at-law John Blake—they had engaged in activities particularly offensive to the anti-Ricardian Appellants. The spectacle of 1388 would, even so, have proven excruciating to him, and until the parliamentary condemnations had run their course he could not have been sure that he was among those to be spared. The question is whether his departure at the end of the 1386 Parliament, and his highly convenient absence from London and Westminster in 1387–89, should be credited to his shrewd foresight and refined sense of tactics, or whether his Kentish sojourn actually arose from circumstances beyond his control.

Certainly, in retrospect, Chaucer appears to have been highly prescient. He escaped the woes surrounding the Merciless Parliament and positioned himself for a brief rehabilitation when Richard reasserted his royal authority in 1389–90. But if he was in fact acting prudently in his own behalf, he was the only one; many of Richard's other followers continued their normal activities well into 1387, unaware of their king's extreme unpopularity and their own vulnerablity. They continued in royal service, or even intensified their ties. Usk became an out-and-out Ricardian henchman by accepting the position of undersheriff of Middlesex in 1387 and set about harassing Richard's enemies on his behalf. Chief Justice Robert Tresilian (with whom Chaucer had at least indirect contacts as justice of the peace for Kent) would join with a group of eminent jurists who concluded, upon Richard's request for a determination in 1387, that the Parliament of 1386 had overreached its authority, perhaps even treasonously so. Nicholas Brembre strode irreversibly forward, traveling in Richard's entourage and making frantic but vain efforts to persuade Londoners to swear an oath of loyalty to the king. All three, together with others, would be condemned to death in 1388. Chaucer's location somewhere outside the vortex of the breaking storm would spare him their fate and we can only congratulate him for it. But factors other than simple judgment in his own interest appear to have been at work.

Several different strands of evidence suggest that, in and around the parliamentary season of 1386, Chaucer had fallen seriously out of favor and may even have been regarded with hostility by his former allies. One of these strands concerns his inability to disassociate himself from the incautious actions of his close associate Brembre. Another was growing dissatisfaction with his collectorship of customs; if not dissatisfaction with Chaucer individually, at least with the position itself, and with the confluence of interests that had placed him there. Another concerns the circumstances of his departure from Aldgate, including evidence of possible tension between Chaucer and the aldermanic faction in whose gift the residence lay. Considered together, these strands of evidence suggest that his decisions at the close of the 1386 Parliament were not just voluntary and self-interested, but resulted also from hostile pressure, including pressure from some of his own previous allies.

Brembre's Collapse. In the crucial years 1386 and 1387, Brembre had been acting in an increasingly headstrong and factionally injudicious way. Even as the Gloucester faction's opposition to Richard was gathering serious steam, and Brembre's mayoral successor Nicholas Exton and a majority of London aldermen were inching toward a policy of nonalignment, Brembre was plunging headlong into a personal policy of support for the beleaguered king. One aspect of this support was a series of personal loans to Richard in 1384, 1385, and possibly thereafter, not just to the exchequer but directly to Richard's personal chamber, an independent mechanism that permitted the king more flexibility in partisan expenditures. When Richard made an ill-advised and ultimately unsuccessful attempt to gather support from his judiciary in Reading in 1387, Brembre was at his side. More consequentially still, Brembre took the lead in enlisting support for Richard, cajoling citizens in 1387 to subscribe to an oath supporting the embattled king—significantly, at the very moment when his mayoral successor, Exton, and the aldermen were declaring neutrality in this accelerating contest.

Brembre was still presiding as mayor when Chaucer was removed from his dwelling, but as a lame duck: nine days later (on October 13, 1386) he would be replaced in that office by Exton. Brembre continued for several more months in many of his posts, including collector of customs and mayor of the Westminster Staple, although these were royal rather than civil appointments. Despite such appearances of continuity, the foundations of Brembre's authority were crumbling. His staunch and invariable allies in power, Walworth and Philipot, had both recently died—Walworth in 1385 and Philipot in 1384. Exton and the new guard were still Ricardian in their general orientation, but within limits never acknowledged by the headstrong Brembre. As astute readers of the political winds, they were seeking a posture less absolute in support of the king and more respectful of the need to foreground city and mercantile interests no matter who was in power. That Brembre was a king's man was unexceptional, but the extent of his partisanship and reliance upon royal favor were liabilities in a conflictual climate in which London interests would best be served by a reasonable amount of political latitude.

All this came to a boil at a crucial time for Chaucer, right at the beginning of the 1386 Parliament. Richard's own unpopularity and that of Brembre as his principal operative in the city of London converged to create a rumor that swept through Parliament and beyond, to the discredit of both men. This is the "occultus rumor," summarized by Knighton, in which Richard schemed to entrap and kill forty shire knights through the agency of a bogus dinner invitation. Within Knighton's account, Brembre is tagged as Richard's co-conspirator. He says that the plot was formed during the closing days of Brembre's mayoralty and disclosed only when his successor, Nicholas Exton, balked at its implementation:

> It was said that they learned that those who had gone to treat with the king would have been fallen upon by armed men and slain . . . but that Nicholas Exton, the mayor of London, having refused to countenance the evil, a deep and wicked plot was spread about and the scandal gradually uncovered.

Given the sequence of events in Parliament, the revelation of this supposed intrigue must have occurred within days after Exton's election as mayor. The incoming mayor, although of Brembre's own general political persuasion, is portrayed as an honest and aboveboard player who did not scruple to expose his predecessor's hyperpartisan chicanery. Under Exton, London policies, including even modified support of the king, would remain the same, but without Brembre's criminal excesses.

Knighton called this rumor of Brembre's collusion "occultus" in the sense that it was whispered or passed underground—but this is not to say that it was limited in its circulation. A rumor, in medieval terms, is something widely and stridently vocalized, a publicly known matter that sweeps a constituency and has the power to effect change. (The Rising of 1381 was, for example, known in some circles as the Great Rumor.) This particular rumor was highly injurious to Brembre and, together with his extreme partisanship of Richard in London and his attempts to coerce fellow Londoners into sworn support, marked the beginning of the end for him. Perhaps as early as the fall of 1386, and very definitely by the early months of 1387, Brembre's fellow factionalists decided to cut him loose, in order to pursue a less adamant and more opportunistic policy in relation to the struggle between Richard and his aristocratic adversaries.

Anti-Brembre agitation, bordering on hysteria, increased after he left office. In the winter of 1388 a number of craft guilds associated with his old rival Northampton took this opportunity to petition Parliament against him, accusing him of "wrongs, subtleties, and also open oppressions." In a petition exceptionally written in English for added visibility, the Mercers' Company accused Brembre of seizing the office of mayor in 1383 "with strong hand," and then of cinching the 1384 election by packing the guildhall with armed supporters, who rushed upon Northampton supporters crying, "Slay! Slay!" Given the traits they assign to him, the petitioners cannot resist a pun on Brembre's name, describing him as a briar or bramble with a ragged root. According to the Mercers, Brembre set himself up as the king's representative in London and falsely imprisoned any who protested against his policies. He was accused of conspiring even more insidiously in the very month of October 1386—this time in concert with his mayoral successor, Exton—to burn the now lost Jubilee Book, a compilation of the rights of London citizens.

The Mercers were Brembre's longtime rivals, and their accusations, timed to come before Parliament at the very moment of the anti-Ricardian Appellants' accusation against Brembre, represent the tone of a general and mounting anti-Brembre climate. More surprising than the existence of such a climate are its intensity and pervasiveness. Brembre found himself almost completely isolated in the months approaching his trial, and during the trial itself, shunned by former friends as well as longtime foes. It would appear that, despite his decade-long sway as the effective leader of the royal party in London, he never enlisted the loyalty or affection of his followers, virtually all of whom deserted him in the end.

In the winter of 1388, when he stood accused by the Merciless Parliament of treason for his immoderate support of the king, not a single MP spoke on his behalf. But the record, closely observed, is even worse than that. Brembre's successor, Nicholas Exton, and the four London representatives to the Merciless Parliament were all previous Brembre allies, members of what had amounted, between 1384 and 1387, to the Ricardian faction in London. Exton stayed with Brembre as long as he could, until March 1387, but deserted him decisively after that date. When the accusations against Brembre came down, not a single one of these former associates rallied to his support.

Brembre's only defender in the trial of 1388 was certainly not the right one: King Richard himself—the very party who was, via his proxies, on trial. Richard "offered a large number of different arguments in exculpation of Sir Nicholas," only to be shouted down by his adversaries. The *Westminster Chronicle* says:

> Before the king in full parliament all the Lords Appellant threw down their gauntlets and then and there all the peers of the realm and many of the knights and esquires, by likewise fling-

ing down their gauntlets before the king to the number of 305 and refusing to take them back, wagered battle that the said Nicholas is a false traitor.

Such histrionics aside, the trial moved swiftly on. A panel of twelve prominent lords offered hesitant support, finding no occasion for the death penalty, but then shirked responsibility for their own conclusion by calling in Mayor Exton and select aldermen, asking them whether they supposed Brembre to be aware of the treasonous acts with which he was accused. Their incriminating reply was that "they supposed he was aware rather than ignorant of them" [*putantes pocius de hujus scire quam nescire*]. This betrayal by his own former allies and associates was the unkindest cut. It was completed by another previous ally, the recorder of the city of London, to whom the lords now turned for his judgment of the law: "Without doubt," he told them, "anyone who, having knowledge of such matters, concealed instead of disclosing them, would be, and would deserve to be, punished by the loss of his life." And so, on February 20, 1388, Brembre was condemned to a common and ignoble death, drawn on a hurdle to Tyburn and hanged, refused even the relative honor (bestowed upon fellow defendant Simon Burley) of a more chivalric beheading on Tower Hill. His goods were confiscated (including a warehouse full of woad, the last of his monopolistic schemes, enough to dye the whole country blue), his estates sold off or regranted, his wife to remarry. He lived on in collective London memory as a figure of strife and division; as late as 1391 Londoners were forbidden by statute to speak of him or his previous struggles with mayoral rival John Northampton.

Brembre's downfall had unavoidable repercussions for his previously close associate Chaucer. From the autumn of 1386 onward Brembre had too many problems of his own to spare much thought for Chaucer's situation. Nor were Exton and other members of Richard's previous faction in London, now engaged in an anxious repositioning that would preserve the city's neutrality in the struggle between Richard and the followers of Gloucester, free to spend much energy on such problems. Indeed, having so recently been hand in glove with Brembre, Chaucer could only have seemed a liability in their quest for a new neutrality. Not only had Chaucer lost a crucial supporter, but his previous involvements with Brembre had become an undeniable liability.

Removal from Aldgate. Of his major life adjustments at the end of 1386, some may be viewed as personal choices. His request for a deputy in customs suggests some measure of personal dissatisfaction with the post, and his experience in Parliament must have been disagreeable from any perspective. But one adjustment suggests the disturbing and stringent possibility that a significant group of his previous allies might have become dissatisfied with him, or his performance, or both. This is the loss of his Aldgate lease. Those acting against him in this matter were not Gloucester partisans and opponents of the king, or oppositional guildsmen of the old Northampton faction, but rather an aldermanic body dominated by people who might have been supposed his closest allies.

Here is the sequence of events. By an action of the mayor and aldermen of London enrolled on October 4, but probably occurring several days before that date, it was agreed that no future grants should be made of dwellings over the gates of the city, or of gardens or vacant places adjoining the gates, but that such properties should henceforth remain in the hands of the city. Whether prompted by fears of a French invasion or other considerations, this resolution seems clear-cut enough and suffi-ciently explanatory of Chaucer's relocation. How surprising, then, that by an action on the *very next day*, recorded on Octo-ber 5, the same parties granted the dwelling over Aldgate to one Richard Forster, and for the term of life! Nor does anybody but Chaucer appear to have vacated his dwelling as a result of the October 4 resolution, nor does the city then cease granting other lifetime occupancies. In short, Chaucer appears to have been the sole object of this initiative.

The whole situation would be comprehensible if a change of city administration had brought in a new political party; Chau-cer's friend Ralph Strode had lost his gatehouse apartment when the populist party of John Northampton gained power between 1381 and 1383. But this is not the case. Chaucer's traditional allies controlled the levers of power. Moreover, his successor, Richard Forster, appears to have been a member of his own faction, serv-ing earlier as an esquire to Edward III, and in fact was an asso-ciate of Chaucer's, having previously acted as his personal attorney. Why then did the common council, on behalf of the mayor, aldermen, and commonalty of the city, single Chaucer out in this awkward and possibly disrespectful way? This action of October 4, followed by reassignment of the lease on Octo-ber 5, looks disturbingly like an attempt to be rid of Chaucer, an attempt countenanced or even initiated by his fellow factional-ists. He appears to have become persona non grata to a number of his previous London allies.

A Petition. Frustrating as the events of the 1386 Parliament had been, Chaucer's frustrations were those of an onlooker viewing the slow-motion train wreck that was befalling Rich-ard's kingship. Yet remaining was a final twist, in which an on-looker found himself a reluctant participant. It involves a parliamentary petition, adopted by the body and read out (in Chaucer's presence) on Parliament's last day.

Petitions were to be delivered during a parliament's opening days; October 3 was the date for this one. Petitions were received by a group of specially chosen knights, who then handed them over for fuller consideration by a more eminent group of magnates, high clerics, and legal justices known as the "triers" of petitions—acting in consultation with the chancellor, treasurer, steward, and chamberlain. Petitions might be filed by individuals (as "singular" petitions) or might represent a more general interest, as that of a trade or a community of the realm (as "commons" petitions). Whatever their origin, after screening by the triers, all petitions became commons petitions in the more formal sense of being avowed or embraced by the parliamentary commons of shire knights and burgesses. By tradition, magnates, or peers of the realm, acted separately on petitions, but in exceptional circumstances a joint session might be arranged in which commons and magnates sat together to hear the responses of the king. The 1386 Parliament was exceptional in this sense. Lords and commons met as a single body in the White Chamber, Geoffrey Chaucer among them.

One of these petitions touched upon matters too close for comfort. With increasing stridency, Parliament had been forming the view that collectors of customs were prevalently corrupt and were bleeding the country of needed revenues, and also that controllers of customs were failing to observe their responsibility to hinder those depredations. In 1379 Parliament had petitioned to replace collectors and controllers of customs annually (citing a precedent of one-year terms for county sheriffs), reasonably citing the substantial portion of the realm's revenue derived from the wool subsidy as the source of their concern.

During the Parliament of 1385, in one of the many petitions subsequently ignored by de la Pole and the king, they raised the volume, arguing that the subsidy on wools and woolfells could be increased if only the controllers of customs and other officials were appointed "from good and loyal persons" and retained or removed according to merit rather than considerations of influence.

In 1386 they raised the argumentative bar once again by taking direct aim at controllers of customs and resolving:

> All controllers of the kingdom's ports who hold their offices for the term of life by grant of the king, because they perpetrate great oppressions and extortions against the people in their offices, be dismissed and removed; and that no such office be granted for the term of life in time to come.

In a strictly technical sense, this petition did not apply to Chaucer. The terms of his appointment, back in 1374 during the reign of Edward III, were open-ended. Yet absence of a stated term limit nevertheless implied a life appointment. Chaucer had served for twelve years—a considerably longer term than was common for controllers—and he had become, in effect, a kind of de facto life controller.

Although the wording of the parliamentary petition did not absolutely *require* that Chaucer vacate his post, the timing and tone of it would certainly have shaken him. Richard, in keeping with his refusal to be pressed on such issues, temporized in response, agreeing only that incumbents might be examined before his council, and that "those who are found to be good remain in office, and the others be removed." Apparently this examination never occurred, but Chaucer was left with matters for serious reflection, sharpened by evident disdain for his position among the fellow parliamentarians with whom he had mingled for those two tumultuous months.

A Constrained Choice. Chaucer's withdrawal from his home and job and city may best be described as a matter of constrained choice. He was leaving a familiar neighborhood and rent-free apartment, a demanding job but one in which he had recently gained the right of assistance by a permanent deputy, and a parliamentary "safe seat" that conferred prestige and undeniable advantage—all for highly uncertain prospects. This was a choice, indeed, but a choice made in difficult and pressured circumstances.

When Chaucer resigned his positions and left town, it was without a send-off or any kind of golden parachute. None of his previous sponsors were available to soften the blow with an enhanced living, or a piece of Kentish property, or any other kind of final financial reward. As far as the records go, he was something of a wanderer in Kent, with no fixed job and insufficient income. This was his time of crisis, the lowest ebb of his fortunes. But the time had also come for him to follow his own advice: to make virtue of necessity. Events had revealed him as a politician of limited gifts, and not much of a factionalist either. Fortunately for him, and certainly for us, his riposte to these new and difficult circumstances wouldn't be a political or factional one; it would be literary instead.

CHAPTER FIVE

The Other Chaucer

One can immerse oneself in the extensive *Life-Records* without learning that Chaucer was a writer at all. This does not mean that he wasn't writing, but only that his writing occurred beneath, or at least outside, the attention of the record keepers. Records were kept for many reasons, involving governmental and bureaucratic receipts and expenditures, appointments and rewards, but completion and circulation of poems would not normally have attracted their notice. Chaucer could have been quietly building a literary reputation without any disturbance of the written record at all. But a good deal of emphasis must fall on the word "quietly." Even in midcareer he would have been better known to most Londoners as a practical functionary—a man with suspiciously good court connections and a compliant partner of Nicholas Brembre and other city connivers—than for his literary accomplishments. In the pivotal year 1386, at the mature age of forty-two or forty-three, Chaucer was a man of literary accomplishment, standing on the brink of his decision to write the *Canterbury Tales.* Yet his recognition as a writer was confined to a small circle of intimates, without extending to Londoners at large.

Chaucer the writer was, in effect, an "other" Chaucer, shielded from public view and pursuing his craft less as a public performance than as a private avocation. This Chaucer wrote as a matter of personal choice and not for acclaim or reward. Well into midlife, he treated his poetry as essentially a private matter to be shared with like-minded friends in intimate circumstances rather than as an engine of personal fame. Temperamentally, he disdained self-promotion, regarding Tuscan eminences like Dante and Petrarch as particularly egregious offenders. Nothing interested him less than the idea of broadcasting his writing to an absent and anonymous clientele.

Chaucer's withdrawal to Kent at the end of 1386 gave him time, if nothing else, to think about his literary career. The 1380s were a crucial decade for literary change in England, and Chaucer's literary situation was as volatile as everything else in his world. New ideas about writing, authorship, audience, circulation, and personal renown were in the air. Writing in English—an unusual decision when Chaucer made it in the 1360s—was taking hold, and demand for works in the native language beginning to grow. Technologies of literary circulation were in rapid development, encouraging the copying and circulation of manuscripts to larger and farther-flung audiences. Chaucer's literary contemporaries were beginning to think differently about claiming credit for their work. Taken together, these developments began to suggest new ways of being a writer, new stagings of a literary career. His just-completed *Troilus* registers the first signs of a shift; that poem's conclusion expresses a welter of confused and disturbing new literary ambitions and desires.

Before turning to the departures of 1386, though, some attention is owed to his earlier accomplishments, to the substantial literary labors that had brought him to this point of change.

The Poet in 1386

Chaucer had been writing steadily throughout his adult life. By 1386 he had completed well over half of his literary oeuvre, including his first undoubted masterpiece, his *Troilus and Criseide*. This was a body of work more than sufficient to establish him as the most eminent English writer before Shakespeare. But then enterprising actor, playwright, and sometime poet Shakespeare was not immediately recognized as "Shakespeare" with all that the name now implies, and struggling civil servant Geoffrey was not immediately recognized as the Chaucer we know today.

Many of his writings, and especially early ones, are now lost. Owing to accidents of preservation, medieval manuscripts have gone missing for a thousand reasons in the best of circumstances, and the younger Chaucer appears to have been casual if not downright negligent with regard to matters of preservation. A surviving scrap of a poem written to admonish his scribe and copyist suggests that he did, at least, have copies made of some poems, after composing them in the first instance on wax tablets or inferior parchment, but these were probably single copies for his own use, either as scripts for reading occasions or as exemplars for later revision. Many of them seem to have been scattered in the course of his frequent later life relocations. In the "Retraction" attached to the end of his *Canterbury Tales*, he expresses regret for having written "many songs and lecherous lays," of which no examples now exist. Chances are that, in the multilingual but primarily French-speaking courts sponsored by Philippa of Hainault and Anne of Bohemia and their entourages, these poems were written in French rather than English, and no trace of them now remains—unless a French-language manuscript suggestively entitled "Poems of Ch—" includes a few of them. And then there are other works lost outright, such as the tantalizing "Book of the Lion" that he also mentions in the "Retraction": a version, perhaps, of *Yvain* by the refined French author Chrétien de Troyes?

But an astonishingly comprehensive body of work, completed by 1386, survives. Several of his earlier poems were written under the influence of a formidable group of fourteenth-century French poets, most notably Guillaume de Machaut (also a distinguished composer of polyphonic music). These poems are written in a form now called the dream vision, since sleep and dream psychology might be involved in one form or another, but in the fourteenth century they were simply considered visions, or *visiones*. In these poems the narrator (who, suggestively, in Chaucer's case, usually turns out to be a version of the poet) is faced with a worldly problem, and the problem is in turn addressed at a different level of reality, in a vision or dream. One of them, the *Book of the Duchess*, was composed in 1369 or 1370, after the death of Blanche of Lancaster and probably prior to John of Gaunt's marriage to Constanza of Castile in 1371. A consternated narrator is caught up in a kind of troubled sympathetic identification. He then dreams, encountering a grieving knight who pours out a testimonial to his deceased lady "White." The knight's talking cure, under the narrator's gentle, if slightly obtuse, probing may represent one of Chaucer's very few attempts at poetic ingratiation with an influential figure through the agency of a poem. If so, no evidence of any particular success survives. (Chaucer's eventual headway with the Lancastrians would appear to have depended far more on the Swynford connection than on anything he wrote.) Two other visionary poems, composed in the 1370s or early 1380s but stubbornly evasive with regard to more precise dating, are his *Parliament of Fowls* and *House of Fame*. Each may be seen, in hindsight, to predict aspects of the *Canterbury Tales*, but neither points toward that work in a way that would necessarily have been evident at the time. These poems display a metrical mastery, a range of literary

styles and tones, a clever deployment of a limited, or socially obtuse, narrator, and a knowledge of French and Italian literary
precedents that alone would have marked him as one of the
three or four most significant English writers of the fourteenth
century.

And where, besides, did he possibly find the time and incentive to translate that wellspring of medieval philosophical and
theological reflection, Boethius's *Consolation of Philosophy*? This
labor would pay poetical dividends when he incorporated
Boethian sentiments in other writings, such as his *Troilus* and
his "Knight's Tale," but he appears to have been motivated by a
keen interest in Boethius himself rather than any ideas about
subsequent literary adaptation. Together with other medieval
writers, such as Jean de Meun in France and Brunetto Latini in
Italy, Chaucer possessed what T. S. Eliot would, in speaking of
the metaphysical poets, call "a mechanism of sensibility which
could devour any kind of experience." This mechanism has since
commonly been described as a unified sensibility, a refusal to
accept conventional or arbitrary distinctions between different
categories of knowledge, be they literary, philosophical, or scientific. Thus, such moments as the antic pedantry of the pomp-
ous Eagle's speech on the diffusion of sound and the confusions
of speech and flatulence in his *House of Fame*, in which he de-
ploys knowledge from Boethius and Vincent of Beauvais to poetic and humorous effect. Most conspicuous in this regard will
be a later work, on which he must, rather astoundingly, have
worked concurrently with the *Canterbury Tales*, his *Treatise on
the Astrolabe*, a practical guide to the use of this instrument, addressed to "little Lewis my son" and based on accepted scientific
sources of the day.

Moreover, by 1385–86 he had completed the awesomely accomplished *Troilus and Criseide*, a free and creative adaptation of Boccaccio's *Filostrato*. Chaucer had a typically medieval attitude toward completion, in which works were valued even in fragmentary form, but this is the major poem that he *did* complete, and triumphantly so. It is a tale of love unsought, found, deferred, celebrated, lost, and finally—with exquisite pain—traduced and betrayed. Chaucer constantly holds his whole poem in view, announcing its sorrowful conclusion in its opening lines, then for a time allowing his reader the balm of a certain forgetfulness, then returning with full force to its unsparing conclusion. Its narrator's—and, behind its narrator, its author's—play of attitude and opinion toward the tale and its characters is unceasingly varied but always under full control. It is a masterpiece of mixed style, ranging from Troilus's flights of unmodulated idealization through Criseide's practical ruminations to Pandarus's crude but ingenious opportunisms. At the end, Troilus's lost love is converted into an emblem of every impermanent earthly object, and the narrator veers wildly between extremes of flippancy, dismissal, sentimentality, scorn, and dubiously placed piety. But these are artistically managed extremities, which express emotional disarray without yielding to it and urgent feeling without loss of artistic poise.

Despite these accomplishments, few people in 1386 knew Chaucer as anything other than a middling bureaucrat struggling to stay afloat in Westminster and London's troubled factional waters. This is the paradox: By 1386 he had written a body of poetry sufficient to undergird a lustrous literary reputation, but none of it appears to have gained circulation, to have left his hand and immediate oversight in written form. Chaucer in 1386 was eminently fame-worthy . . . but certainly not famous yet.

His London Circle

Of course the younger Chaucer had an audience, and poetry would have seemed to him meaningless or impossible without one, but it was personally selected and local rather than national or international in scope. During his years of residence in London Chaucer was blessed with the presence of a supportive literary circle, an audience loyal and responsive even if numerically small. It consisted mainly of personal friends and people with whom he enjoyed circumstances in common. Its members encountered his poetry in intimate settings, read aloud, in most cases by the author himself, rather than in written form. "Audience" in the fourteenth century meant something different from what it means today. A modern audience might very occasionally gather for a reading in which a writer (most often a poet, who feels obliged by the contemporary rules of the game to be rather dismissive of the whole occasion) performs his or her work. But this is the exception. Works are more often read in solitude, in book or other written form or, more recently, on a computer screen or electronic tablet. Whereas a fourteenth-century audience consisted of those for whom the work was audible, those who gathered, usually in modest numbers, to hear it recited or read aloud. Poetry in the later fourteenth century was not "oral," in the sense of being improvised or composed in the course of a performance but was "aural" in the sense that it was privately composed and written out in manuscript form for presentation, aloud, to an audience gathered to hear it. This was certainly the case with Chaucer. He embraced the idea of manuscript circulation only latterly, and few manuscripts were in circulation among readers outside his immediate circle in his lifetime—particularly few or even none by 1386. Only after his death would manuscripts of his poems be commissioned in significant quantity, at first bespoken and eventually speculatively prepared for circulation to absent readers.

Chaucer appears to have formed some literary attachments during the years 1367 through 1374, when he served as an esquire in the court of Edward III, and carried them forward into his London years. Among Chaucer's courtly associates we may count Thomas Clanvowe, a courtier of distinction whose poem "Cuckoo and the Nightingale," written in the 1380s, contains lines borrowed in tribute or in theft from Chaucer's own "Knight's Tale." (His poem was in fact so "Chaucerian" that it was confidently included in early editions as one of Chaucer's own.) Henry Scogan, who would tutor the sons of Henry IV and would write a deeply Chaucerian "Moral Balade," is a somewhat younger friend, whom Chaucer addresses intimately in a jesting "Envoy" situated among his undated shorter poems. Scogan is an esquire of the king's household in the 1390s, and Chaucer—probably during his years in Kent—addresses him as if from afar, and as a prior acquaintance who might do him a favor, saying that Scogan "kneels at the stream's head of grace" ("*knelest at the stremes hed / Of grace*"), but that, as for himself, "At the end of which stream I am as dull as dead" ("*In th'end of which strem I am dul as ded*"). Manuscripts of Chaucer's poem addressed to Scogan include marginal glosses of the stream's head as "Windesor" (or the court) and the stream's end as "Grenewich," Chaucer's possible Kentish location. Another intimate poem, written on what might have been a "bachelor party" occasion, addresses comic strictures against marriage to Sir Peter Bukton, a knightly member of the royal household, who obviously possessed a compatible sense of humor. Other jesting lines, punning on "vache" / "cow" are added in an envoy to an otherwise serious Boethian poem, urging Sir Philip de la Vache, another knight in royal service, out of his worldly "stall" and into trust of God.

Another crucial literary friend was Ricardian chamber knight and international diplomat Lewis Clifford, intermediary between Chaucer and contemporary French poet Eustache Deschamps. Though it is doubtful that Deschamps actually read any of Chaucer's writings, the French poet composed a ballade, to be delivered by the hand of Clifford, hailing him as a "great translator" and promising to send along some of his own work so that Chaucer can "plant" it in his poetic garden. Deschamps rather aloofly describes himself as a self-authorizing poet (as one of those who authorizes himself, "*de ceus qui font pour eulx auctorisier*") as opposed to Chaucer's more derivative activities. The one concrete thing he seems to know about Chaucer does involve an act of translation: his involvement in an early and now lost rendering of the thirteenth-century French *Roman de la Rose*. This is a fact that Deschamps—who otherwise praises Chaucer for general traits, as a philosopher like Socrates and a moralist like Seneca—could easily enough have learned from their mutual friend Clifford. Thus, although Deschamps's ballade to Chaucer is sometimes cited as evidence of Chaucer's international reputation, I am inclined to take it in a different sense, but still an important one: as evidence of Clifford's loyalty and partisanship, first sparked in court circles and continuing into the years around 1390, when Clifford would most likely have been in Deschamps's company in France.

Latterly joining these courtly participants was a diverse and talented London contingent.

A peripheral (and self-nominated) London member was a dodgy fellow writer and political shape-shifter named Thomas

Usk, already mentioned as a less cautious factionalist than Chaucer and one of the Gloucester faction's political victims. Usk is an intriguing figure in his own right, a self-educated, self-made scribe, hedge lawyer, sometime author, and ceaseless striver. He was a late convert to the Ricardian cause, when it suited his advantage; after ceaseless efforts he gained a patronage position as undersheriff of Middlesex in 1387—just in time to be condemned and put to death by the Merciless Parliament for the extremity of his partisan efforts in that post. He enjoys the distinction of being the first English person—and the only one prior to the autumn of 1386—to cite Chaucer's work. His allusion occurs in his 1385 *Testament of Love*, at once a work of Boethian philosophy and unrestrained factional pleading. There, when Usk tackles issues of necessity and free will as part of his argument for the voluntary nature of the political choices he has made, he cites Chaucer's treatment of similar issues in the fourth book of his *Troilus*. Love, Usk's interlocutor, salutes "my own true servant the noble philosophical poet in English . . . who in a treatise that he made of my servant Troilus has touched this matter and fully resolved it." Usk would have had good cause to associate himself with Chaucer, and to tag him textually besides. But his reference to Chaucer is general enough that it might have been based on hearsay rather than direct acquaintance or on membership in Chaucer's literary circle. Usk was a would-be insider and proven snoop, a man who had founded his whole career on being in the know. He might be considered an aspirational member, aware that a Chaucer circle exists and wishing to claim membership in it. Fortunately, to his rather anomalous case may be added some more solid evidence of Chaucer's core audience.

Chaucer reveals two of its members at the end of his *Troilus*, when he submits his poem to the stewardship and judgment of "moral Gower" and "philosophical Strode." Gower is John Gower, a prolific poet in Anglo-Norman French and Latin and, perhaps nudged by Chaucer's own earlier decision to write in English, author of his own tale collection in their native tongue. Concurrently with Chaucer's decision to launch the *Canterbury Tales*, and perhaps even some months before, he began his own English-language *Confessio Amantis*, in which a poetic version of himself confesses his worldly sins and misbehavior to a priest named Genius. He was, like Chaucer, a claimant for King Richard's good opinion (until he switched sides to cultivate the future king Henry, a move that Chaucer would also make, but several years later, in the last year of his life, once Richard was dead and Henry already on the throne). He may be considered something of a friendly rival, as jibes about his work by Chaucer in the prologue to the "Man of Law's Tale" appear to confirm. He was a bit Chaucer's senior, and undoubtedly more somber in his views—as Chaucer's "moral Gower" would suggest—but he must certainly be thought well abreast of Chaucer's poetical productions. So too with "philosophical Strode." Ralph Strode has been identified with a learned Oxford philosopher of the same name, the supposition being that he switched careers in middle age and moved to London, where he became a common pleader—a civil employee and legal officer. There's a possibility that the London Strode simply happens to be the philosopher's namesake and that Chaucer is teasing him with the moniker "philosophical" . . . but, in any case, Strode was a smart and competent professional, a fellow Ricardian factionalist within the city who, like Chaucer, depended on the Brembre faction for advancement, and he even lived nearby, in a city property over another city gate. Whether or not a trained philosopher, he was certainly Chaucer's worthy friend.

Given the unusual insularity of London's different literary and intellectual communities, it would seem that some contemporary writers of importance may not have known Chaucer at all, or only by sight or chance encounter. They include William Langland (author of the brilliantly satiric *Piers Plowman*, and in and out of London during Chaucer's years there) and the anonymous poet of *Sir Gawain and the Green Knight* (whose possible temporary residence in London in the 1370s and early 1380s might have overlapped Chaucer's). Langland's friends inhabited a demimonde of minor ecclesiastics and churchy intellectuals, and the *Gawain* poet retained closer ties to baronial courts in Cheshire or Lancashire than any he would have formed in London. But other, aspirant, writers would have reason to seek Chaucer's acquaintance or, retrospectively, to claim it. The exchequer employee and poet Thomas Hoccleve, a devotee and admirer of Chaucer's work, claims to have known him personally, although, some twenty-five years younger and barely twenty in 1386, he would presumably have been on the outside looking in.

This small cluster of names and associations does not exhaust Chaucer's audience, but—augmented with female members, whose presence is signaled by sly digs and jokes Chaucer throws their way—suggests its contours. I'm calling it an audience and a circle rather than a literary public at this stage, because it hasn't reached anything close to the numerical size or the breadth of appeal we might associate with the latter phrase. But this is hardly to minimize the importance of an intimate audience or circle to a medieval poet.

Why Audience Matters

A writer's sense of audience plays an under-acknowledged role in literary creation. Although mystics and romantics have from time to time (and usually unpersuasively) claimed otherwise, the normal condition of the writer is not pure solitude but rather embraces an awareness of those whom he or she is addressing, their interests and likely responses, their generic expectations, what they can be supposed to know and not to know, their sympathies, their endurance . . . I agree with those who believe that a written or spoken communication is held in common by its writer or speaker and its audience. Sitting at one end of what might be thought a communicative bridge or chain, the audience has a tacit but constant influence on the form of the final work. Always a factor, the audience's influence on the work is all the more pronounced in the medieval period, owing to the normal circumstances of literary performance.

The medieval writer, and certainly Chaucer before 1386, imagines reading aloud to an audience gathered for the occasion. So pervasive were medieval assumptions about oral performance that even those alone in a room with a manuscript normally constituted themselves as an audience of one, reading the work aloud and essentially performing it for themselves. In his *Confessions*, Augustine comments with amazement that Ambrose, bishop of Milan, customarily read to himself in silence; that

> his eyes scanned the page and his heart sought out the meaning, but his voice was silent and his tongue was still. Anyone could approach him freely and guests were not commonly announced, so that often, when we came to visit him, we found him reading like this in silence, for he never read aloud.

Even in the late fourteenth century, silent readers like Ambrose were the exception rather than the rule. Whether one was read to or read to oneself, reading was an oral performance.

Troilus—the last of the works Chaucer completed before the *Canterbury Tales*—abounds in evidence of intimate author-audience interaction. *Troilus* is richly arrayed in references to an alert and reactive listening audience, and a climate of lively exchange, and occasional badinage, pervades the poem. One imagines *Troilus* read aloud, and that each of its five books might have lent itself to a long afternoon's or evening's enjoyment. It even includes a reading scene, or an allegory of its own presentation. In book 2, Pandarus goes to visit Criseide and finds her in a "paved parlor," or enhanced garden setting, with a maiden reading aloud to her and other companions from a romance of Thebes. An ambitiously executed illustration to one of the sumptuous editions of *Troilus* produced in the decade after his death has Chaucer reading his poem aloud to a courtly audience consisting of Richard II (whose face is rubbed out, presumably by a disapproving later partisan of the new king Henry IV) and his queen Anne and other persons of refinement. This illustration, designed to compliment Chaucer and attract interest in his work, is almost certainly a fanciful one; he probably never actually read aloud to the king and queen. But the fact of oral performance, for a listening public, is more firmly grounded, and would have definitely been the way that Chaucer expected to present his poem.

In the poem's early sections, where optimism about love's prospects is permitted to prevail, Chaucer playfully addresses "ye lovers," representing them as experts and, characteristically, himself as a fumbler in the game. He speaks familiarly of what his hearers suppose, or know, about love, and he also implies a kind of solidarity from his audience, reflecting on assumptions they share or points on which they agree (how it seems to "us" or what *"us thinketh"*). He even enlists his audience as collaborators in the narrative enterprise, speaking of what his story still needs for completion (*"us lakketh noght but . . ."*). He pauses, on occasion, to jest with female members of his audience. At the moment of Troilus and Criseide's consummation, he speaks of his hero's joyous release from previous sorrows, and observes in sly provocation that sexual capitulation is the best overall policy for womankind: "For love of God, may each woman take heed / And thus conduct herself in time of need." (*"For love of God, take every womman heede / To werken thus, if it comth to the neede."*) He even engages (with doubtful propriety) in a moment of playful self-promotion, capping his reflection on Diomede's betrayal with a suggestion that women nevertheless reserve some trust for the poet, urging them to be wary of men but listen to what he says: "Beware of men, and harken to what I say" (*"Beth war of men, and herkneth what I seye!"*). Sensing possible audience dissatisfaction in the way a narrative that begins as a romance devolves into a tragedy of betrayal and loss, he engages in a playfully transparent repositioning, characterizing himself as a bystander of his own story: "Men say—I know not—that she gave him her heart" (*"Men seyn—I not—that she yaf him hire herte"*).

To lose "audience"—the attention of a circle of hearers, within the circuit of one's own voice—was a wrenching, even disastrous experience. In his "Tale of Melibee" Chaucer himself takes note of the destitution of a speaker who loses audience. A home invasion has occurred, and the householder, Melibee by name, is taking consultation among his friends and neighbors about what kind of revenge he should seek. He is eventually straightened out on this matter by his aptly named (and partially allegorically conceived) wife, Prudence, who counsels forgiveness. Among his advisers are young hotheads, who recommend war, and then an older, wiser man, who raises his hand to request audience. This wise man's cautionary remarks involve the uncertainties of war, and he seeks to underscore his words (*"to enforcen his tale"*)—through examples. At this point, the hotheads interrupt: "Practically at once they rose to interrupt his tale, and bade him often to abridge his words" (*"Wel ny alle atones bigonne they to rise for to breken his tale, and beden hym ful ofte his wordes for to abregge"*). Chaucer as narrator—for this is one of the two tales he tells in his Pilgrim persona—concedes that nobody enjoys unsolicited advice: "For truly, he that preaches to those who prefer to not hear his words, only annoys them with his speech" (*"For soothly, he that precheth to hem that listen nat heeren his wordes, his sermon hem anoieth"*). But he then sympathizes with this old wise man in his loss of audience, or at any rate allows him this retort:

And when this wise man saw that he lacked an audience, he shamefacedly sat down again. For Solomon says, "When you don't have an audience, restrain yourself from speaking." "I see well," said this wise man, "that the common proverb is true, that 'good counsel is lacking when it is most needed.'"

(And whan this wise man saugh that him wanted audience, al shamefast he sette hym doun again. For Salomon seith: "There as thou ne maist have noon audience, enforce thee nat to speke." "I see wel," quod this wise man, "that the commune proverbe is sooth, that 'good conseil wanteth whan it is moost nede.'")

So the old man gets in his parting shot, a final assertion of the value of his words. But this is wounded pride, a vain attempt to bolster his dignity in a situation of extreme affront. Having no

audience, no immediate listening public, is emotionally distressing, whether for an aged counselor or a not-quite-so-aged poet.

Chaucer registers this matter of a "broken tale"—a stream of
spoken exposition interrupted—throughout his writing career.
He will return to it again and again in his tales of Canterbury
that, after all, recount a tale-telling competition in which feelings frequently run high and often culminate in attempts at interruption. Some would-be troublemakers are rebuffed. When
the Pardoner breaks in on the Wife of Bath's account of tribula-
tion in marriage (in order to advance the doubtful proposition
that he had been considering wedlock), her simple but commanding "Abide" or "Wait a while" (*"Abide!"*)—secures his silence. And when the Friar and the Summoner interrupt the
Wife's narration with their quarrel, a formidable alliance of
Harry Bailly and Dame Alice promptly silences them. But several Canterbury tales are broken, and audience lost, with accompanying perturbation and disappointment.

One of them, as it happens, is Chaucer's own. The tale he will
assign to his "Pilgrim self," or persona, provokes a painful interruption. After 227 grueling lines of Sir Thopas, the parodic popular romance Chaucer has wryly assigned to his Pilgrim self, master
of ceremonies Harry Bailly can stand no more and interrupts:

"No more of this, for God's dignity,"
Said our Host, "for you make me
So weary of this utter ignorance
That . . .
I have an earache from your worthless speech."

(*"Namore of this, for Goddes dignitee,"*
Quod oure Hooste, " for thou makest me

So wery of thy verray lewednesse
That . . .
Mine eres aken of thy drasty speeche.")

And lest his point be missed: "Your wretched rhyming isn't worth a turd!" (*"Thy drasty riming is nat worth a toord!"*)

Nobody likes to be interrupted, or to be cut off in full flow, or (in the terms already discussed) to lose audience. What Chaucer here suggests, albeit comically, is that this is a problem of which he is not unaware. The emotional damage of the interrupted tale and lost audience persist as themes of the pilgrimage. Although he bears his predicament more aloofly and less complainingly than the Pilgrim Chaucer, the Monk has to endure the interruption of his series of "tragedies" by no less an eminence than the Knight. Though the Squire seems mainly to be his own nemesis—by attempting an overcomplicated tale—he too is interrupted, or in this case rescued, by the diplomatic Franklin. Concern with the rights of the tale-teller to speak, and the obligations of the listening audience, leave no doubt that Chaucer was intensively concerned with what might be called the dynamics of presence in the literary situation.

Writing is, after all, a social medium, and communication between writer and audience is a two-way street. In the heightened conditions of live contact, within which Chaucer normally presented his poems, this collaborative aspect of the poetic springs even more vividly to view. Some of his apparent asides to a live audience may be invented—simulated rather than real—but their abundance leaves no doubt about the interactive aspects of his poetry. Chaucer's audience, as portrayed and implied within his poetry, must compel our admiration. It may be granted a share of credit as virtual co-creator of his works.

Even so, this is the very audience from which the crisis months of 1386 were about to sever him. This severance from his accustomed audience and writing situation was the greatest of all the dislocations he was about to suffer. Chaucer has, in the political and civil events I have recounted, sometimes seemed at the mercy of external events. He was, after all, subject to the whims and schemes of powerful and headstrong men, a petitioner and recipient rather than an architect of favor. But with respect to his art—his unflagging productivity and pursuit of his literary objectives regardless of circumstances—he was nobody's pawn or fool. He would find a way to keep writing in this new and unsettled situation. And because a sense of audience was vitally important to his creative process, he would soon be seeking a new, or at least a radically reimagined, one.

CHAPTER SIX

The Problem of Fame

In his earlier moment of self-assessment in his *House of Fame*, Chaucer's stand-in, Geffrey, claims to be self-sufficient, to be the sole judge of his personal and artistic successes and failures:

> I'm the one who best knows how I stand;
> For what things I endure, or what I think,
> I'm the one who'll swallow all that drink.

> (*I wot myself best how I stonde;*
> *For what I drye, or what I thinke,*
> *I wil myselven al hit drinke.*)

This is, of course, mainly bravado. Chaucer's audience was always important to him, although this bit of swagger might help to explain his contentment with an intimate audience of friends and familiars, as opposed to any more general quest for celebrity or personal fame. A pronounced skepticism about fame, and its costs and effects, recurs within Chaucer's poetry, not only in his *House of Fame* but elsewhere in his earlier poetry as well. But with the progress of years he betrays an ambivalence, a softening of his position on the subject, especially in his *Troilus*, the poem he completed on the brink of the 1386 crisis. Just at this moment, when external events were about to compel a reconsideration of his audience relations, he was rather torturously pursuing some of his own new thoughts on the matter.

Fame

Some of Chaucer's European counterparts—and especially north Italian intellectuals and men of affairs like Dante, Petrarch, and Boccaccio—had shown themselves quite adept at building their literary reputations. The situation still lagged in England, however, in part because of writers' own reluctance to cultivate, or seem to be cultivating, literary fame. English writers throughout most of Chaucer's lifetime display something between nonchalance and stubborn refusal to name themselves in their writings, or only name themselves in veiled ways. Forthright self-naming seems to have been considered a brazen or boastful practice. Chaucer's brilliant contemporary, the author of *Sir Gawain and the Green Knight*, doesn't name himself at all. His friend and rival John Gower omits himself from his first poem, *Mirour de l'Omne* (composed in the 1370s). He only obliquely names himself by means of a cipher in his *Vox Clamantis* or *Voice of One Crying* (early 1380s), explaining that he does not write for personal fame. His controversial fellow Londoner Thomas Usk writes his *Testament of Love* to improve his personal standing with King Richard's (and Chaucer's own) political faction, but, even in a work blatantly intended to attract attention to himself and his predicament, names himself only in an elaborate acrostic that wasn't deciphered for five hundred years (during which most people who knew his text assigned it to Chaucer!). William Langland, author of the popular and satiric *Piers Plowman*, identifies himself only with a glancing reference to his narrator as "Long Will," a pun on his presumed name . . . although his actual name was veiled to most readers of his poem, and one is still 99 percent rather than 100 percent sure that a person named William Langland actually strode the earth. Chaucer permits a character in his *House of Fame* to address him as "Geffrey," and with typically wry humor he has a Canterbury Pilgrim, the Man of Law, denounce one "Chaucer" as an absent third party, a crude but prolific poet who has muddied the narrative waters by getting to all the best tales first. But these are broad hints rather than overt acts of self-naming. Authorial identity in the later fourteenth century might be described as a half-open secret, known to close associates and a few others of a highly inquiring disposition, but taken for granted or cheerfully ignored by most hearers or readers of a poetic or fictional composition.

This idea of modest self-restraint extended, in fact, to the very concept of authorship itself. An *auctor* in the fourteenth century was an authority, a classical writer, or a writer committed solely to the production of Latin verse according to accepted literary models. Chaucer never actually calls himself an author, nor would he. "Compiler" is as close as he comes, saying in the prologue to his *Treatise on the Astrolabe* that "I am only an unlearned compiler" (*"I n'am but a lewd compilator"*) of the work of others. Fifteenth-century scribes and editors take him at his word, calling him "compilator" in the headnotes and endnotes of his poems; the idea of Chaucer as an author is strictly a creation of his admiring followers in the fifteenth century.

This is not just a pretense of modesty, however, or one of those artful tropes where the audience is being coaxed into a ringing affirmation of the very authorship that the writer has just denied. Ample evidence in Chaucer's earlier poetry suggests, if not actual modesty, then something close to it: a genuine contempt for fame-seeking writers and the pursuit of fame.

This is, in fact, the subject of his *House of Fame*, a poem of his midcareer written, among other motives, to twit his illustrious predecessor Dante as a fame-seeking windbag.

The entire edifice of Fame, which Chaucer (in his naive and truth-seeking persona Geffrey) visits in this poem, is itself faulty, founded on a *"feble fundament,"* or uncertain foundation of ice, the half of which—together with the honor roll of names inscribed upon it—is melting away. The great authors and artists honored within as supporters of fame turn out upon closer acquaintance to be in envious competition among themselves. Worse yet, even the unquestioned greats like Virgil and Ovid are plunged into a hubbub of dubious entertainers, including jugglers and magicians, witches and sorceresses, and their poetic productions are all but lost in a babble that the confused Geffrey compares to the noise of a rookery. Fame herself turns out to be entirely arbitrary in her rewards, infected by every bad aspect of what Chaucer already knew as a culture in which seekers of personal advantage endlessly (and often fruitlessly) petitioned and scrambled for favor. A change of venue doesn't help. Geffrey progresses from her palace to its annex—a spinning wicket called the house of rumor—and matters there are even worse.

The reader arrives at Fame's house through a celestial journey evocative of Dante's own journey in his *Divine Comedy*—a work at once pillaged and mocked within the inventive contours of Chaucer's own poem. The rhetorically heightened invocations with which he launches his poem's sections are clearly parodic of Dante's, especially the invocation to Apollo, the god of science and of light with which he begins his final section. He seeks inspiration, even as he engages in exaggerated apology for his own frivolous and unlearned *("light and lewed"*) verse, and declares that he cannot hope for more as a poet than to capture the general sense of things. If he succeeds, he says, he will rush to the next laurel tree he sees and kiss it, since it is Apollo's tree. Here he imitates *Paradiso* 1.13–27, with a crucial difference. Dante wishes for Apollo's support, not just in honoring the laurel but also in winning it for his own brow. "You shall," he promises Apollo, "see me come to the foot of your beloved tree and crown myself with its leaves"—a laureate aspiration that Chaucer is more inclined to mock than to emulate.

Chaucer's mild amusement at Dante's self-seriousness shifts to outright ridicule in the passages where we encounter his guide to celestial adventure, a giant, golden eagle:

> I thought I saw an eagle soar . . .
> It was of gold, and shone so bright
> That never saw men such a sight.
>
> (*Me thoughte I sawgh an egle sore . . .*
> *Hit was of gold, and shon so brighte*
> *That never sawe men such a sighte.*)

This eagle, snatching Chaucer in his talons and bearing him to Fame's house, stands in for the eagle that bears Dante aloft in *Purgatorio* 9.19–21:

> in a dream I seemed to see an eagle,
> with golden feathers, hovering in the sky,
> his wings spread wide, ready to swoop.

The eagle's interest in Dante, however, initially seems to that poet a mark of distinction. Within his dream he compares himself to Ganymede, a favorite of the gods, whereas Chaucer's eagle is derisive from the outset. He turns out to be a loquacious busybody, lecturing Geffrey as he goes. One of his subjects is Geffrey's personal inadequacies. Helpless in the eagle's clutches, the poet is berated for his lack of social skills, his solitary bookishness, and, by implication, his weight problem. The eagle's, and Jove's, aim is to raise Geffrey's spirits by granting him access to information, or "tidings," in the House of Fame. But even this promise is undercut by the fact that the tidings reaching Fame's dwelling are borne upward by sound, and the eagle's learned explanation of sound waves turns out to be a ribald one. For,

> Sound is only air that's broken;
> And every speech that's ever spoken,
> Loud or private, foul or fair,
> Consists of nothing but of air;
> For as flame's but lighted smoke,
> Just so, sound is broken air.

> (*Soun is noght but eir ybroken;*
> *And every speche that is spoken,*
> *Lowd or privee, foul or fair,*
> *In his substaunce is but air;*
> *For as flaumbe is but lighted smoke,*
> *Right soo soun is air ybroke.*)

Sound, and speech itself, turns out to be "broken air," or nothing but a form of farting, revealing what one might call the fundamental unseriousness of the whole account.

No wonder that in his *House of Fame* Geffrey declares a determination to chart his own course, and pronounces himself his own best judge. As he says, in a passage quoted earlier in this chapter, he'll mix and swallow his own drink, thank you, especially with respect to matters touching upon his own artistry. With respect to fame, or acclaim, he is not one of those laurel-seeking Tuscans like Dante or Petrarch but will live outside the limelight as a matter of choice.

Fame Revisited

The year 1386 was a watershed, after which nothing in Chaucer's life would be the same. The political developments of October through December 1386 would deprive him of his dwelling, his living, and, most relevantly for his poetry, access to the intimate audience on which that poetry had always depended. These external events would force him to reconsider his whole attitude toward writing and reception. But concurrent signs suggest that he was ready for a reconsideration, that by 1386 he had already begun to modify his ideas about literary circulation, and even his previously adamant attitude toward fame. This new attitude first emerges to view at the end of *Troilus*, which he completed late in 1385 or early in 1386, and it marks a new preparedness to embrace fame, together with its unsettling potentialities.

At the end of *Troilus*, Chaucer responds in an agitated way to an idea that appears to have just occurred to him, or that is striking him with unprecedented force: He has written a poem deserving of broad admiration, a poem that may circulate to present and future audiences in manuscript form, and thus be read without his superintending presence and beyond his personal control. This possibility arises in a complicated way and is expressed as a collision between several different states of mind. One involves an ambivalent mistrust of manuscript circulation, or any other kind of circulation that might lead to the enjoyment or scrutiny of his works away from his own presence and oversight. Another implies his recognition that the possibilities for such circulation were now increasingly at hand. Yet another involves a modification of his previous, adamant rejection of fame and fame seeking, founded on the undeniable fact that with his *Troilus* he has just written an absolutely major poem, a poem that might entitle him to a share of celebrity and literary renown.

All this occurs in his leave-taking to his own completed poem, a farewell to his "little book" ("*litel bok*"). He expresses the hope that, having completed a tragedy, he may have grace to write a comedy someday. Then he appends a caution that also verges on a boast, or at least a modest man's muted near-boast:

Go, little book . . .
But little book, don't envy others' poems,
Subject yourself to all of Poetry;
And kiss the steps upon which poets walk:
Virgil, Ovid, Homer, Lucan, Stace [Statius].

(*Go, litel bok . . .*
But litel book, no making thou n'envye,
But subjet be to alle poesye;
And kis the steppes wher as thow seest pace
Virgile, Ovide, Omer, Lucan, and Stace.)

The enlargement of Chaucer's expectations is immediately signaled by this dramatization of his book's send-off, a form of envoi stretching back to Ovid and the classical greats, and revived in the Middle Ages by Boccaccio and others. Boccaccio, in the case of one shorter work, even previews Chaucer's affectation of modest self-diminution, with his "O my little book . . . go" (*"O picciolo mio libretto . . . va"*), with *"picciolo libretto"* equivalent to *"litel bok."* The fact that Chaucer, previously so reticent with his manuscripts, speaks even obliquely of sending this one off to seek its fortunes already signals a massive shift of attitude.

One sign of Chaucer's new attitude is a considerable surge in the scope of his literary ambitions. In his *Inferno* Dante imagines himself welcomed by the classical greats in limbo. So too does Chaucer, even while modestly protesting his unworthiness, allow himself a presumptuous accompanying speculation. Declaring himself a reverent follower of Virgil, Ovid, and the other greats, he also floats the implicit suggestion that he might not only be their devotee but also their worthy successor. This is an exciting idea, but also a frightening one. It is tantamount to declaring himself an author, the bold assertion he would never make for himself in so many words. An author lays claim to a readership in posterity, which means a readership that will encounter his work in written form, beyond his immediate oversight or surveillance. This leads, in turn, to the second aspect of Chaucer's unease: the liabilities of manuscript circulation itself. Manuscript circulation introduces the possibilities of scribal error and bad transmission, and also those of misunderstanding or bad interpretation by an audience located beyond the writer's advice and control:

> And since there is such great diversity
> In English, and in writing of our tongue,
> I pray to God that none miscopy thee,
> Or mangle meter from knowing not the tongue;
> And, wherever you be read or sung,
> That thou be understood, I pray to God!

(*And for ther is so greet diversitee*
In Englissh, and in writing of oure tonge,
So praye I God that noon miswrite the,
Ne the mismetre for defaute of tonge;
And red wherso thou be, or elles songe,
That thou be understonde, God I biseeche!)

"Beseech" is a strong word here: He uses it to say not just that he hopes for understanding but that he urgently and rather abjectly prays for it. And well he might, if the situation that both tempts and consternates him should come to pass: His work might migrate beyond its immediate circle of listeners and companions and into the hands of an estranged readership that will encounter it, possibly in corrupted versions, and draw conclusions of their own.

Having considered these rather dizzying prospects, Chaucer returns at *Troilus*'s very end to a more familiar, and constrained, idea of his poem's circulation. At its closing he invites fellow poet John Gower and the apparently erudite civil servant Ralph Strode to be its recipients and overseers:

Oh, moral Gower, this book I direct
To you, and to you, philosophical Strode,
But grant that you'll correct it when need be . . .

(*O moral Gower, this book I directe*
To the and to the, philosophical Strode,
To vouchen sauf, ther need is, to correcte . . .)

Whether he "directs" the poem to Gower and Strode in the literal sense of sending them copies of the poem for their inspection or whether he is just thinking of them as members of an exemplary audience in a more figurative sense isn't clear. The expense of preparing manuscript copies and his own ambivalence about circulation would suggest the latter, that he is directing the poem to them in a more ideal and theoretical way. Whether or not he actually sent manuscripts to them, his invocation of their names is a conservative gesture. By naming two stalwarts of his earlier public, at least one of whom, moral Gower, may be reckoned a literary conservative, he is returning to an earlier and more personal idea of literary reception. By thinking of such established associates at this point, he holds the idea of harum-scarum, reckless circulation to an unknown readership at bay. But the fame genie is, one might say, out of the bottle. The idea that persons beyond one's circle of intimates might encounter, and respond to, one's poem has taken tentative shape, and will exert itself within Chaucer's future literary career.

Nevertheless, several pieces of evidence do suggest that *Troilus* already marked a turning point in Chaucer's ideas about manuscript circulation. For one thing, whatever else he did with it, he undoubtedly had at least one copy of *Troilus* made. His arrangements with his copyist (or scrivener) are known from a poem preserved in a fifteenth-century manuscript, under the title "Chaucers Wordes unto Adam, His Owne Scriveyn." In it, he chides the hapless Adam:

> Adam the scribe, if you are ever asked
> To copy out Boethius or Troilus anew,
> I wish you maddening itch under your curls,
> Unless you reproduce my verse more true;
> So many times a day I must renew your work,

In its correction I must rub and scrape,
And all is through your negligence and haste.

(*Adam scriveyn, if ever it thee bifalle*
Boece or Troylus for to writen newe,
Under thy long lokkes thou most have the scalle
But after my makyng thow write more trewe;
So ofte adaye I mot thy werk renewe,
It to correcte and eke to rubbe and scrape.
And al is thorugh thy negligence and rape.)

Chaucer's authorship of this little poem, preserved in a mid-fifteenth-century manuscript supervised by a scribal entrepreneur named John Shirley, has been called into doubt. Certainly, its title was composed by Shirley rather than Chaucer himself. Nor was this scrivener—since identified as one Adam Pinkhurst—exactly Chaucer's "own" scribe, since he worked on commissions for others as well. In my view, this is still a genuine poem. This poem's expressed concerns seem intimately related to Chaucer's own, with its unease about the possibility of scribal error chiming closely with the anxieties about being "miswritten" expressed at the end of *Troilus*. Additionally, this poem's subtle but telling effect of elevating Chaucer's own literary activities by separating them from those of the scribe upon whom he must depend—its sense of himself as poet rather than mere copyist or transcriber—accords well with his growing authorial ambitions in the mid-1380s. Whether the copy to which he alludes was made for his own use or for broader circulation cannot be known. But he suggests ("if you are ever asked / To copy out Boethius or Troilus anew") that he may be coming back to Adam for more copies in the future.

Meanwhile, other evidence has come to light, suggesting that *Troilus* did indeed circulate beyond Chaucer's immediate circle. Historians Martha Carlin and Caroline Barron recently announced discovery of a legal document concerning a Southwark innkeeper and scrivener named Thomas Spencer. In 1405 testimony bearing on the matter of a disputed debt, Spencer says that on November 4, 1394, he settled the debt with Agnes Goodgroom of Guildford, a part of the settlement being "a certain book called *Troilus*, valued at 20s." Spencer himself may or may not have been its scribe; his role in scribal culture together with his vocation as an innkeeper would have situated him as a possible middleman of one sort or another. In any case, here we have a copy of *Troilus* changing hands between two persons situated well beyond the boundaries of Chaucer's own customary literary circle. The valuation of the manuscript at 20s. is itself an important piece of data in the discussion of early manuscript books and their circulation and cost. It indicates a valued manuscript, although probably not an extensively decorated or illuminated one; a manuscript suitable for circulation in a comfortably situated—though not necessarily elite—readership. Above all else, though, this is the first, and only, evidence ever discovered of a poem by Chaucer having circulated prior to his death in 1400. It need not be, and surely was not, the only such instance. But it is an important and singular counterpart and corroboration of the new ideas about literary circulation that Chaucer was forming in the course of the year 1386.

Following upon *Troilus*, Chaucer even permits himself a daydream of celebrity, an indulgent notion that his poem has come to the attention of King Richard and Queen Anne and has even scandalized them a bit. It occurs in his *Legend of Good Women*, an unfinished poem that followed *Troilus*, and on which he may have worked intermittently in the remaining years of his life. In this poem he whimsically supposes that his portrayal of Criseide's faithlessness has attracted the negative notice of the God of Love and his queen, Alceste. The God of Love accuses him of having translated the "Romance of the Rose" (a now lost version of the poem in which Jean de Meun engages in an antifeminist tirade) and also of having defamed Criseide while slanting the case against women:

Have you not made as well the English book
Of how Criseide Troilus forsook
To show how often women go astray?

(*Hast thow nat mad in English ek the bok*
How that Crisseide Troilus forsook
In shewynge how that wemen han don mis?)

Alceste pleads for him, citing a bibliography of his past literary accomplishments (itself an indulgence in a kind of self-promotion that a younger Chaucer would probably have avoided) and promising that he will write a new legend, or a collection of saintly stories, honoring women true in loving all their lives. The God of Love and Alceste have been generally understood (and were probably understood by Chaucer's original audience) to allude to the testy young king Richard II and his elegant wife Anne of Bohemia. Chaucer's oblique suggestion is that *Troilus* might have attracted royal notice, even if notice in the slightly literal-minded and crotchety form in which the God of Love expresses it. Under the cover of a disavowal—that his Richard figure disapproves rather than approves of his poem—he allows himself a very bold surmise about the outer circumference of

Troilus's readership. This imagined circle was, moreover, closed early in the fifteenth century, when a sumptuous manuscript of *Troilus* was prepared, probably for presentation to Henry IV or a member of his circle. The manuscript is prefaced with an elaborate frontispiece depicting Chaucer at a podium and in formal if not priestly garb, reading his poem aloud to the court of Richard II. Too bad that Chaucer didn't live to see it. Although undoubtedly fanciful, it embodies a dream of acceptance and approval, a dream cautiously or even timorously expressed at the end of *Troilus*, comically inflated and indulged in the *Legend of Good Women*, and finally, after Chaucer's lifetime, come audaciously true.

Ambition—and specifically literary ambition—seems suddenly in the air. Chaucer's fellow poet Gower was apparently also breathing it. He has a fantasy of royal reception too. His account of royal interest and approval is probably no less fictive than Chaucer's, although he reports it as an actual experience. He claims in his long English poem *Confessio Amantis* that King Richard himself commissioned it. He describes himself rowing on the Thames and being espied by Richard, who invited him onto the royal barge:

> Spying me, he bade me come
> Out of my boat into his barge
>
> (*Out of my bot, whan he me syh,*
> *He bad me come in to his barge . . .*)

Once there, Richard charged him to make a book consisting of "some new thing" ("*som newe thing*") as a favor to himself. Gower later canceled these lines, but not out of modesty; in the later years of Richard's reign, Gower would cover his bets by dedicating a revised preface to Henry of Derby, who would indeed then supplant Richard on the throne in 1399. This notion that one's writings might attract the attention of a king, or kings, was a heady one. But his claim, or fantasy, about royal sponsorship is not completely personal or idiosyncratic; it suggests the more general emergence of new and less disguised ambitions around the previously less assertive enterprise of writing verse in English. (Although of course the far more modest and elliptical Chaucer, suggesting that Richard and Anne in the persons of the God of Love and Queen Alceste might have noticed his *Troilus*, amusingly records their reaction as one of complete disapproval.)

John Gower's tendency, in literature as in life, was to present in more evident, or even more blatant, form some of Chaucer's more muted aspirations. Gower's own ascending curve of literary ambition is certainly more boldly proclaimed than Chaucer's own. When he died in 1413 the aged Gower was buried in a monumental setting, now displaced from its original location and reinstalled, but its essentials still visible in Southwark Cathedral. In a scheme probably planned by Gower himself and possibly completed during his lifetime, he is represented as reclining with his head on the three major volumes he wrote during his lifetime, and with the legend "Gower Arm. Angl. Poeta celeberrimus"—"Gower, esquire: highly celebrated Poet of England." Even though Chaucer never calls himself either poet or author, contenting himself with the more humble *"compilator"* or "compiler" of the works of others . . . what if he had lived another thirteen years? Had he lived into the next century, and a time when the Lancastrians were encouraging the writing of poetry in English, and the idea of fame was more accepted, perhaps he would have countenanced such an epitaph.

Another Italian

Chaucer's newly unsettled attitude toward fame undoubtedly possessed a competitive edge. He had no real domestic competitors. Some of his fellow Englishmen, and especially the author of *Piers Plowman*, were writing accomplished poems in what is known as alliterative verse (in which three of the four stressed syllables of a line begin with the same consonantal sound) and Chaucer pauses in his *Tales* to have his Parson brush aside such "rum, ram, ruf" versifying. Closer to home was John Gower, and Chaucer allows his Man of Law to make some fun of this undeniably moral man by twitting him for telling "cursed stories" of incest and other abominations. Among writers from abroad he had no choice but to take Dante and Petrarch seriously, but he still didn't need to think of them as his personal competitors. Dante wrote in vernacular Italian but on incontestably high themes, and Petrarch's impeccable Latinity made him the equal of the greatest classical authorities. Chaucer could and did mock them a bit, but as august forebears rather than as challenging contemporaries.

Another Italian author of broad accomplishment nevertheless presented a more direct and less avoidable spur and challenge. This was Boccaccio, a near contemporary (barely a generation older) and a master of narrative in his own vernacular Italian tongue. Boccaccio's reputation had swept Florence and Milan, and was strongly established among the Italian merchant classes with whom Chaucer would have interacted, not only on two trips he had taken to Italy, but also in and around the wool custom. Chaucer's contacts put him in a unique and rather privileged position with regard to Boccaccio's vernacular Italian writings. He certainly knew and enjoyed access to several of them, including the *Teseida* (of which Chaucer's "Knight's Tale" is a respectful adaptation) and the *Filostrato* (the incentive and direct inspiration of his *Troilus*, his own greatest work to date). Moreover, he was either the *only* native English writer or literary enthusiast of the 1380s to know these works, or one of very few. This knowledge might be construed to confer a kind of responsibility as custodian of Boccaccio's English literary reputation. If so, he was notably derelict in this responsibility's exercise.

Whatever his ambivalences, Chaucer names Dante and Petrarch within the body of his own work. But although far more reliant upon Boccaccio than on either of them, he altogether omits his name. In fact, in the course of his *Troilus*, he drops the names of several precursors whom he does *not* use—Dares and Dictes—and even jestingly but also craftily invents and mock credits a source in the writings of one "Lollius." But his heavy reliance upon Boccaccio is uncredited and, it must be said, willfully concealed.

One can admire Chaucer immensely and still grant that his relationship to Boccaccio was problematic; productive, in that Chaucer learned all kinds of things from him about the staging of a longer narrative poem, but also fraught with unmistakable symptoms of envy. Compounding all this was the fact that Chaucer would undoubtedly have heard about a work he might not actually have read, Boccaccio's *Decameron*, a tale collection narrated not by the author himself but by a company of young Florentine gentlefolk traveling about the countryside to avoid an outbreak of the plague. The suggestion is sometimes made that Chaucer knew the *Decameron* firsthand, but it is not necessarily so. Several of the *Canterbury Tales* have close counterparts in the *Decameron*, but their similarities appear to have derived from common ancestry rather than Chaucer's use of Boccaccio as a direct source. The *Decameron* seems to have spurred Chaucer simply by the fact of its known existence. He may never have held a copy in his hand, but it incited him as a work of rapidly growing reputation by a near competitor, in his native tongue rather than in Latin, with mingled motives of entertainment and instruction similar to his own.

In the fall of 1386, Chaucer confronted a welter of emergent problems and tantalizing possibilities: his forced relocation and separation from his audience; a hesitant but growing interest in the prospect of expanded literary reputation; and—as a final component—a concealed but highly active sense of rivalry with his better established Italian competitor, Giovanni Boccaccio. All these latent possibilities constitute a kind of tinderbox or storehouse of combustible materials and incentives. In Kent, the necessity to forge new audience relations will be the spark that falls among them.

CHAPTER SEVEN

Kent and Canterbury

C haucer's withdrawal to Kent after the 1386 Parliament was
disruptive in every way. Events and the passage of time had
already alienated him from most of the vivid and influential
people with whom he had associated in recent years, and the
move to Kent would drive a further wedge. In the spring of 1387
his wife, Philippa, only in her early forties, was to die of unknown causes. Her sparkling and frisky sister Katherine, to
whom Chaucer was obliged for his Lancastrian connections,
was becoming devoutly religious; she would eventually end her
life as a crucial benefactor of the chapter of Lincoln Cathedral
and live out her last years within the cathedral close. John of
Gaunt returned from Spain in 1388 a discredited and effectively
broken man; he married Katherine in order to legitimize their
Beaufort offspring and effectively disappeared from court and
the politics of the realm. The seemingly invulnerable Nicholas
Brembre was on the ropes, striving without success to rally London followers on Richard's behalf; he was accused of treason in
the autumn of 1387 and executed a few months later. Just when
he most needed it, Chaucer's political and personal support system was stripped away.

His potential area of new assertion, his writing career, was
threatened too. Exactly at the moment when he was beginning
to think about expanding his audience, the forced relocation interrupted his ties with the audience that had previously sus-

tained him. Nor does Kent, as it existed in 1386, appear to have been a promising place (or even a possible place!) in which to commence the search for a new one. Suppose, though, that the move to Kent might be viewed in a different way. The move to Kent, with all its dislocations, will prove a catalyst and crucial spur in Chaucer's search for a new kind of author-audience relation.

In Kent

Where in Kent did Chaucer go to ground, and under what circumstances? He appears to have had nothing we might think of as a fixed address. He had some Kentish connections, but not necessarily people with whom he was on easy terms. These were mainly fellow factionalists whom he first met in 1385, when he was appointed as one of nine justices of the peace for the county of Kent, filling a vacancy created by the death of a reliable Ricardian party man there. But, typically, he would have found himself by far the least qualified among the justices with respect to rank, influence, land ownership, or any other criteria for service. Justices of the peace sat four times yearly, in the county of their appointment, to hear and make preliminary disposition of indictments for felony and trespass, as well as to accept guarantees in local complaints involving the keeping of the peace. Although such duties were often of a mundane character, those sitting to hear them were the county's most conspicuous worthies. Most were resident landowners, of knightly rank or the judicial equivalent of knightly. Those appointed in 1385 and 1386, while Richard was still enjoying relatively untroubled sway, were of a decidedly loyalist character. Others reappointed in 1385 were a comparably distinguished group, including: Sir Simon de Burley (constable of Dover Castle), staunch Ricardian condemned by the Merciless Parliament in 1388; Lord John Cobham (justice of the King's Bench, member of the king's council, and prominent Kentish landowner); Sir Robert Belknap (sergeant-at-law, Kentish landowner), exiled by the Merciless Parliament; John Devereux (lord of Penshurst, garter knight, and member of the king's council); Thomas Culpepper (knight, of a distinguished Kentish family); Sir Thomas Fogg (Ricardian and constable of Calais; succeeded Geoffrey as MP for Kent); Walter Clopton and Sir William Rickhill (distinguished barristers and sergeants-at-law); Sir Arnold Savage (country sheriff and lord of Bobbing); and Hugh Fastolf (a prominent Ricardian who would be named sheriff of London in 1387). Added in 1386 was Sir Robert Tresilian (chief justice of the King's Bench, later condemned by the Merciless Parliament).

What we have here, in short, is a virtual honor roll of active Ricardians, mostly consisting of lords and landholding knights, mostly (excepting several of the jurists) prominent within Kent, and all exceeding Chaucer's modest station. Only two—William Topcliffe (steward to the archbishop of Canterbury) and Fastolf (prosperous merchant of Great Yarmouth, London alderman, and ally of Nicholas Brembre)—lacked knightly standing, but each possessed other indices of rank. Aside from three of the justices, who were judged by other criteria, and Devereux and Fastolf (highly influential factionalists), all were Kentish landowners. Although insistence on residence as a condition of service on peace commissions did not gain statutory approval until 1388–89, it was just around the corner and already amounted to a de facto requirement—one that Chaucer, typically, did not meet.

Similarly, his initial election as a shire knight had been beholden to people better situated than himself—in particular, to the county sheriff responsible for his appointment. Sir Arnold Savage, who as sheriff of Kent received the writ of election in August 1386, was a man of considerable distinction: a frequent parliamentarian and the speaker of commons during the reign of Henry IV. He would have presided at the session of the shire court, in Rochester or Canterbury, at which Chaucer was selected. Although Savage proved flexible, weathering the different power transfers between Richard and the Appellants from 1387 to 1389 and the usurpation of 1399, his identifications in 1386 were primarily those of a king's man. He presided over his father's estates in Kent, including his principal seat at Bobbing, two miles west of Sittingbourne. Bobbing appears to be tagged in the *Canterbury Tales* as Bobbe-up-and-doun, the village where the Manciple abuses the Cook and then tells his tale. A nod to Savage would have been appropriate, since he was the man of position and authority who had placed Chaucer in Parliament despite his lack of residence or other normal qualifications.

Savage's manor house is one of the few places in Kent where Chaucer can be imagined seeking some kind of Kentish refuge. Fortifying this possibility is the fact that Savage seems to have had some literary interests besides. He was an executor of John Gower's will in 1408 and, while his administrative experience would have recommended him for such a post in any case, a personal interest in literature might have been the basis of his connection with this otherwise modestly situated esquire of a neighboring county. But Savage's manor at Bobbing might be described as comfortable rather than grand, and would certainly not have had the space or resources of those great magnate households that customarily housed and patronized literary figures. Chaucer more probably remained a shadowy figure to such worthies as Savage, and very possibly a puzzling one: a king's man, as most of them were, but a king's man temporarily on the shelf. These are not conditions in which magnate hospitality customarily flourished.

Another, and completely different, possibility of haven presents itself. Had Chaucer wished to maintain as many London ties as possible, he might have considered the villages of Deptford or Greenwich, four or five miles downriver from the Wool Wharf and easily communicable by skiff or water taxi. In the 1380s they were simple fishing villages without urban amenities, and hardly places for a polished cosmopolite like Chaucer to love, hardly places where a water taxi would bother to call. Even so, some suggestive evidence of his presence in those environs does survive. On November 13, 1386, two weeks before Parliament's end, Chaucer stood surety for the court appearance of one Simon Manning in a case of alleged debt. Manning was a resident of Cudham (Codham), Kent—a small village near the border with Surrey—but also had Greenwich ties of a suggestive sort.

A fugitive story, probably more a matter of fanciful tradition and less of historical fact, would strengthen the tie. Manning's wife, Katherine, who had owned property in Greenwich, is identified in a document of 1619 as "sister to Chawcer, knight, and most celebrated of English poets." Chaucer was far from knighthood and no fourteenth-century records suggest that he even had a sister. But this notion of Chaucer living among relatives, perhaps even rent-free, in the area of Deptford or Greenwich, or in a rural village of western Kent, would go a long way toward explaining the absence of any other record of his Kentish whereabouts. What it *wouldn't* explain is how he was ever to form a new set of literary relations.

Here was Chaucer with all kinds of time to write. For the next three years his nightly and personal avocation might become his daily and principal vocation. But for whom was he now writing? Aside from the possibly incidental connection between Savage and Gower, nothing suggests that his associates in Kent were any sort of literati. His customary expectation of a responsive literary circle remained to be addressed. Launching a literary work without its accompanying circumstances of telling and hearing, performance and response, approval and disapproval, enjoyment and controversy would have remained problematic for a poet accustomed to a full measure of such actions and reactions. Whatever else it did and didn't afford him, his sojourn in Kent would give him incentive and occasion to address this problem. It would be addressed, and memorably so.

No Audience? Invent One.

This is when Chaucer follows his own favorite advice by making virtue of necessity. He confronts his new circumstances by reconceiving the entire matter of his audience relations and, in the process, discovering a new and unprecedented form for his poetic endeavor. He needs a situation of direct address—he cannot imagine mobilizing a narrative without one—and he will satisfy this requirement with a dazzling act of imagination. He will keep on writing—but *for an audience of his own invention.* Its members will be the vivid portrait gallery of Canterbury Pilgrims—hearers, tellers, judges, and occasional victims—a body of ambitiously mixed participants suitable for a collection of tales unprecedented in their variety and scope. It will live within the boundaries of his work, perennially available as a resource for the telling and the hearing of tales. Above all else, it will be a portable audience, enabling Chaucer to create a work of art that will triumph over catastrophe by placing itself beyond the vagaries of time and circumstance.

This is Chaucer's bold stroke, his sudden grasp of a new principle that permits an artistic breakthrough. The ancients used to explain such moments of artistic inspiration with the visit of a muse, and perhaps they weren't so wrong. Chaucer seems, at least provisionally or wryly, to believe in such a thing, if the invocations to various muses with which he introduces the five books of his *Troilus* are taken to heart. His character Pandarus entertains a compatible belief, that an idea or a plan comes to you suddenly and complete; that you grasp it entirely and all at once. Pandarus, a bit of an author and artist figure in his own right, argues that he and Troilus must have a complete plan to seduce Criseide before they can begin. A person who wants to build a house, he says, doesn't rush straight to the task (*"Ne renneth nought the werk for to biginne / With rakel hond"*) but waits a while until he has grasped it whole, formed a plan within his heart that will achieve his purpose (*"but he wol bide a stounde / And send his hertes line out fro withinne / Alderfirst his purpos for to winne"*). With respect to his new work, the *Canterbury Tales*, Chaucer has such a plan. He grasps its design, its total form, simultaneously and whole. The idea starts with a mixed company of Pilgrim tale-tellers. From this mixed company issues the form of the work: It will be serial, multivoiced, stylistically mixed, many-themed, and contentious.

The idea of a tale collection was not, in itself, new. Medieval literary culture was awash with poetry anthologies, sermon collections, compilations of saints' lives, collections of aphorisms and literary excerpts called "florilegia," exemplifications of vices and virtues, and the like. The *Canterbury Tales* even includes one such collection within its bounds, in the Monk's tragedies.

Chaucer's contemporary John Gower was working on his collection of moral or exemplary tales, the *Confessio Amantis*, or the *Lover's Confession*, in which a poetic version of Gower himself receives narrative instruction.

Nor was Chaucer the first to hit upon the idea of including an audience, and its responses, within the body of a work. Back at the beginnings of Western literature, Homer's *Iliad* includes a scene where Achilles consoles himself by listening to a bard recount his own exploits. The *Odyssey* includes a scene in which an audience, including Odysseus himself, listens to a poetic account of his deeds. The *Thousand and One Nights* contains a keenly attentive audience of one, the autocrat for whom Scheherazade spins her tales. Medieval works of religious homily and instruction often include a description of the devotional listeners at which they are aimed; medieval collections of saints' lives contain frequent references to their intended audiences and what those audiences are expected to learn from them.

But no audience as varied as Chaucer's Pilgrims had ever been implied or imagined within a literary work. Prior to Chaucer, imagined literary audiences tend to be homogeneous or consistent in their composition. Uniformity in the composition of a work's audience encourages a comparable consistency in the narrative or narratives the work contains. Gower's *Confessio Amantis* relies upon the presence of a spiritually obtuse version of himself who listens to, and comments upon, the edifying tales that Genius tells him. The presence of a single listener whose spiritual deficiencies persist from tale to tale encourages a tone of somber didacticism throughout the many tales he will be told, just as the presence of a single teller, Genius, supports Gower's quest for a stylistic "middle way." Even in Boccaccio, where we encounter multiple tellers and hearers, and narrative responsibility circulates in a manner analogous to the *Canterbury Tales*, the social uniformity of his company, or *brigata*, encourages a broadly congenial middle style that Boccaccio describes as a *piano*, or level plain. Similarly, although Boccaccio gathers all different sorts of tales for his collection, he aims to assimilate them into a new and inclusive category of *novelle*, seeking out qualities of stylistic similarity and likeness rather than dissimilarity and divergence. Closely as Boccaccio anticipates Chaucer's artistic plan for communal tale telling, he has not hit upon the other critical component of the Pilgrim company: its inner variety and commitment to stylistic difference.

The idea of a socially mixed body of Pilgrim hearers and tellers originated with Chaucer, as an imaginatively lavish stroke with a variety of consequences. One is, of course, the creation of the Pilgrims as an end in themselves as a band of vividly realized characters whose pronounced personalities and entertaining shortcomings continue to engage readers seven centuries after their creation. Another is their suitability to an artistic ambition that Chaucer has increasingly entertained: to establish himself as a writer of incomparable versatility who can create a heady and utterly unpredictable grab bag of tales at all levels of taste and style. Even as he will mix gentle characters and bourgeoisie and lowlifes, so will he give us idealizing romances, moral tales, and scurrilous fabliaux, not to mention advice literature, parody, edifying examples, religious homilies and devotions, adventures, an animal fable, orientalist fantasy, knavery, dolorous tragedy, a sermon—God's literary plenty indeed, all within a single work's capacious bounds. And a final consequence is that this expansively imagined Pilgrim band may be taken as an emblem of Chaucer's growing ambition for an enlarged literary public—not as an exact blueprint for that public but as a measure of his increasingly inclusive ambitions.

The Pilgrim Company

Back in his *House of Fame*, his character Geffrey visited the House of Rumor, a spinning wicket where "tidings," gossip, and tall tales restlessly circulate in search of speakers who might tell them. The tales are finally united with their tellers, a ragtag bunch of shipmen and pilgrims and other celebrated liars; now that the tales have found someone to tell them they can issue forth into the world. This was prophetic, since Chaucer, arriving in Kent, brought a grab bag of uncirculated tales with him (ranging from his chivalric "Knight's Tale" through his pious "Second Nun's Tale" to his politically admonitory "Monk's Tale") and a considerably larger number of highly varied tales in mind that he still wanted to write. What he needed was tellers, but not just bland or faceless or monochromatic tellers. He needed tellers vivid enough in character and varied enough in social station to provide an apt counterpart for the cornucopia of genres and styles that he had in mind. And he needed characters who would enable him to enter imaginatively into the presentational situation he had left behind: into a climate of intimate and attentive and appreciative (if sometimes contentious) exchange, in which tales would be recited, given close attention, praised, or blamed. He could start with his own idea of shipmen and pilgrims and liars, but it would require a good deal of expansion.

Enter the Canterbury Pilgrims. Chaucer's varied cast of rogues, pitchmen, scammers, sincere and insincere divines, social snobs, humble toilers, and the rest was, in its day, a miracle of imaginative inclusion. Galleries of such highly varied characters may be found here and there in literature and art just before and just after Chaucer, but only if we go looking for them. Prior to Chaucer, a category of learned satiric poems known as "estates satire," written mainly in Latin and for limited circulation, reviewed the different ranks of society and castigated their moral shortcomings. But these were aloof in perspective and were wanting in the impartial generosity of Chaucer's vision. In the fifteenth and sixteenth centuries, a macabre genre called the "Dance of Death" imagined all the different ranks of categories of society being led to judgment by mocking skeletons, but again for bluntly moralizing purposes rather remote from Chaucer's own. For Chaucer's contemporary readers, seeking out a literary experience of mixed entertainment and instruction written in their native tongue, the inclusiveness of his social vision and the gently pointed equanimity with which he views his characters would have been a revelation indeed.

Chaucer is not a photorealist or a social geographer. His ultimate purpose is to achieve the best possible mix of tale-tellers rather than accurate social description or ethnography for its own sake. If he were, for example, aiming at social accuracy, the actual conditions of medieval society would have required him to include twenty-four or twenty-five peasants and agricultural workers among his thirty-odd pilgrims. He chooses instead to make do with a single, rather idealized Plowman—and a rather prosperous professional plowman who sells his services on the open market rather than a serf bound to the land. Even then, his Plowman (along with the Five Guildsmen and a couple of servants and attendants) is the only character for whom he fails to dream up a tale. Similarly, at the high end of the scale, he gives us no great aristocrats, but only his gentle and relatively companionable Knight, together with his pretentious (but perhaps only quasi-gentle) Prioress. His great interest is in what may be called the "middle strata" of his society, the professionals and entrepreneurs and artisans and scrambling in-betweeners normally ignored in the formal medieval social theory that emphasizes the three estates of knighthood, priesthood, and peasantry. His interest is drawn to some two dozen possible forms of life and vocation hardly noticed in medieval social theory at all, ranging *between* the peasantry and the gentry. He gives us worthies (a distinguished jurist in the Man of Law, an early moneyman in the Merchant, an aspiring shire knight in the Franklin, an austere and antifeminist scholar in the Clerk), poseurs and social climbers (the self-consciously genteel Prioress, the socially ambitious Guildsmen), scammers and scramblers (the duplicitous Pardoner, the sex-pest Friar, the conniving Manciple), and rural workers (the boisterous Miller, the choleric Reeve).

The Prologue to his *Tales* is a dazzling tour de force. Imagine asking any reader to sit still for an initial rendering of twenty-two static portraits (treating the five guildsmen as a single entity and omitting the Prioress's entourage and Chaucer himself). He achieves it with a mix of revealing and constantly varied detail (the Knight's rust-stained tunic, the Prioress's indulged canines, the Wife of Bath's gapped teeth, the Pardoner's long and thinning hair, the Miller's door-busting head . . .) and by the sheer audacity of the enterprise.

When he's through he has a pilgrim company ready to indulge, support, and further the widest possible range of literary tastes. Incidentally, Chaucer knows full well that the actual connection between a person's social position and literary tastes is more complicated than he is making it out to be. He embraces the convenient but simplifying premise that knights like romances, that millers tell bawdy stories, that monks keep tragedies in their cells, that social-climbing franklins like tales illustrative of gentle conduct, that devout nuns tell saints' lives, and that even the slightly less devout enjoy highly accented miracles of the Virgin, that parsons sermonize . . . and so on. This connection is reasonable enough on its face but never exactly borne out in practice. Consider the example of the Knight telling a "noble storie" laced with elements of chivalric ceremony and high romance, as compared with the Miller's immediately following bawdy peasant's, or "churl's," tale. In point of fact, mercantile audiences of Chaucer's day were avid consumers of romance and all aspects of knightly culture. Nothing in life so pleased Nicholas Brembre as his knighthood, and the first thing most prosperous London merchants did with their money was buy country estates. The first collection of romances in English, the so-called Auchinleck Manuscript, was most definitely aimed at a London or bourgeois audience, as were fifteenth-century Arthurian tales such as those written by Lovelich and Malory. Even more surprisingly, the bawdy French fables (or fabliaux), which provided the precedents for those of the Miller and the Reeve, turn out to have been fancied mainly by aristocratic audiences and secondarily by socially mixed audiences with aristocratic and gentle components.

Although Chaucer makes his tale assignments along deliberately simplified class lines, he is too great an artist to rest complacently within this agenda. The voice and tone of his tales never strictly confine themselves to the character of their imagined teller, but ranges more widely than that. His "Knight's Tale" punctuates its high seriousness with rough and rather decidedly ungentle joking about Arcite's death, rather flippantly saying that when Nature is against him and medicine won't work, the time has come to get the funeral started. (*"And certeinly, ther Nature wol nat wirche, / Fare wel physik! Go ber the man to chirche!"*) Just as, by contrast, the "Miller's Tale" pauses in its account of sexual hijinks to gaze down upon the spontaneous Alison from an aloof social height (comparing her to a fresh wildflower fit "For any lord to lay down in his bed, / Or yet for any good yeoman to wed" ("*For any lord to leggen in his bedde, / Or yet for any good yeman to wedde*"). This kind of migration of artworks from their ostensible moorings is familiar to us today, when grade-B movies, daily newspaper comics, rap music, and street graffiti move up, as well as down, the scale of social consumption. It is no less true in the fourteenth century, when an art form's imagined point of social attachment, and its actual audience, may not nearly coincide.

If Chaucer's premise that different styles and subject matters have strong vocational and class affiliations is more premise than reality, it remains an immensely productive one. His social and vocational mix of Canterbury Pilgrims, even though unrepresentative of actual pilgrimages, permits him to get on with his actual business, which is to gather a collection of wholly unprecedented variety. In this sense, Chaucer's invented audience does double or multiple duty. Not only does his invention give him what he lacked—an audience—but it gives him the kind of audience that will support his staging of the most internally varied tale collection existing before or since.

Perhaps most important of all, the created Canterbury audience will give Chaucer something vital that has just gone missing from his actual life: an environment of avid interest in literature and its effects. Whatever its other spiritual and recreational objectives, this pilgrimage is above all else a literary occasion, and a highly interactive one. This is hardly to say that the Canterbury Pilgrims are all literary connoisseurs: They frequently go far off the track. But tales and tale telling are always at the center for them, and (save for a few moments of disappointment or pique, as when the Monk refuses to carry on after the Knight's interruption) their interest is unflagging.

Tale telling is, after all, the whole purpose here. Once the pilgrims have constituted themselves as a group and have chosen the genial Harry Bailly as a kind of master of revels, he sets things in motion by instituting a tale-telling competition, with a reward for the pilgrim who tells the most instructive and enjoyable tale. The telling of tales—their uses and responsibilities as well as their enjoyment—will never be displaced as this group's central activity. For their part, the pilgrims not only join the enterprise of tale telling with good will, but also surround it with an enlivened climate of commentary and opinion.

The Knight no sooner concludes his initial story than the body of pilgrims rush to praise it—especially, as Chaucer wryly observes, the "gentle" ones. The counterreaction is almost as swift, as the drunken Miller interrupts the order of tellers with his rejoinder, a bawdy fable that will pay back or requite (*"quite"*) the Knight's more stately romance. When the Reeve responds to the Miller with his own comic tale of revenge, the Cook enjoys it so viscerally that he feels like the Reeve is scratching his back (*"For joye him thoughte he clawed him on the bak"*). The Friar critiques the Wife of Bath's admittedly long prologue (*"this is a long preamble of a tale"*), and takes incidental note of the learning (*"scole matere"*) compacted within her otherwise earthy diatribe. When the Friar uses his tale to score points on Summoners, the Summoner is so angered that he quakes like an aspen (*"lik an aspen leef he quook for ire"*). Harry Bailly would rather his wife heard the Clerk's tale than have a barrel of ale, and he pays stricken tribute to the Physician's account of the death of Virginia, saying that his heart is lost for pity of the maid (*"Min herte is lost for pitee of this maide"*). Not that Harry lacks occasional severity; the Pilgrim Chaucer's own stumbling parody of a popular romance so annoys him that he declares it *"nat worth a toord."* The Prioress's rather drastic miracle of the Virgin sobers the entire company, but such consensus is rare. The Knight, exasperated by the Monk's tragic recitals, cuts him off in midstream with his preemptory *"namoore of this!"*

Chaucer doesn't intend that his Pilgrims' judgments be on the mark; quite the contrary, in most cases. They constantly overpraise and underpraise one another, miss the point, get the moral wrong, pursue unrelated quarrels, introduce arrant irrelevancies. But the interactive climate, mingling narrative action and audience response, is what he is looking for and what he achieves. There's an underlying rationale here. At precisely the most estranged (and presumably lonely) moment of his life, Chaucer actively sets about the imaginary creation of a fellowship, a *felaweshipe* of pilgrims formed by chance but one that enters into strenuous and conflicted intimacy. All the more poignant that, at this moment of Chaucer's separation from his London audience, this is a literary fellowship as well, one in which tale telling is central and really matters.

A generous inclusivity, a receptiveness to different voices, has been a benchmark of literary accomplishment in English from Shakespeare through Joyce. With the creation of the Canterbury pilgrimage, and its cacophony of competing speakers, Chaucer stands at its wellspring. He seizes every opportunity to throw elite and ordinary people into one another's company, to mix "high" and "low" literary styles, to place apparently incompatible sorts of narrative side by side. His varied group of hearers and tellers anchors an altogether new work of literature, a tale collection founded on a preference for diversity over similarity, for variety rather than consistency of subject matter, viewpoint, and style.

Laureate Chaucer

B eginning with an ambitious idea about tale-telling pilgrims, and already possessing a few tales in draft that he could adapt to his purpose, Chaucer still had a long way to go. He appears to have worked on his project rather intensively during the years 1387 to 1389, when he was in political exile, then less when he enjoyed a brief rehabilitation in royal service as clerk of works from 1389 to 1391, then sporadically until his death in 1400. The *Canterbury Tales* would eventually be "finished," in a manner of speaking, but not in his own lifetime.

He died just ten months after moving into his first really settled residence since Aldgate, a retirement property within the grounds of Westminster Abbey that his well-connected son Thomas probably arranged on his behalf. His itinerant life of the preceding fourteen years had been radically unsuited to the careful transportation and preservation and collation of a jumble of finished and less finished writing. There in his lodging would have been a tangle of completed works copied out on parchment, some corrected and some not; personal drafts and jottings on parchment; and other provisional scratchings on wax tablets awaiting transcription.

Among these materials were ten different fragments of the as-yet-untitled work that we know today as the *Canterbury Tales*. Each is called a fragment because its relation to the other nine remains unfixed, though each is internally whole. One of the ten fragments Chaucer left behind is, most crucially, a prologue to the entire work, in which the impetus to pilgrimage is explained and its starting point established as the Tabard Inn in Southwark, and the twenty-nine initial Pilgrims introduced to the reader. This prologue was probably not the first of the fragments to be written, since some of the tales—such as the "Knight's Tale" and the "Second Nun's Tale"—had probably been written before Chaucer got the idea of collecting them. It was, however, written fairly early on, because it contains a bold announcement of plans for the total volume that Chaucer would later modify. The original plan, as explained in the Prologue, is startlingly ambitious, involving the staggering goal of some 120 tales. As Harry Bailly tells it, in his initial briefing of the Pilgrims:

> Each of you, to speed us on the way,
> In this journey shall tell us all two tales,
> Toward Canterbury, I mean that this be so,
> And then, returning home, another two.

> (*Ech of yow, to shorte with oure weye,*
> *In this viage shal telle tales tweye*
> *To Caunterbury-ward, I mene it so,*
> *And homward he shal tellen othere two.*)

This is one of those unfinishable schemes in which the Middle Ages abounded. (Chaucer embeds such another impossible scheme within his own manuscript: his "Squire's Tale," in which the teller gets himself involved in a plan of narration so convoluted, and so overambitious, that he finally has to be interrupted by the merciful Franklin.) This aspect of the medieval sensibility may still be viewed in a dozen different medieval cathedrals, with plans so ambitious as to be protracted across centuries, representing the work of many hands and many different conceptions—never entirely finished but worthy of the highest admiration for the achieved portion of the original design. If executed, Chaucer's announced plan would have resulted in a volume more than four times the length of its present manuscripts; given the weight of parchment, fond owners would have had to haul it around in wagons. Of course the plan had to be abandoned, and from the evidence of his ten fragments Chaucer had, over the course of the 1390s, quietly done so. The main indication of his revised and scaled-down intentions is that, of the twenty-four tales he did complete (with only the Yeoman, one or more Guildsmen, and the Plowman outside the fold), each is assigned to a single Pilgrim, and no Pilgrim is assigned more than one tale. In other words, Chaucer had quietly modified his scheme into a new one in which each Pilgrim would tell a single tale. This would be a one-way pilgrimage rather than a round-trip, with only the Southwark-Canterbury segment of the journey to be described.

Chaucer additionally signaled his acceptance of the one-way premise by composing a fragment that could serve as an ending to the work. This fragment includes the "Parson's Tale"—a fitting conclusion to a spiritual journey, and the Parson is given extra time and space to describe the necessity and urgency of the penitential process. This fragment does not actually introduce the Pilgrims into the city of Canterbury, or into the cathedral and Becket's shrine, but it does bring them to the outskirts of the town. We are told (by both clock and natural time) that the day is late, that it is now four in the afternoon, and that haste must be made. Harry Bailly announces that his plan is fulfilled, with only one tale lacking (*"Now lakketh us no tales mo than oon"*). To the Parson's tale, Chaucer, evidently personally stirred by what he has just written, then appends a very final-sounding statement, or "Retraction," in which he expresses late-life regret for some of his frivolous writings, as well as satisfaction with some of his more devout and theological pieces.

Even if the pilgrimage doesn't quite make it to Canterbury, matters have certainly been brought round to an apparent ending, though an ending on a spiritual rather than geographical plane. And this is in fact the Parson's—and presumably Chaucer's—final point: The pilgrimage is to be spiritually regarded as a journey not to Canterbury but to "the celestial Jerusalem." By establishing his pilgrimage's beginning and its end, together with some provisional ordering of the tales between, Chaucer provided a blueprint for his masterwork's completion, a blueprint that other persons devoted to its completion could follow, even as, by jettisoning three-quarters of his original plan, he radically improved the prospects for his work's circulation. If he was not to see it in his own lifetime, he could at least die with the reasonable hope that it might be circulated soon after, in something approximating his revised design.

By modifying his plan to one now nearly complete, Chaucer signaled a concern for his own posthumous literary reputation. He was sending the same signal in other ways as well. On two occasions within the tales—as well as another in the nearly contemporary *Legend of Good Women*—he steps into the gap as a temporary bibliographer of his own work, seizing upon varied pretexts to preserve a list of his completed writings. His Man of Law, in the prologue to his Canterbury tale, complains about this prolific "Chaucer," who has preempted him by writing numerous tales of love, including the *Book of the Duchess* and the unfinished *Legend of Good Women*. And, in *Legend*, Chaucer has his God of Love accuse him of misspeaking against women in a (now lost) translation of the *Romance of the Rose*, and especially in his depiction of Criseide in his *Book of Troilus*. The Queen of Love then responds with a list of all the poems he has written that are favorable to love, including the *Book of the Duchess*, the *Parliament of Fowls*, the story of Palamon and Arcite (which would become his "Knight's Tale"), and many other works, including his Boethius and a now lost translation of Pope Innocent. This enumerative impulse also plays out in another and surprising place: in the penitent statement appended to the "Parson's Tale." There he includes a longish list of poems he is sorry he has written (including those tales of Canterbury that promote sin) as well as others that still comfort him (including Boethius and works of morality and devotion). All this concern with listing his personal oeuvre, in the latter case even at cross-purposes with his motive of self-accusation, suggests that Chaucer has come to care a great deal about his literary legacy.

Although he died with the *Canterbury Tales* unfinished, the plan of his completion and his hopes for it were effectively inscribed within the DNA of the surviving fragments. The task of sorting them into a plausible-looking "Book of the Tales of Canterbury," as it would be called by its first scribes and editors, was a formidable one, but the signals of his intentions were sufficiently clear that it could be achieved. Its earliest manuscripts announce themselves as books, have the appearance of finished books, and modern editions, fortified with editorially added headnotes, endnotes, and titles, strike readers that way today.

The first enactment of Chaucer's wishes appears to have been the work of the scribe to whom he had earlier addressed a short poem of amiable exasperation over errors of neglect and haste, one Adam Pinkhurst. Adam was a professional scrivener, apparently a fully qualified master and an independent entrepreneur. He worked regularly, though not exclusively, with the Mercers' Company on their records and papers (including that petition defaming Nicholas Brembre), and also had a second specialization in literary manuscripts, including some by Gower and others as well as by Chaucer.

Adam would eventually have more responsibility than he could have imagined; upon Chaucer's death he would be enlisted to address the problem of turning fragments and other scattered writings into the first, and most authoritative, versions of the *Canterbury Tales*. Upon his shoulders, and that of the poet's friends or admirers who subsidized and oversaw his efforts, rested Chaucer's reputation in posterity. Adam is known today only by his handwriting, Chaucer's little poem, and his signature in the records of the Scriveners' Company. Had he failed in his responsibility, Chaucer's name would still have a place in literary history, but he would be less vividly known than he is to us today.

Adam's job upon Chaucer's death was to shape his uncompleted manuscript fragments into something resembling the book that Chaucer had in mind. This task would have been eased by previous knowledge of Chaucer's habits of work and, probably, his literary intentions as well. (In one indication of special knowledge, Adam adds after the incomplete "Cook's Tale" that "Of this Cook's Tale Chaucer wrote no more" ["*Of this Cokes tale maked Chaucer na moore*"], in distinction from other subsequent scribes who, lacking such information, left space in the hope of obtaining more of the tale.) Even so, Adam would not simply have pitched in on his own. As a professional scribe working for hire, he would have needed financial assurances before undertaking so formidable a task as assembling and writing out the whole of the *Canterbury Tales*. Exactly who these interested parties might have been remains in some doubt. Possibly Chaucer's son Thomas—a Lancastrian stalwart—and others close to the new king Henry IV, who had captured the throne in the last year of Chaucer's life, were responsible. Unlike Richard II's mainly French-speaking court, the new Lancastrian dynasty was supportive of the use of the English language in both practical and literary contexts, and the new king had shown additional interest in encouraging the domestic literary arts. In any case, Adam and his shadowy supporters were spectacularly successful. The result was two closely related, and impressively finished, examples (known to specialists as the Hengwrt and Ellesmere manuscripts), each executed at a very high level of refinement, and the latter illustrated with portraits of the Pilgrims, including one of Chaucer himself.

Leaving behind the ten fragments of a nearly finished book, together with what amount to clues for its completion, Chaucer has come a long way toward abandoning his inhibition about manuscript circulation. He anticipates an enlarged audience for his new work, and he seems at peace—if still a bit ambivalent—about the idea that it will encounter his work in manuscript form. He offers one small clue of his revised outlook in the bachelor-party poem composed for his friend Bukton, sometime after Philippa's death and after the *Canterbury Tales* was under way. He admonishes Bukton to heed his warnings and that, if his friend remains in any doubt on the matter, he should consult the Wife of Bath: *"The Wyf of Bathe I pray yow that ye rede / Of this matere that we have on honde."* Bukton is presumably hearing, rather than reading, this poem, and has probably heard others as well, but Chaucer now imagines his friend's access to a written version of the *Tales*. An even more revealing moment, within the body of the *Tales* themselves, occurs in his mock apology for the rude speech of his "Miller's Tale." There he seems first to imagine the kind of listening audience he would always have enjoyed, but then modifies or corrects himself to include the absent, reading audience he now imagines. He says that whoever would rather not *hear* the tale should turn over the *leaf*, or *page*, and choose another one (*"whoso list it nat yheere, / Turne over the leef and chese another tale"*). Here his imagined listening public, which he supposes might shrink from hearing the tale, is suddenly converted to a new audience of absent page-turners who, rather than closing its ears to his work, will simply turn over the manuscript page and begin reading something new and more congenial. Inviting his absent readers to share responsibility by making choices for themselves, Chaucer claims a new kind of personal and artistic freedom to go ahead and say whatever he wants to say. But at the same time he is making a concession, granting an absent audience an autonomy and scope different in character from that of his earlier and more intimate circle of listeners and friends.

Modeling a Literary Public

That Chaucer should imagine the circulation of his written texts among a widely dispersed audience seems entirely reasonable to us; that is, after all, how we know them. But for him to imagine such an audience in posterity would have required formidable powers of visualization, as well as an ability to foresee the contours of future developments from barely visible clues in the present. We live at a moment of rapid technological change, in our case away from the printed book and toward various forms of electronic delivery. But these delivery systems have morphed so rapidly, even in the past few years, that we would be overbold to suggest that we know exactly what form the reading experience will assume, even a few years from now. Even though the pace of change was less rapid in Chaucer's day, and measured in decades rather than years or months, he lived in a similarly transitional moment. As with writers of today, Chaucer and his contemporaries were forced to imagine the contours of the reading experience in their own near future. Their problem of extrapolation, guessing at the emerging form of literary circulation from varied and telltale signs, was similar to ours.

They wouldn't have guessed at the most striking change less than a century away: the arrival in England by 1473 of capacities for setting type and printing books. But significant changes in manuscript production and circulation evident in their own day were uncannily predictive of the larger changes to come. One is the acceptance of English as a literary language. Until the mid-fourteenth century English had been almost entirely sidelined by Latin (as the language of record keeping and theological disputation), Anglo-Norman (as the language of courts and the law), and Continental French (as the literary language of the cosmopolitan English court). Suddenly, though, exactly in the 1380s, use of English surged. It gained ground as the language of domestic dispute (including proclamations, political broadsides, and other texts, such as the Mercers' petition against Nicholas Brembre). Simultaneously, it began to win new respect as a literary language, chosen not only for writings by Chaucer and John Gower, but also by figures like Thomas Usk, who argued in his 1385–86 *Testament of Love* for setting down "our creations in such words as we learned from our mothers' tongue" (*"let us shewe our fantasyes in suche wordes as we lerneden of our dames tonge"*). Hand in hand with this development was an expansion of literacy itself. Sir Thomas More claimed in the early sixteenth century that six in ten English persons could read the language at some level, and a figure of about a third would not be amiss for the later fourteenth century. Reading circles and reading aloud remained popular in the fifteenth century, but the possibility of a readership sitting down with a manuscript on their own behalf was clearly at hand. Another development almost as revolutionary as printing itself was the development of papermaking, as an alternative to far more expensive vellum and only slightly less expensive parchment. Imported paper was in frequent use in the fourteenth century, in forms of which Chaucer would have been aware, and was domestically produced on a large scale in the fifteenth. Without even waiting for the printing press, the possibilities of increased manuscript circulation surged with the coming of paper, even as paper was, in turn, prerequisite for the arrival of printing in the following century.

Other changes were afoot in scribal culture. Professional scribal culture had its origins in the ancient world and was present throughout the Middle Ages, but the second half of the fourteenth century also witnessed enormous strides in scribal productivity and the organization and accessibility of scribal labor. In earlier medieval centuries, the scribal system existed mainly to address pragmatic necessities of record keeping and statute writing and the circulation of Bibles, homilies, and other religious texts, though literary texts might be copied too. The production of such texts was arduous and required settled circumstances, predictable funding, and provision for education. Such preconditions were best met institutionally: within religious foundations, noble households, and governmental bureaucracies. Manuscript production by individual scribes on their own initiative, as a speculative and entrepreneurial enterprise, was certainly known but remained rare before the mid- and late fourteenth century. In Chaucer's own lifetime independent scribes, binders, illustrators, and other book producers began truly to flourish, and to take the first steps toward constituting themselves as members of an independent trade.

A London ordinance of 1357 addresses conditions of work for scriveners or scribes of the "court letter" (working on legal and other documents) and scribes of the "text letter" (copying works of popular devotion, instruction, and other literary texts). These scribes, or scriveners, were (like Chaucer's Adam) available to copy individual manuscripts, whether for writers who wanted a fair copy or copy for presentation purposes, or occasionally as a commissioned production for an interested client. During Chaucer's lifetime these literate entrepreneurs and vendors of their own services had begun to live and work in neighboring quarters more conducive to the coordination of their activities. Emerging as the principal center for text production was the vicinity of St. Paul's, and especially a series of small shops along Paternoster Row. Gathered there were text writers (or scriveners), bookbinders, illuminators, parchment makers, and perhaps most significantly, stationers. A stationer could coordinate the various activities essential to the production of a manuscript, pamphlet, or book, and, equally important, could arrange matters of distribution and sale. Stationers addressed the needs of an expanding and literate lay market, exceeding the more limited requirements of religious foundations, governmental bureaucracies, and aristocratic patronage networks that had preceded them.

During Chaucer's lifetime the great majority of books produced under such auspices continued to be "bespoken"—that is, ordered in advance by a particular customer. But the possibility of book production on speculation for opportunistic sale was close to hand, and would be realized as the fifteenth century progressed. Many of the fifty-five surviving manuscript copies of the *Canterbury Tales* would be produced in that way—speculatively, in anticipation of sale to a diversifying literary public. And in this way Chaucer's book can be seen not simply as a beneficiary of the new technology but as a driver of it, as one of the volumes around which the new trade would organize itself. Significantly, just three years after his death, the guilds of text writers and manuscript illuminators, together with other Londoners involved in binding and selling books, would organize themselves into a single fraternity of book artisans, eventually to become known as the Stationers' Company.

This cluster of coordinate developments could not have failed to influence Chaucer's view of the kind of audience he might seek and the means by which he might address it. Present here are the preconditions for the creation of a new kind of audience, an audience with freer access to books and less restricted in its ways of interpreting and enjoying them. These developments were spurs and incentives to a new idea, that of an enlarged reading public, a diverse cross section of English society devoted to letters and avid for tale telling, and particularly receptive to books written in the English tongue. Chaucer wasn't the only author to reach out to such an audience; Usk and Gower were writing for it too, and the reformist and proto-Protestant Lollards were busily engaged in a collective English translation of the Bible. But Chaucer's imagination of this new public was a particularly vivid and energizing one, and in the composition of his Pilgrim band he signals the breadth and ambition of his endeavor.

The Pilgrims are not a replica or scale model of the public Chaucer imagines. As a gathering, in a single time and place, the company of Pilgrims was a practical unlikelihood; so socially varied a group interacting in civil (if occasionally irascible) terms would have been a rarity, if not an impossibility. Yet they embody an idea, a literary public *in potentia*, a dream of an inclusive national readership ready to support an ambitious literary design executed in the English tongue. Things have to be imagined before they can be achieved, and here we see Chaucer's brave imagining of a new horizon of literary production and consumption, an enlarged fellowship of discourse not yet existing in the world. The Pilgrims enact the role of a present audience, an audience of tales they hear and tell. But they also serve as intermediaries between Chaucer and the extended public he has begun to imagine. They enable him to stage his tales in the old way—that is, convivially and socially—but for the enjoyment of a new readership in new and even unpredictable circumstances.

The circulation of Chaucer's poetry to an expanded readership and on a large scale had to await the first decade after his death. The years 1400 to 1410 saw a surge in the creation of manuscripts of his poetry intended for circulation to absent readers, including four surviving copies of the *Canterbury Tales* (and probably a dozen more now lost), together with several copies of *Troilus*. Some of these, such as the Ellesmere manuscript of the *Canterbury Tales* and the Corpus Christi MS 61 *Troilus* (with its fanciful but grand frontispiece of Chaucer reading aloud to the court of Richard II), were sumptuously executed, plainly intended for presentation to illustrious patrons. But less finely finished manuscripts, suitable for more ordinary circulation, were produced as well. Chaucer's early fifteenth-century audience appears to have grown at both ends of the social scale. Jean, count of Angoulême, brother of the poet Charles d'Orléans, was such an enthusiast that he had a manuscript prepared for his own use and added notations of his own, but other copies found their way to such relatively marginal readers as John Baron of Amersham, an accused heretic, and John Brinchele, tailor of London. By the midcentury, Chaucerian texts were being circulated for speculative sale by scribal entrepreneur John Shirley and others. With the origin of print, in what now seems a foregone conclusion, Caxton would place the *Canterbury Tales* early on his list of English publications and take it through two printings (in 1478 and 1484).

Man of Letters

Chaucer didn't start writing for advancement or profit but because he wanted to. His activity was personal and, as yet, rather peculiar, unframed by any particular vocational track. In a later century he might have aspired to be a man of letters but, as with the concept of a reading public, no such thing could yet be said to exist. Writing could only be an avocation, a pursuit conducted alongside, or behind the shelter of, one's actual vocation or career. Religious establishments and universities supported the work of learned practitioners like Richard of Bury writing principally in Latin on learned or philosophical subjects, but the idea of a secular author making his way in the world via writings in vernacular English was all but unknown. Italy, with Dante and Brunetto Latini and Petrarch and Boccaccio, had been home to some literati celebrated for imaginative writings likely to appeal to noncloistered audiences, and French writers such as Guillaume de Machaut (also a prolific composer of music) and Jean Froissart (who boldly presented a copy of his love poems to

Richard II) had made strides in that direction. Breaking into such a circle presented a daunting challenge, and the more so for an English poet writing in a vernacular and non-Latinate tongue.

Nevertheless, the *Canterbury Tales* are marked by signs of increasing ambition: for an enlarged and diversified audience, for new kinds of circulation, and even for himself as a literary figure. He never called himself an author, and he seems never even to have called himself a poet either. Nor would he have remotely aspired to crown himself with laurel, in the manner of the Italians. The idea of laureation was unavoidably rife in Italy throughout Chaucer's lifetime; although most of his knowledge of Italian affairs was secondhand, he could not have failed to know the importance of this status to his Italian counterparts. Petrarch was crowned laureate by the Roman Senate in 1341, and when Boccaccio visited him in Milan in 1359 the two of them sportively cultivated a laurel bush in Petrarch's garden as a mark of their mutual self-estimation. Chaucer's reserve on such matters is epitomized by his Clerk who, in the prologue to his Canterbury tale, pays tribute to "Francis Petrarch, the laureate poet" ("*Fraunceys Petrak, the laureat poete*") but dryly adds that "He is now dead and nailed in his chest" ("*He is now deed and nailed in his cheste*"). Any suggestion that he might personally come to be regarded as some kind of laureate would probably have caused Chaucer to laugh outright . . . but he might have been surreptitiously pleased and intrigued by the idea too.

That, at any rate, is what happened. His renown so accelerated in the decade after his death that his eager followers and disciples raised the stakes by routinely declaring him a poet, and even by introducing the previously unthinkable subject of laureation. The only public reference to Chaucer as a literary figure prior to 1386 was Thomas Usk's elliptical comment about his philosophical prowess—and that without mention of his proper name, and in a manuscript that appears never to have been circulated prior to its revival in the sixteenth century. Then, in the closing years of his life, and especially in the decade after his death, the floodgates suddenly open. John Gower declares him a poet in the 1390 version of his *Confessio Amantis*. Then John Lydgate, eulogizing Chaucer soon after his death in a poem entitled the "Flower of Courtesy," pushes ahead to imply laureate status:

> Chaucer is dead, who had such a name
> For fair writing, that was no doubt
> Fairest in our tongue, just as the laurel's green.

> (*Chaucer is deed that had suche a name*
> *Of fayre making that [was] without wene*
> *Fayrest in our tonge, as is the Laurer grene.*)

This becomes a recurrent theme. In his "Life of Our Lady" (around 1410), Lydgate claims that he "worthy was to have the laurel of poetry and the palm attain" ("*worthy was the laurer to haue of poetrye, / and the palme atteyne*"). Others, including his follower Thomas Hoccleve (who claims to have met Chaucer in his youth) are similarly idolatrous; attesting Chaucer his "*maister,*" Hoccleve arranges to have a portrait inserted in his own poem, *Regement of Princes*. No wonder that the matter of Chaucer's status is settled by the time we get to Caxton at the end of the century. Caxton commissions a florid Latin tribute to Chaucer in which he is called *vates*—a kind of exalted poet/prophet—and declares in his second edition of the *Canterbury Tales* that

Chaucer's philosophical profundity and ornate writing merit "the name of a laureate poete."

Flying partially blind, on hope and instinct, Chaucer pointed the *Canterbury Tales* to eventual success and himself into a posthumous literary career that hadn't existed in his own lifetime, as England's first widely acclaimed literary celebrity. In his lifetime, some hundreds of people might have known him as a poet, but (in my view) probably not more than that. Thousands would know him before the fifteenth century was out, and, of course, many millions (especially if we count those who know him as a poet without actually reading him) now.

For Chaucer, on the skids in Kent in the winter of 1386–87, the idea of attaining literary celebrity for the new poem he was hatching, or gaining notice as anything other than its humble anthologist or compiler, would have been a stretch at best. He was unused to the limelight and constitutionally hesitant in seeking it. He was surrounded by magnates and other players more vivid and puissant than he ever supposed himself to be. These others have receded now. Philippa and Katherine and the stylish Hainaulters are mostly forgotten (although Katherine has been a subject of romantic history and biography). Nicholas Brembre, who bestrode London for nearly two decades, is remembered, if at all, for his factional struggles with his democratizing rival John Northampton and for a walk-on role in support of Richard II during the Rising of 1381. Richard II is remembered as a feeble and petulant king, mainly by virtue of Shakespeare's decision to portray him. Henry of Derby and eventual Henry IV had been a man of sparkling promise in his youth but shrunken accomplishment as king. Even the great Gaunt now looks rather silly, strutting his vain pretensions as king of Castile. Surpassing them all in collective memory is a rather self-contained and private-minded civil servant: time server in customs, member of diplomatic missions but head of none, lost in the crowd at the moment of his wife's social apotheosis, least qualified shire knight in his parliamentary term, expendable factionalist in the civic broils of 1386 . . . Through his own precocious talent and his personal determination to make virtue of necessity, this overworked and underpaid civil servant achieved permanent prominence as Geoffrey Chaucer, a founder and, by most reckonings, *the* founder of English letters.

NOTES AND FURTHER READING

Abbreviations of Works Frequently Cited

Close Rolls
Calendar of Close Rolls, 1327–99. Numerous volumes, cited by year (London: Stationer's Office, 1892–1927).

DNB
Oxford Dictionary of National Biography. www.oxforddnb.com/public/index -content.html.

Fine Rolls
Calendar of Fine Rolls, 1307–99 (London: Stationer's Office, 1912–29).

Froissart
Oeuvres de Froissart, ed. Kervyn de Lettenhove (Brussels: V. Devaux, 1867–77).

Gower. Complete Works
Complete Works of John Gower, ed. G. C. Macaulay, 4 vols. (Oxford University Press, 1899–1902).

History of Parliament
J. S. Roskell et al., *The House of Commons, 1386–1421, The History of Parliament*, 4 vols. (Stroud: Alan Sutton, 1992). http://www.historyofparliamentonline.org.

Knighton's Chronicle
Henry Knighton, *Knighton's Chronicle 1337–1396*, ed. G. H. Martin (Oxford University Press, 1995).

Letter Books
Calendar of Letter Books of the City of London. Electronically available from British History Online. www.british-history.ac.uk/subject.aspx?subject=7&gid=58. (Each volume cited by initial—G, H, etc.—pertaining to the period of time it covers; *Letter Book H* covers the period 1375–99.)

Life-Records

Martin M. Crow and Clair C. Olson, *Chaucer Life-Records* (Oxford University Press, 1966).

Memorials

Memorials of London Life, ed. H. T. Riley (London: Longmans, 1868). Electronically available from British History Online, http://www.british-history.ac.uk/.

Patent Rolls

Calendar of Patent Rolls, 1327–99 (London: Stationer's Office, 1891–1916).

Plea Rolls

Calendar of Plea and Memoranda Rolls, ed. A. H. Thomas, 6 vols. (Cambridge University Press, 1926–61).

Riverside Chaucer

The Riverside Chaucer, 3rd. edition, ed. Larry D. Benson (Boston: Houghton Mifflin, 1987).

Rolls of Parliament

Parliament Rolls of Medieval England. CD-ROM and print. Ed. Chris Given-Wilson (Woodbridge, Suffolk: Boydell Press, 2005). Electronically available from British History Online http://www.british-history.ac.uk/.

St. Albans Chronicle

St. Albans Chronicle (the *Chronica Maiora of Thomas Walsingham*), vol. 1, ed. and trans. John Taylor, Wendy Childs, and Leslie Watkiss, vol. 1, 1376–94; vol. 2, 1394–1422 (Oxford University Press, 2003). (Alternately available in a spirited English translation as *Thomas Walsingham, Chronica Maiora*, trans. David Preest [Woodbridge, Suffolk: Boydell, 2005]).

Social Chaucer

Paul Strohm, *Social Chaucer* (Harvard University Press, 1989; 1994).

Turbulent London

Ruth Bird, *The Turbulent London of Richard II* (New York: Longmans Green, 1949).

Westminster Chronicle

Westminster Chronicle 1381–94, eds. L. C. Hector and Barbara Harvey (Oxford University Press, 1966).

Introduction: Chaucer's Crisis

Modern English translations of Chaucer are my own. The accompanying passages in his original Middle English are based on the *Riverside Chaucer*, but with substitution of the modern character "i" for the Middle English "y" for ease of interpretation.

This book concentrates on a single turning point in Chaucer's life. For those interested in supplementing it with an account of his whole life, I recommend Derek Pearsall, *The Life of Geoffrey Chaucer* (Oxford: Blackwell, 1992). Also of interest is Donald Howard, *Chaucer: His Life, His Works, His World* (New York: Dutton, 1987). A conveniently available and authoritative map re-creating the London of the 1520s, but still applicable in most respects to places and events in Chaucer's own London, is *Historical Map of Tudor London*, c. 1520 (London: Shire Books, 2013).

In researching this book I have relied constantly on the definitive collection of *Chaucer Life-Records*, drawn from varied historical sources and edited by Martin M. Crow and Clair C. Olson. Records covering the events mentioned in my rapid survey of Chaucer's adventures and misadventures are to be found in *Life-Records*, pp. 1–12 (mercantile origins), 23–24 (capture in France), 67–93 (marriage), 29–66 (journeys), 144–47 (residence above Aldgate), 344–46 (*raptus* of Cecily Champagne), and 477–89 (robbery by highwaymen). These and other persons and events mentioned in this introduction will be treated, with full references, in following chapters.

In the "Knight's Tale" the wise Theseus, offering his consolation to those grieving the death of Arcite, urges, *"Thanne is it wisdom, as it thinketh me, / To maken vertu of necessitee."* Chaucer repeats this sentiment on three other occasions in his poetry.

W. W. Skeat is the scholar who thought that the strident wake-up call must have come from Chaucer's wife; for references to his and other interpretations of the passage, see the *Riverside Chaucer*, p. 982, note to *House of Fame*, ll. 561–62. An important and useful article on the status of first-person statements made within the boundaries of stories or poems is Leo Spitzer, "Note on the Poetic and Empirical 'I' in Medieval Authors," *Traditio*, 4 (1946), pp. 414–22.

The subject of an author's "circumstances" as a suitable emphasis in biographical inquiry has recently and trenchantly been addressed by Charles Nicholl, "Ben Jonson's Chair," *The Guardian*, 4 (July 2013).

Congenial thoughts on the applicability of present experience to the past are expressed by Ian Mortimer in *The Time Traveller's Guide to Medieval England*

(London: Bodley Head, 2008). This book also serves as a useful introduction to fourteenth-century English life and culture for those new to the period.

Chapter One: A Married Man

Documents bearing on Chaucer's family background and his and Philippa's household appointments and associated rewards through 1377 are found in *Life-Records*, pp. 1–143. The prior lease for Chaucer's dwelling to Walter Parmenter and his wife Joanna exists in *Letter-Book G* (f. 20v, p. 24); I am grateful to Caroline Barron for drawing my attention to it.

Background on the de Roets, including Thomas Swynford's inheritance in Hainault, is found in J. M. Manly, *New Light on Chaucer* (New York: Henry Holt, 1926).

Gareth's social predicament is delineated in all major editors of Malory's works, including *Le Morte d'Arthur* (University of Michigan, 1997); http://quod.lib.umich.edu/C/cme/MaloryWks2/1:9, p. 219.

The basic life of John of Gaunt remains that of Sydney Armitage-Smith, *John of Gaunt* (London: Constable, 1904; frequently reprinted). See also Anthony Goodman, *John of Gaunt* (Harlow, UK: Longman, 1992). Some observations on Chaucer's social standing are based on my own *Social Chaucer*. The duties of king's esquires are described in *The Household of Edward IV: The Black Book*, ed. A. R. Myers (Manchester: University of Manchester Press, 1959).

Valuable background information on the Hainault connection is found in Henry Stephen Lucas, *The Low Countries and the Hundred Years' War* (Ann Arbor: University of Michigan Press, 1929) and Ardis Butterfield, *The Familiar Enemy: Chaucer, Language, and Nation in the Hundred Years War* (Oxford University Press, 2009). The disparaging comment on male fashion in the court of Edward and Philippa is from the *Eulogium Chronicle*, *Eulogium Historiarum sive Temporis*, ed. F. F. Haydon, vol. 9, nos. 1–3 (Rolls Series, 1858–63), vol. 9, no. 3, pp. 230–31. The rage for "crakowes" or peaked shoes is further described by John Stow, *A Survey of London* (Stroud, UK: The History Press, 2009), p. 299. On the *frike* ladies of Philippa's court, see *The Life of the Black Prince*, eds. Mildred K. Pope and Eleanor C. Lodge (Oxford University Press, 1910); also available in translation as http://www.yorku.ca/inpav/chandos_pope.pdf.

Marriage ages in the medieval and early modern periods are discussed in Peter Laslett, *The World We Have Lost* (Cambridge University Press, 1965).

Gaunt's surviving records, including his gifts to Katherine, are gathered in John of Gaunt's *Register*, pp. 372–76 (Camden Society, 3rd series, vols. 20–21) and 1379–83 (Camden Society, 3rd series, vols. 56–57). Other gifts to Katherine are also conveniently summarized in Armitage-Smith, pp. 462–63. On the 1371–72 English campaign in Aquitaine, and Gaunt's involvement, see Goodman, pp. 47–49.

For Froissart's *Chronicles* I rely on Kervyn de Lettenhove's *Oeuvres*. Volumes of particular importance for this chapter include: vol. 1, part 1 (introductory material); vol. 2 (marriage of Edward III and Queen Philippa, her court, and Froissart's assessment of her and her countrymen's impact on English manners and culture); vol. 15 (for the marriage of Gaunt and Katherine Swynford, scandalized commentary by ladies of the court, and Froissart's own tempered comments, see pp. 239–40). For Gaunt flaunting his illicit relationship all over the countryside, see a textual variant printed with the *St. Albans Chronicle*, vol. 1, p. 970. The contemptuous reference to Katherine as *alienigena* appears in *Knighton's Chronicle*, pp. 236–37. For the description of Gaunt's temporary repentance, see *St. Albans Chronicle*, vol. 1, pp. 556–67. For Walsingham's comment on her unsuitability for marriage to a man so eminent, see *St. Albans Chronicle*, vol. 2, pp. 38–39. The confirmation of Katherine's right to Kettlethorpe is noted in *Patent Rolls, 1381–85*, for the year 1383, p. 317, as is evidence of local disturbances around her property and the useful services rendered by Sir William Hawley, pp. 501, 507. Katherine's successful petition to enclose land at Kettlethorpe is recorded in *Patent Rolls, 1381–85*, p. 317. Evidence of the rebels' detestation of Gaunt in 1381 is conveniently available in R. B. Dobson, ed., *The Peasants' Revolt of 1381*, 2nd. ed. (New York: Macmillan, 1983), pp. 33, 69, 75, 128, and 279. Goodman, *John of Gaunt*, summarizes the terms of Katherine's loan to Gaunt, p. 379; it is datable either to 1386 or 1387, but more likely the former, in view of Gaunt's financial necessities prior to his departure for Castile. Unsparing denunciations of Katherine are found in *The Anonimalle Chronicle*, ed. V. H. Galbraith (Manchester: Manchester University Press, 1927), p. 153, and *St. Alban's Chronicle*, p. 79.

Available information about Katherine, and her sanctified ending within the precincts of Lincoln Cathedral, is conveniently gathered in pamphlet form: Anthony Goodman, *Katherine Swynford* (Lincoln, UK: Honywood Press, 1994). Records of the induction ceremony at Lincoln Cathedral, at which Philippa was honored and Katherine was a behind-the-scenes presence, are printed in *Life-Records*, pp. 91–93. Katherine's gifts to Lincoln Cathedral, including twenty-four copes adorned with her emblem of three wheels, are detailed in H. Bradshaw, *Statutes of Lincoln Cathedral* (Cambridge University Press, 1897), p. 262.

John of Gaunt's gifts and annuities to Philippa and to Geoffrey are detailed in the *Life-Records*, pp. 85–91 and 271–74. The warrant for payment of Philippa's annuity in Lincolnshire is in *Life-Records*, p. 87. Evidence bearing on Chaucer's children is presented in *Life-Records*, pp. 541–46.

Chaucer's frequent return to the subject of marriage in his poetry, and especially in what he calls the "Marriage Group" of *Canterbury Tales*, was first observed by G. L. Kittredge in "Chaucer's Discussion of Marriage," *Modern Philology*, 9 (1911–12), pp. 435–67. On Chaucer's late-life move to Westminster Abbey see *Life-Records*, pp. 535–40.

On Chaucer's reliable activities as go-between, picking up the absent Philippa's annuity cheques and delivering them to her by his own hand, see *Life-Records*, pp. 77–78.

Chapter Two: Aldgate

General conditions for housing and occupancy in Chaucer's London are described in John Schofield, *Medieval London Houses* (London: Paul Mellon, 1994), and Schofield, *The Building of London from the Conquest to the Great Fire* (London: Collins, 1984).

W. R. Lethaby reports his archaeological investigations, including his measurement of the footprint of the towers, in "The Priory of Holy Trinity, or Christ Church, Aldgate," *Home Counties Magazine*, 2 (1900), pp. 45–53. Also reproduced there is an excellent rendering of the sixteenth-century sketch map of the Holy Trinity grounds, including the north tower of Aldgate. The sketch map itself is beautifully reproduced in John Schofield and Richard Lea, *Holy Trinity Priory, Aldgate*, monograph 24 (London: Museum of London, 2005). The manuscript of Symonds's sketch map is located in Hatfield House (Herts), the library of the Marquis of Salisbury: CPM I/10, I/19. The Agas engraving of 1561–70 is printed in Schofield and Lea, *Holy Trinity Priory, Aldgate*, p. 20. Valuable information on Westgate, Canterbury, is contained in Tim Tattin-Brown, *The Westgate* (Canterbury: Canterbury Archaeological Trust, 1985). For other information on the Westgate, see *Close Rolls*, 1385–89, pp. 120–21. Special thanks to Craig Bowen and Julian Spurrier of the Canterbury Heritage Museum for arranging and supervising my access to Westgate.

For Chaucer's lease, together with related documents, see *Life-Records*, pp. 144–47; for a translation of the Latin lease see *Memorials*, pp. 377–78. On the terms of his occupancy, and profiles of other persons living over city gates after 1374–75, see Ernest P. Kuhl, "Chaucer and Aldgate," *PMLA* 39 (1924), pp. 101–22. On Strode's compensation for his lost lease, see *Letter-Book H*, p. 245. Stow's sixteenth-century comments about the deeper history of Aldgate, and also his observations about the neighborhood, are taken from his *Survey*, pp. 132–42.

The Bastard of Falconbridge's assault on London, and the lowering of Aldgate's portcullis, is most fully described in *The Arrivall of Edward IV* (edited from British Library Manuscript Harley 543) by John Bruce, Camden Society, series 1, no. 1 (London, 1838). On the muster of 1386 and its reference to Aldgate, see *Close Rolls*, 1385–89, p. 264. The erection of "barbykanes" is described in *Letter-Book H*, pp. 64–65. The passages on invasion fears are from *St. Albans Chronicle*, vol. 1, pp. 792–93. Contents of the carts rumbling through Aldgate are from the *Letter Books*, especially *Letter-Book F*, p. 173, and *Letter-Book H*, p. 54.

My observations on Chaucer's failure to claim London citizenship are informed by conversations with Caroline Barron.

Regulations governing the London Watch are found in *Letter-Book C*, p. 85. London ward arrangements, and ward politics, are described by Caroline M. Barron, *London in the Late Middle Ages* (Oxford University Press, 2004), esp. pp. 121–26, 130–31. Other valuable material on the London wards is in Bird, *Turbulent London*, passim.

On all matters related to Holy Trinity Priory and its history, see Schofield and Lea, *Holy Trinity Priory, Aldgate*. Records of the city's temporary jurisdiction are cited in *Patent Rolls*, 1379–81, p. 599. The Agas woodcut's rendering of the Aldgate neighborhood is reproduced in Schofield and Lea, p. 20. The priory's property holdings are detailed in the *Cartulary of Holy Trinity Priory, Aldgate*, ed. G. A. J. Hodgett (Leicester, UK: London Record Society, 1971).

Information on Aldgate inns and taverns is contained in *Plea Rolls*, 1381–1412, mem. A27, pp. 83–85. The centrality of the parish in religious life, and the importance of parish burial, are described by Ellen Rentz in her forthcoming *Imagining the Parish in Late Medieval England* (Ohio State University Press, in press).

On narrativity within medieval documentary archives, see Natalie Z. Davis, *Fiction in the Archives: Pardon Tales and Their Tellers in Sixteenth-Century France* (Cambridge University Press, 1987), and Joel T. Rosenthal, *Telling Tales: Sources and Narration in Late Medieval England* (Pennsylvania State University Press, 2003). For the scandalous case of Margaret and Maud, see *Select Cases in the Court of King's Bench*, ed. G. O. Sayles, vol. 7, no. 23 (London: Selden Society, 1971). For Elizabeth and Johanna, see *Letter-Book H*, pp. 271–72.

Chaucer's testimony about an encounter on Friday Street is reprinted in *Life-Records*, pp. 370–74.

Langland's rendition of London street chatter occurs in *Piers Plowman*, ed.

Derek Pearsall (Exeter, UK: Exeter University Press, 2008). For regulations on punishment of courtesans, see *Liber Albus*, p. 395.

On the bells of St. Botoph's, see William Baldwin, *Beware the Cat*, ed. William A. Ringler Jr. and Michael Flachman (Los Angeles: Huntington Library, 1988), p. 55. Wymbissh's Holy Trinity bell is described in *Letter-Book D*, p. 287. For translation, see *Memorials*, p. 287. Lincoln bell peals and other aspects of the daily service are described in Christopher Wordsworth, *Notes on Medieval Services in England* (London: T. Baker, 1898). For the peals of St. Mary on the Hill, see *The Medieval Records of a London City Church*, ed. Henry Littlehales (London: Early English Text Society, 1905). Other aspects of the daily service are usefully considered by J. C. Dickinson, *Monastic Life in Medieval England* (London: A. and C. Black, 1961). Valuable observations on liturgical time in a medieval monastery are found in Barbara Harvey, *Living and Dying in England, 1100–1540* (Oxford University Press, 1993); see also Harvey, *Westminster Abbey and Its Estates in the Middle Ages* (Oxford University Press, 1977). For regulation of the London curfew by bells, see *Letter-Book C*, p. 85; also see *Liber Albus*, p. 240, and Riley, *Memorials*, p. 21. The cycle of liturgical times and services is described in Harvey, *Westminster Abbey and Its Estates in the Middle Ages*.

Chapter Three: The Wool Men

The chronology of events bearing on Chaucer's appointment to the controllership is based on *Life-Records*, pp. 112, 148–52, 271. The most useful previous analysis of the circumstances of his appointment appears in J. R. Hulbert, *Chaucer's Official Life* (Menasha, WI: Collegiate Press, 1912; reprinted New York: Phaeton Press, 1970).

Matthew Hale's "Treatise in Three Parts" is published in Francis Hargrave, *A Collection of Tracts* (London and Dublin: E. Lynch, 1787).

For rules governing treatment of Lorrainers and other foreign traders, see *Liber Custumarum*, ed. H. T. Riley, Rolls Series 12:2 (London, 1861). On the case of Johannes Imperial, see Paul Strohm, "Trade, Treason, and the Murder of Johannes Imperial," *Theory and the Premodern Text* (University of Minnesota Press, 2000).

Observations on the general site of the customhouse and its riverside location, as well as a subsequent description of the customhouse itself, are based on "Excavations at the Custom House Site, city of London, 1973," Tim Tatton-Brown et al., *Transactions of the London and Middlesex Archaeological Society*, vol. 25 (1974), pp. 117–219; vol. 26 (1975), pp. 103–70. The documents pertaining to

Churchman's Custom House are digested in the *Patent Rolls, 1381–85*, pp. 149, 249. For discussion and analysis, see Mabel H. Mills, "The London Customs House," *Archaeologia*, 83 (1933), 307–25. She quotes the full description of the addition from the original patent roll entry: "*nos pro eo idem Johannes preter dictam domum pro tronagio ordinatam & preter solarium super eande domum pro dicto computatorio dispositum nobis concesserit quandam camerulam pro latrina dicto computatorio annexam necnon solarium desuper computatorium predictum . . . in quo quidem solario sunt due camere & vnum garitum. . . ."*

For Wyngaerde's sketch map, see Antonis van den Wyngaerde, *The Panorama of London circa 1544*, drawing 9, publication 151 (London: London Topographical Society, 1966). The custom house may also be present, in a highly idealized form, in a well-known manuscript illumination of the fifteenth century, British Museum Manuscript Royal 16E ii f 73. For this illumination, with notes by Sonja Drimmer, see *Royal Manuscripts: The Genius of Illumination* (London: British Library, 2011), pp. 376-77. The identification of the idealized building in MS Royal 16E as an evolved version of the medieval customhouse has been suggested by Julian Munby, "A Note on the Medieval Buildings," in Tatton-Brown et al., vol. 26, p. 113. His identification is supported by the arcaded character of the building in the MS Royal illumination. A contending identification holds that this building is a new and arcaded city market just constructed in 1460 in Billingsgate with public funds. The argument for this alternative is presented in *Hugh Alley's Caveat: The Markets of London*, ed. Ian Archer, Caroline Barron, and Vanessa Harding (London: London Topographical Society, 1988), pp. 53, 84. Readers with a particular interest in the customhouse and in evolving conceptions of late medieval London may wish to seek out the Royal illumination, and also to compare the arguments of Munby and Archer et al.

For Gower's acerbic remarks on the wool trade see *Mirour de l'Omne, Complete Works*, vol. 1, lines 25, pp. 357–500. The *Mirour* is also available in translation as *Mirour de l'Omne (Mirror of Mankind)*, ed. and trans. William Burton Wilson (East Lansing, MI: Colleagues Press, 1992).

Total crown revenues are notoriously difficult to compute, but general figures may be found in James H. Ramsay, *A History of the Revenues of the Kings of England, 1066–1399*, vol. 2 (Oxford University Press, 1925). More specific information on the "income" side is to be found in Anthony Steel, *The Receipt of the Exchequer, 1377–1485* (Cambridge University Press, 1954). On the crown itself as security for loans, see Paul Strohm, *Politique: Languages of Statecraft Between Chaucer and Shakespeare* (Notre Dame, IN: Notre Dame Press, 2005), p. 221 and note. For perspective on the development of institutions of public finance and on the relation of "consent" in taxation to the origins of Parliament, see Sydney Knox Mitchell, *Taxation in Medieval England* (Yale University Press, 1951) and, especially, G. L. Harriss, *King, Parliament, and Public Finance in Medieval England to 1369* (Oxford University Press, 1975).

An excellent overview of the English wool trade in the later fourteenth century is included in J. L. Bolton, *The Medieval English Economy, 1150–1500* (London: Dent, 1980), esp. pp. 294–97. For particulars, and especially for the complicated history of the English Staple, the monopoly that benefited the London capitalists, see T. H. Lloyd, *The English Wool Trade in the Middle Ages* (Cambridge University Press, 1977).

Both Lloyd and Ruth Bird, in *Turbulent London,* discuss the indictment of Lyons and de Bury in the "Good Parliament" of 1376. For additionally detailed information on London political alignments in the 1370s see Pamela Nightingale, *A Medieval Mercantile Community: The Grocer's Company and the Politics and Trade of London* (Yale University Press, 1995). Information on Brembre's loans is also to be found in Steel, *Receipt*, together with further information on his associations, finances, and accumulated property and wealth in Ruth Bird, *Turbulent London*. Loans to Edward III are intensively studied by Roger Axworthy, *The Financial Relationship of the London Merchant Community with Edward III, 1327–77*, 2 vols., thesis, University of London, 2001. (His data, drawn from receipts and issues of the exchequer, includes loans from Philipot and Walworth and many others but contains no notice of any loans from Brembre during Edward's reign.) The *Dictionary of National Biography* contains informative entries on Brembre (by Andrew Prescott), Walworth (Pamela Nightingale), and Philipot (Pamela Nightingale). Lloyd addresses the subject of Brembre's wool shipments. For evidence of bribery by Italian merchants in Southampton, I am indebted to A. Ruddock, *Italian Merchants and Shipping in Southampton 1270–1600* (Southampton, UK: Southampton University Press, 1951).

For Brembre's appointment and reappointment in the wool custom, see *Fine Rolls, 1369–77*, pp. 245, 293; and for *1377–83*, pp. 7, 132. His 1375 termination is recorded in *Close Rolls, 1374–77*, pp. 166–67. His 1371 loan to Edward III is recorded in *Letter-Book G*, pp. 275–76. On his participation in the collective 1374 loan to Edward III, see *Patent Rolls, 1374–77*, p. 36. His first substantial loan to King Richard is recorded in *Patent Rolls, 1374–77*, p. 24 (including repayment from customs and subsidies). Among loans after 1377, see September 1378, *Fine Rolls, 1377–83*, p. 41 (particularly important for its provisions bearing on direct repayment from revenues of the wool custom). On outright gifts to Richard see Bird, *Turbulent London*. The Mercers' Petition against Nicholas Brembre is printed in *A Book of London English, 1384–1425*, eds. R. W. Chambers and Marjorie Daunt (Oxford University Press, 1931), pp. 33–37. On Brembre's downfall and 1388 trial and execution, see the *Westminster Chronicle*, esp. pp. 312–15. Parliamentary complaints against Richard Lyons are detailed in *Rolls of Parliament* for 1376.

On the imposition of wool duties in 1275 and early policies on division of the cocket seal, see *Fine Rolls, 1272–1307*, pp. 47, 60–61. For the quoted terms of the 1374 loan, see *Patent Rolls, 1374–77*, p. 36.

On the responsibilities of collectors and controllers of customs see E. M. Carus-Wilson and Olive Coleman, *England's Export Trade, 1275–1547* (Oxford University Press, 1963). Carus-Wilson's conclusions about the general reliability of customs accounts must be qualified by the far more jaundiced study of Robert L. Baker, whose detailed review of the crown's futile attempts to ensure honest collection of the wool custom in the midcentury have informed several aspects of my analysis: *The English Customs Service, 1307–43* (American Philosophical Society, 1961). See Baker, also, for the reformist legislation of 1331, which he transcribes in full on p. 23. Baker also relates the case of the fraudulent Ipswich collectors, p. 21. Similarly dubious about the integrity of the wool custom and its processes is Carus-Wilson's collaborator, Olive Coleman. Her trenchant and worldly wise observations are to be found in "The Collectors of Customs in London Under Richard II," *Studies in London History Presented to Philip Edward Jones*, ed. A. E. J. Hollander and William Kellaway (London: Hodder and Stoughton, 1969), pp. 181–96. In this essay, Coleman details instances in which Brembre was on both ends of the transaction, holding the two halves of the cocket seal. My discussion of further malfeasance at Ipswich is based on the research of Isabel Abbott and Roland Latham, "Caterpillars of the Commonwealth," *Speculum* 30 (1955), pp. 229–32. For the satiric verses against bribery in the exchequer see C. H. Haskins and M. Dorothy George, "Verses on the Exchequer in the Fifteenth Century," *English Historical Review* 36 (1921), pp. 58–67.

Crow, *Life-Records*, continues to be indispensable, here for detailed information on the terms and language of Chaucer's grants and letters of appointment, persons appointed to posts in customs and their terms of office, numbers of cargoes handled by Chaucer, records of the wool custom during Chaucer's tenure, and also supplementary texts touching upon oaths taken by controllers, the case of the offending wool packers, and the honest controller Thomas Prudence. Andrew Prescott, a leading theorist of the medieval archive, has suggested in conversation that Chaucer's own handwritten exchequer accounts may have been spirited away by a souvenir hunter; none of these have survived, although many other comparable accounts of the period have.

George Lyman Kittredge's keen insight is from his superb *Chaucer and His Poetry* (Harvard University Press, 1915), pp. 45–47.

For actions for debt against Chaucer, 1388–90, see *Life-Records*, pp. 384–90; on the end of Philippa's annuity, *Life-Records*, p. 78; on his sale of his exchequer annuities, *Life-Records*, pp. 336–39.

Chapter Four: In Parliament

A general outline of parliamentary procedures in the second half of the fourteenth century, including the social stratification of its membership, is provided by the contemporary *Manner of Holding Parliament*, edited by Nicholas Pronay and John Taylor in *Parliamentary Texts of the Later Middle Ages* (Oxford University Press, 1980). Further comments on the summons to Parliament and electoral practices are based on the introductory discussion of J. S. Roskell, *The House of Commons, 1386–1421* in *History of Parliament*, vol. 1. Chaucer's own summons to Parliament is printed, like so many other central documents, in Crow, *Life-Records*.

Authorities differ on the matter of Chaucer's own residence. J. S. Roskell's study in the *History of Parliament* finds that of the 252 known members in 1386, all but nine were residents, and he counts Chaucer among the nonresident nine; yet the carefully researched biography printed elsewhere in the same series takes his residency for granted.

For the proceedings of the Parliaments of 1385 and 1386, see *Parliament Rolls*. The influential conclusion that the crown made no special effort to pack the Parliament of 1386 appears in Crow, pp. 366–67. On Chaucer's fellow MPs Organ and Hadley, see the *History of Parliament*. Also see the *History of Parliament* for the biographies of individual shire knights of 1386, especially the commendable efforts of Carole Rawcliffe and L. S. Woodger, upon which I rely for my conclusions about the relative strength of the court party versus Gloucester's oppositional alignment. The Gloucester party in the Parliament of 1386 can be reconstructed from hints in biographies of the seventy-four shire knights. Those knights opposed to Richard II and Chaucer's faction can be identified by their signs of extra-parliamentary loyalty to the Duke of Gloucester and to his associates, the earls of Arundel and Warwick. Other clues to membership in this dissident faction include support for Richard's eventual supplanter Henry of Derby, as well as other activities on behalf of the house of Lancaster. Finally, among those MPs who survived until 1397–98, former dissidents self-identify by scurrying to seek immunity when Richard sought long-delayed but savage revenge against Gloucester and his followers. Following such criteria, thirty to thirty-two shire knights of 1386 may be reckoned hard-core supporters of the Duke of Gloucester and his anti-Ricardian faction. A roughly equal number of shire knights were still hesitating at the opening of Parliament, waiting to see which way the balance would tip. It would tip decisively in the course of the session, and even from its opening gavel.

For data and interpretative discussion concerning fourteenth-century Westminster, I am indebted to Gervase Rosser, *Medieval Westminster, 1200–1500* (Oxford University Press, 1989); Rosser translates the story of the unfortunate Whalley. Regulations of the Southwark stews, including attempts to close them during sessions of Parliament, are printed in J. Post, "A Fifteenth-Century Customary of the Southwark Stews," *Journal of the Society of Archivists* 5 (1974–77), pp. 418–28.

The London MPs' 1389 reimbursements are printed in Riley, *Memorials*. The original is found, in manuscript, in *Letter-Book H*, folio ccxlv. Hoccleve's verses on the Westminster taverns are to be found in his "Male Regle," a poem of personal misgovernance, in *Hoccleve's Works: The Minor Poems*, ed. F. Furnivall, Early English Text Society, Extra Series, vol. 61 (1892). The jaundiced (and extremely well-informed) description of malingerers in Parliament is from "Richard the Redeless" in *The Piers Plowman Tradition*, ed. Helen Barr (New York: Dutton, 1993).

The most satisfactory general survey of time, clocks, and their effect on sensibility is Gerhard Dohrn-van Rossum, *The History of the Hour: Clocks and Modern Temporal Orders*, trans. Thomas Dunlap (University of Chicago Press, 1996). Particularly helpful to me has been Caroline Barron's unpublished paper "Telling the Time in Chaucer's London," which was delivered at the New Chaucer Society Congress in London on April 19–20, 2007; this paper includes the information on parliamentary timekeeping first noted by Robert Ellis. Jacques le Goff makes a valuable distinction between church's time (sacred or liturgical time) and merchants' time (practical and measured time) in *Time, Work, and Culture in the Middle Ages* (University of Chicago Press, 1982). The shift from liturgical time to clock time was inexorable but uneven. Edward III installed his great clock in Westminster, but also hedged his bets: in 1366–67 he spent £246 16s. 8d. for three bells, the largest of them weighing over four tons. The entries concerning Edward III's clock and bells are found in Pipe Roll 41 (1366–67), British National Archives. Logonier's clock agreement is printed in *Archaeological Journal*, vol. 11 (1855).

The parliamentary outcry captured in the Bill of 1385 is available as an appendix to J. N. N. Palmer, "The Impeachment of Michael de la Pole in 1386," *Bulletin of the Institute of Historical Research* 42 (1969), p. 101.

The late fourteenth-century locations of Parliament are carefully adduced in Ivy M. Cooper, "The Meeting-Places of Parliament in the Ancient Palace of Westminster," *Journal of the British Archaeological Association*, 3rd series, vol. 3 (1938), pp. 97–138. Specifics of the Painted Chamber are reconstructed by Paul Binski, "The Painted Chamber at Westminster, the Fall of Tyrants and the English Literary Model of Governance," *Journal of the Warburg and Courtauld Institutes*, 74 (2011), pp. 121–54. An earlier, and partially superseded, study by Binski, *The Painted Chamber at Westminster* (London: Society of Antiquaries, 1986), contains an excellent discussion of the symbolism of the royal bed. On the Canterbury Pilgrims' efforts to interpret the cathedral's stained-glass windows, see *The Tale of Beryn*, ed. F. J. Furnivall, Early English Text Society, Original Series, vol. 105 (1901).

One aspect of the 1386 Parliament's business is treated in detail in J. S. Roskell, *The Impeachment of Michael de la Pole Earl of Suffolk in 1386* (University of Manchester Press, 1984).

On the device of the "commune" or "common" petition, see Doris Rayner, "The Forms and Machinery of the Commune Petition in the Fourteenth Century, Parts I and II," *English Historical Review* 56 (1941), pp. 198–233, 549–70. The significance of Richard's absence from Parliament, and also the implications of his direct address (*par sa bouche demesne*) to the gathered body at the end of the session, are discussed by Phil Bradford, "A Silent Presence: The English King in Parliament in the Fourteenth Century," *Historical Research* 84 (2011), pp. 189–211.

On Chaucer's decision to vacate his posts and withdraw to Kent, see Paul Strohm, "Politics and Poetics: Usk and Chaucer in the 1380s," *Literary Practice and Social Change in Britain, 1380–1530*, ed. Lee Patterson (University of California Press, 1990), pp. 83–112. My earlier discussion of these matters placed somewhat more emphasis on his personal discretion and somewhat less emphasis on the elements of coercion surrounding his decision than the current discussion. On Richard Forester, see *Life-Records*, pp. 54, 99, 146. Brembre's ill-timed gestures of all-out support for Richard, including his cash gifts directly to Richard's Chamber, are detailed in Anthony Tuck, *Richard II and the English Nobility* (London: Edward Arnold, 1973), pp. 18–19, 110–11. For Nicholas Exton's cagey relations with Brembre in 1386, see *DNB*. On the London representatives to the Parliament of 1388, see *History of Parliament*, vol. 2, pp. 128–31; vol. 3, pp. 773–76; vol. 4, pp. 343–46, 733–35. The grim circumstances of Brembre's arraignment and betrayal by his fellow London merchant capitalists are detailed in *Westminster Chronicle*, pp. 312–15.

Chapter Five: The Other Chaucer

The suggestion that Chaucer juvenalia might have included poems in French is pursued by James Wimsatt, *Chaucer and the Poems of "Ch,"* Chaucer Studies, no. 9 (Cambridge, UK: D.S Brewer, 1982). T. S. Eliot's comments on unified sensibility are found in "The Metaphysical Poets," *Selected Essays* (New York: Harcourt, Brace, 1932).

The Usk reference is to *The Testament of Love*, ed. R. Allen Shoaf (TEAMS: Middle English Texts, 1998), book 3, chap. 4, lines 559–64. Details of Usk's career, and emulation of Chaucer, may be found in Paul Strohm, "Politics and Poetics: Usk and Chaucer in the 1380s," *Literary Practice and Social Change in Britain, 1380–1530* (University of California Press, 1990). Deschamps's ballad and Gower's admonition that Chaucer write a testament of his own are conveniently available in *Chaucer: The Critical Heritage*, vol. 1, ed. D. S. Brewer (London: Routledge, 1978). See also Gower, *Complete Works*, vol. 3, lines 15–16. On Chaucer's and Gower's interactions, the definitive account is John H. Fisher, *John Gower: Moral Philosopher and Friend of Chaucer* (New York University Press, 1968). For Hoccleve's claim that the older Chaucer was available to instruct him in his verse—*"fayn wolde han me taught"*—see his *Regement of Princes*, line 2078, and J. A. Burrow, *Thomas Hoccleve*, Authors of the Middle Ages Series (Aldershot, UK: Variorum, 1994), p. 10.

The matter of Chaucer's literary circle is taken up in my *Social Chaucer*, esp. pp. 47–83, with documentation of his interactions with Clanvowe, Scogan, and others mentioned here. A recent essay by Derek Pearsall argues that the *Canterbury Tales* were nurtured by a supportive London audience; his and my views of Chaucer's London public are congenial, although, as readers will see, I am inclined to connect Chaucer's works before 1386, rather than the *Canterbury Tales*, with his access to a London circle. See Pearsall, "The *Canterbury Tales* and London Club Culture," *Chaucer and the City*, ed. Ardis Butterfield (Cambridge: D.S. Brewer, 2006), pp. 95–108. The fascinating subject of Lewis Clifford as cultural intermediary between Chaucer and the French poet Eustache Deschamps has often been discussed, most notably by James I. Wimsatt, *Chaucer and His French Contemporaries* (University of Toronto Press, 1991), pp. 242–72, and Ardis Butterfield, *The Familiar Enemy* (Oxford University Press, 2009), pp. 143–55. Butterfield provides the best and most authoritative transcription and translation of the ballade Deschamps addressed to Chaucer, upon which I have relied here. She explains the hostility in Deschamps's positioning of translation as a derivative activity (versus his own practices of original composition) and also (with the Hundred Years War still in progress) his view of French-English translation as a typical act of aggressive appropriation. We differ, though, in our estimate of Deschamps's acquaintance with Chaucer's English writings; my own view is that all Deschamps knew of Chaucer's writings were things he might have been told by Clifford.

On the imaginary character of writers' representations of audiences and audience relations, see Walter J. Ong, "The Writer's Audience Is Always a Fiction," *PMLA: Publication of the Modern Language Association* 90 (1975), pp. 9–21. My comments on the utterance as a bridge between speaker and hearer are indebted to V. N. Voloshinov, *Marxism and the Philosophy of Language* (Harvard University Press, 1986), p. 86. The aurality of medieval literature and the medieval author's particular reliance upon an intimate circle are discussed by Joyce Coleman, *Public Reading and the Reading Public in Late Medieval England and France* (Cambridge University Press, 1996); in this discussion I subscribe to her view. On St. Ambrose's habits of silent reading, see Augustine, *Confessions* (Oxford University Press, 1991), bk. 6, pp. 92–93.

Chapter Six: The Problem of Fame

A rewarding discussion of self-naming by medieval authors is Anne Middleton, "William Langland's Kynde Name," *Chaucer, Langland, and Fourteenth-Century Literary History* (Farnam, UK: Ashgate Variorum, 2013).

Gower advances his ambitious suppositions about Richard II's encouragement in Gower, *Complete Works*, vol. 3, p. 4.

Purgatorio 9, lines 19–21 is quoted from Dante Alighieri, *Purgatorio*, trans. Jean Hollander and Robert Hollander (New York: Doubleday, 2003).

The literary tradition of Chaucer's epilogue to *Troilus* is authoritatively discussed by J. S. P. Tatlock, "The Epilog of Chaucer's 'Troilus,'" *Modern Philology* 18 (1921), pp. 625–29.

Chaucer's literary relations with Boccaccio have been discussed often, most recently and persuasively by David Wallace, *Chaucerian Polity* (Stanford University Press, 1997), esp. pp. 9–82. Although Chaucer knew other of Boccaccio's works, his firsthand acquaintance with the *Decameron* remains in doubt. On the lack of evidence for such acquaintance, see Nicholas Havely, *Chaucer's Boccaccio* (Cambridge: D.S. Brewer, 1980), especially p. 12 and p. 197, n. 37.

The discovery of Thomas Spencer's testimony about discharge of a debt with a copy of *Troilus* was announced by Martha Carlin, "Chaucer's Southwark Network," Thirteenth Conference of the Early Book Society, St. Andrews University, July 7, 2013.

Chapter Seven: Kent and Canterbury

Information about Chaucer's fellow peace commissioners is given in *Life-Records*, pp. 348–63; see also the *Dictionary of National Biography* for Belknap, Burley, Clopton, Cobham, Devereux, Rickhill, Savage, and Tresilian. Savage is also treated in the *History of Parliament*. Savage's seat at Bobbing may possibly be referenced in one of the place-names of the Canterbury pilgrimage, "Bobbe-up-and-doun" (fragment 9, l. 2)—although the connection, if granted, would create difficulties for the traditional ordering of the Canterbury tales. On Bobbing, see *Notes and Queries* no. 127 (1932), p. 26—though its author is unaware of the additional strength lent to Bobbing as Chaucer's point of reference by the existence of the Savage connection. On Savage's possible literary interests, as indicated by his service as an executor of John Gower's will, see Gower, *Complete Works*, vol. 1, p. xviii.

On the possibility that Chaucer had a Kentish sister, Katherine, see A. A. Kern, "Chaucer's Sister," *Modern Language Notes* 23 (1908), 52.

For pertinent observations about "tydyngs" in the *House of Fame* and their relation to tale telling and the Canterbury project see Vincent Gillespie, "Authorship," *A Handbook of Middle English Studies*, ed. Marion Turner (Oxford: Blackwell, 2013), pp. 137–54.

Ideas of literary form are usefully discussed in Christopher Cannon, "Form," *Middle English*, ed. Paul Strohm (Oxford University Press, 2007), pp. 177–90. Chaucer's idea of literary form as something simultaneously apprehended may be traced to the medieval rhetorician Geoffrey of Vinsauf, who recommends that a successful composition should be complete in its planner's mind before it is undertaken. Using the analogy of house building, he says, "If a man has a house to build, his impetuous hand does not rush into action. The measuring line of his mind first lays out the work. . . . The mind's hand shapes the entire house before the body's hand builds it." Its mode of being is archetypal before it is actual (*prius achetypus quam sensilis*). For the full passage, see *Poetria Nova*, trans. Margaret F. Nims (University of Toronto Press, 1967).

On various computational and calendar-based arguments for 1387 as the imagined date of the Canterbury pilgrimage, see W. W. Skeat, ed., *The Complete Works of Geoffrey Chaucer* vol. 3 (Oxford University Press, 1894), pp. 373–74.

On the unprecedented nature of Chaucer's varied tale collection, I am in debt to Helen Cooper, whose *The Structure of the Canterbury Tales* (London: Duckworth, 1983) remains fundamental for the study of Chaucer's greatest work. The suggestion that the creation of the Canterbury Pilgrims might have followed, rather than preceded, the composition of the individual tales originates with C. David Benson, *Chaucer's Drama of Style* (University of North Carolina Press, 1986). The enlarged palette of vocational types in medieval satirical poetry is explored by Jill Mann, *Chaucer and Medieval Estates Satire* (Cambridge University Press, 1973).

Epilogue: Laureate Chaucer

On early references to Chaucer, see Caroline Spurgeon, *Five Hundred Years of Chaucer Criticism and Allusion*, vol. 1 (London: Chaucer Society, 1914) and *Chaucer: The Critical Heritage*, vol. 1, ed. Derek Brewer (London: Routledge, 1978).

The discussion of Adam Pinkhurst's role in the production of Chaucer's poems, and especially the Hengwrt and Ellesmere manuscripts of the *Canterbury Tales*, is most tellingly inaugurated by Linne R. Mooney. For an even more ambitious rendering of his importance than I have offered here, see her "Chaucer's Scribe," *Speculum* 81 (2006), pp. 97–138. Although elements of her analysis have been questioned, none have seriously doubted that Pinkhurst enjoyed privileged access to Chaucer's papers after his death, and that his hand is present in these two crucial early manuscripts, as well as a fragmentary *Troilus* and a Boethius. For some thoughtful questions about the origin and status of Chaucer's poem to Adam, see Alexandra Gillespie, "Reading Chaucer's Words to Adam," *Chaucer Review* 42 (2008), pp. 269–83. Also relevant to my discussion is Glending Olson, "Author, Scribe, and Curse: The Genre of Adam Scriveyn," *Chaucer Review* 42 (2008), pp. 284–97. Olson makes the congenial point that the opening lines of the poem "suggest a certain struggle and perhaps audacity on Chaucer's part in asserting himself as an author in the humanist mode."

On the state of Chaucer's papers at the time of his death, and also on the earliest owners of his manuscripts, see M. C. Seymour, *A Catalogue of Chaucer Manuscripts*, vol. 2 (Aldershot, UK: Scolar Press, 1997). With regard to the fifty-six existing whole or partial manuscripts of the *Canterbury Tales*, he contends that "all derive ultimately from one set of unbound or partially bound booklets, put together as one collection in London shortly after Chaucer's death (25 October 1400) in four slightly different editions." The Ellesmere and Hengwrt manuscripts of the *Canterbury Tales* have been accessibly published in facsimile: *The New Ellesmere Chaucer Facsimile* (Los Angeles: Huntington Library, 1996) and *The Canterbury Tales: A Facsimile and Transcription of the Hengwrt Manuscript*, ed. P. G. Ruggiers (University of Oklahoma Press, 1979).

Lancastrian encouragement of Chaucer's works is suggestively treated by John H. Fisher, "A Language Policy for Lancastrian England, *PMLA: Publications of the Modern Language Association* 107 (1992), pp. 1168–80.

The growth of the English reading public is succinctly described by M. B.

Parkes, "The Literacy of the Laity," in *Literature and Western Civilisation, II: The Medieval World*, eds. David Daiches and Anthony Thorlby (London: Aldus, 1973), pp. 555–77. Three excellent surveys of manuscript circulation in the later Middle Ages are: J. Griffths and P. Pearsall, eds., *Book Production and Publishing in Britain, 1375–1475* (Cambridge University Press, 1989); C. F. Briggs, "Literacy, Reading, and Writing in the Medieval West," *Journal of Medieval History* 26 (2000), pp. 397–420; and W. M. Ormrod, "The Use of English: Language, Law and Political Culture in Fourteenth-Century England," *Speculum* 78 (2003), pp. 750–87. For additional material on late medieval literacy, see Paul Strohm, "Reading and Writing," *A Social History of England 1200–1500*, eds. Rosemary Horrox and W. Mark Ormrod (Cambridge University Press, 2006).

The subject of scribal culture and manuscript production in later medieval London is in a period of rapid development right now; one starting point of special interest, because it involves Chaucer's scribe Adam Pinkhurst, is provided by Linne R. Mooney, "Chaucer's Scribe," *Speculum* 81 (2006), pp. 97–138. On other aspects of manuscript production and circulation, see M. A. Michael, "Urban Production of Manuscript Books," pp. 168–94; Julia Boffey and A. S. G. Edwards, "Middle English Literary Writings, 1150–1400," pp. 380–90, both in *Cambridge History of the Book in Britain*, vol. 2, eds. Nigel Morgan and Rodney M. Thomson (Cambridge University Press, 2007). Also see A. I. Doyle and M. Parkes, "The Production of Copies of the Canterbury Tales," *Medieval Scribes, Manuscripts and Libraries* (London: Scolar Press, 1978). An especially valuable essay on early fifteenth-century production of manuscript books is C. Paul Christianson, "The Rise of London's Book-Trade," in *Cambridge History of the Book in Britain*, vol. 3, eds. Lotte Hellinga and J. B. Trapp (Cambridge University Press, 1999). On production of paper in England, see David Christopher Chamberlain, "Paper," *Oxford Companion to the Book* (Oxford University Press, 2010), pp. 79–87, and with particular emphasis on the availability of paper in the fourteenth century, Orieta da Rold, "Materials," in *The Production of Books in England 1350–1500*, eds. Alexandra Gillespie and Daniel Wakelin (Cambridge University Press, 2011).

The story of Petrarch, Boccaccio, and the cultivation of laurel is recounted in Vittore Branca, *Boccaccio: The Man and His Works* (London: Harvester Press, 1976), p. 112.

INDEX

~~~~

Notes and Further Reading are unindexed, although several notes of particular importance, indicated by n, are included here